Toronto

METROPOLITAN PORTRAITS

Metropolitan Portraits explores the contemporary metropolis in its diverse blend of past and present. Each volume describes a North American urban region in terms of historical experience, spatial configuration, culture, and contemporary issues. Books in the series are intended to promote discussion and understanding of metropolitan North America at the start of the twenty-first century.

Judith A. Martin, Series Editor

Toronto

Transformations in a City and Its Region

Edward Relph

PENN

UNIVERSITY OF PENNSYLVANIA PRESS

PHILADELPHIA

Published by
University of Pennsylvania Press
Philadelphia, Pennsylvania 19104-4112
www.upenn.edu/pennpress

Printed in the United States of America on acid-free paper
10 9 8 7 6 5 4 3 2 1

Library of Congress Cataloging-in-Publication Data
Relph, E. C.
   Toronto : transformations in a city and its region / Edward
Relph.—1st ed.
      p. cm. — (Metropolitan portraits)
   Includes bibliographical references and index.
   ISBN 978-0-8122-4542-4 (hardcover : alk. paper)
   1. Toronto Metropolitan Area (Ont.)—History.   2. City
planning—Ontario—Toronto Metropolitan area—History.
3. City and town life—Ontario—Toronto Metropolitan Area.
I. Title.   II. Series: Metropolitan portraits.
F1059.5.T6857R45   2014
971.3′541—dc23
                                        2013015881

Contents

Preface

Toronto was founded a decade after the end of the American War of Independence as a colonial outpost to promote settlement and to protect British interests in what was then known as Upper Canada. Over the next century and a half it developed into a modest industrial city, one of a group of manufacturing cities around the Great Lakes that included Buffalo, Cleveland, and Detroit. Since 1970 it has undergone a remarkable change. Unlike those other cities, Toronto did not go into a decline and its center was not hollowed out as manufacturing moved away. Instead it has boomed as a result of immigration from around the world and the growth of financial services, and it has become one of the largest and most prosperous metropolitan areas in North America. This book is an account of the various landscapes and urban patterns of Toronto, of how the city developed from its origins to the present day, and especially of the transformations over the last fifty years that have turned it from a primarily white, rustbelt city into an intensely multicultural, polycentric metropolitan region that extends across much of south-central Ontario and around the western end of Lake Ontario.

Toronto: Transformations in a City and Its Region has been a very long time in preparation. My idea of a book about the Toronto region originated in 1998 at what was, if I recall correctly, the second meeting organized by Judith Martin to discuss the Metropolitan Portraits series. That was held in Sam Bass Warner's house in Cambridge, Massachusetts, during a dinner with Larry Ford and Carl Abbott, and we all made commitments to write books about our respective cities. Their books in the series were published by 2004, but I had become involved in academic middle management at my multicultural suburban campus of the University of Toronto Scarborough, and I didn't escape my administrative shackles for more than a decade. Judith required each prospective author in the series to give her a tour of his or her city, and in 2008 I finally found the opportunity to show her around Toronto. She encouraged me to get back to writing, but my administrative responsibilities were extended for a further two years; only when those were done was I finally able, after twelve years, to get down to serious work.

I like to think the delays were, in part, for the better, because they allowed me the chance to teach courses about Toronto and to benefit from the insights and feedback of students. Furthermore, in the last decade there have been important changes for Toronto, especially the implementation of three interlocking regional plans for the Greater Golden Horseshoe. Sadly, however, the delays also meant that I was not able to benefit from Judith's renowned advice and editorial skills because she died unexpectedly and much too young in 2011 as I was completing the first draft. This book would not have been thought of, emerged from its dormancy, or brought to completion without her inspiration and encouragement. I cannot acknowledge her contribution too much.

All the photos and sketches in the book are mine. I have also drawn the maps, in some cases adapting the material from various sources that are listed in the captions. Many of the ideas and themes I express about Toronto and its region have emerged through discussions and/or urban explorations with colleagues, friends, and students, in some cases over the course of two decades and in others over just a few days, though I have bent them to my own purposes. I am especially indebted to André Sorensen, Susannah Bunce, Ahmed Allahwalla, Minelle Mahtani, Zack Taylor, and especially Michael Bunce (all from Geography and City Studies at the University of Toronto Scarborough), and also to Bev Sandalack, Brian Banks, Alan Walks, Wayne Reeves, Richard Harris, Bob Mugerauer, Paul Hess, Girish Daswani, Gunter Gad, Larry Bourne, Phil Triadafilopoulos, Lena Mortensen, and Ranu Basu. I have also benefited from the excellent work of graduate and undergraduate students, notably Angela Loder's research on greening cities, Jenny Hall's on heritage and new urbanism, Andrew Blum's about place and electronic media, and Luisa Veronis's on transnationalism. I appreciate invaluable contributions from Noreen Khimani, Mandeep Gulati, Golda Oneka, Edward Birnbaum, Katie Mazer, Nitika Jagtiani, Mark McConville, Christine Lau, Helen Lee, Jason Chang, Aslam Shaikh, Nicole Ristic, and Nadien Awad. At the University of Pennsylvania Press, I am very grateful to Bob Lockhart, who offered sage advice about my very belated manuscript and then shepherded it through the editorial process, and to Rachel Taube, Erica Ginsburg, and Christine Dahlin for their splendid work turning my manuscript into a book. Irene, Lexy, and Gwyn have invariably been sources of inspiration and support. And the youthful enthusiasms of Alex and Isabelle remind me that more transformations are inevitably to come.

Chapter 1

Urban Transformations

In the 1960s Toronto was, by almost any measure, a provincial industrial city. Robert Fulford, a Canadian journalist who grew up there in the 1950s, described it as "a city of silence, a private city, where all the best meals were eaten at home . . . a mute, inward-turned metropolis." At that time it was the second largest city in Canada with a population of about one and a half million, but in almost every way—population, economic clout, fashion, self-image—it remained as it had always been since it was founded in the 1790s, clearly subservient to Montreal.[1]

I arrived in Toronto in 1967 after living for five years in London, so perhaps it was not surprising that my first impressions were that Toronto was not only inward-turned but stuck in the past. There's an imposing statue of Queen Victoria in her imperial dotage in front of the Ontario government buildings in the center of the city, and her matronly royal gaze still held Toronto in its thrall (Figure 1.1). Everything seemed to be coated with old dust, which in itself was not remarkable because most cities in the 1960s had a layer of soot and car exhaust on the outside and a sheen of nicotine inside, but there were also old-fashioned streetcars running along streets lined with wooden telephone poles festooned with wires, residential streets with tired Victorian houses, subway stations named for British patron saints, and a population with predominantly British roots that were tangled up with romantic images of a Britain that no longer existed. A puritan sensibility prevailed; wine for your private meal had to be bought in characterless government stores where all bottles were kept out of sight, then carried home in plain brown paper bags so fellow citizens would not be morally offended by your sinful ways. By most indications Toronto was

Figure 1.1. Queen Victoria's statue outside the Legislature of the Province of Ontario fixes the center of Toronto in her gaze.

an old-fashioned, grimy, strait-laced, and rather dreary Victorian manufacturing city at the edge of what remained of the British Empire.

There were, however, signs that Victoria's gaze was beginning to falter. A recently opened New City Hall, with two sleek curved towers and a Henry Moore sculpture, was locally considered to be Toronto's entry ticket to modernity. In addition, a pair of elegant, black skyscrapers, designed by the modernist architect Ludwig Mies van der Rohe, dominated the skyline and were taller than any office towers then in London. Even more impressive to me, because at the time there were none in Britain, were the expressways leading to Niagara Falls, to Montreal, and north to the lakes and forests on

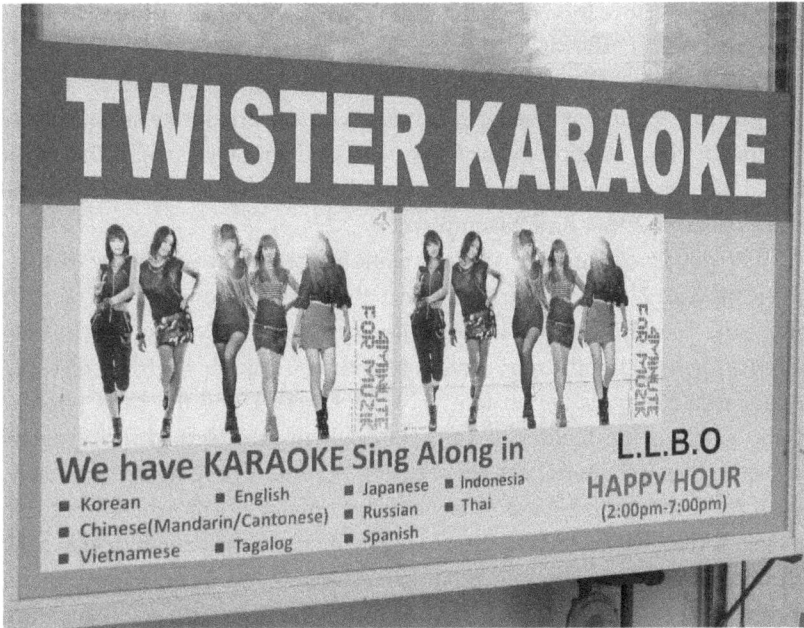

Figure 1.2. Twenty-first-century Toronto. A club in the inner suburb of North York in 2010 offers karaoke in ten languages and a five-hour-long happy hour.

the Canadian Shield. It seemed to take almost no time to escape the city and speed past brand-new suburbs into landscapes of farms and orchards.

Streetcars still rumble along streets lined with old wooden telephone poles, but in almost every other respect Toronto has changed dramatically. Those streets are now lined with patio cafés serving beer and wine, and the city bustles with pedestrians in a way scarcely imaginable in the 1960s. The population overtook Montreal's decades ago. The Mies skyscrapers have been surpassed and surrounded as the skyline has continued to push upward. Sleek condominium towers, some as tall as the office skyscrapers, have replaced factories and warehouses. British influence has waned, and on sidewalks and in shopping malls throughout the whole urban region it is obvious that Toronto is now intensely multicultural and cosmopolitan (Figure 1.2). I didn't know it at the time but I had arrived at the end of the flood of immigrants from the British Isles that had lasted for over a century. Subsequent immigration, at the rate of about eight hundred thousand people a decade, has been from all over the world. Almost half the current population is now foreign born, and almost all that half belongs to what the Canadian Census discreetly refers to as "visible minorities." If, in 1967, Queen Victoria had risen from her tomb to tour the fragments of her empire, she would have found much that was familiar in the still relatively compact, white, Anglo-Saxon, Protestant, and morally upright industrial city. If she were to return now, she would be utterly dumbfounded by the transformations that have taken place.

The details of Toronto's transformations are, of course, locally distinctive, but in a North American context they are also remarkable for their intensity. According to one well-documented website, New York is the only city in the world with more skyscrapers than Toronto. Highway 401, the major expressway, is the busiest in North America, and the city's population density is the highest of any metropolitan area (though Los Angeles sometimes lays claim to both these titles). Toronto's proportion of foreign-born residents is the highest of any city not only in North America but also in the developed world. The continuously built-up metropolitan area now stretches around the western end of Lake Ontario, embracing many old and new urban centers in an urban agglomeration that in 2011 had a population of about 6.1 million, making it by far the largest in Canada and the fifth largest in North America (after New York, Mexico City, Los Angeles, and Chicago, and slightly ahead of Dallas-Fort Worth, Miami, Philadelphia, and San Francisco). More or less in the center of this vast agglomeration, where it butts up against the northern shore of Lake Ontario, is the old city of Toronto that I first encountered in 1967, now much altered and a relatively small part of an extensive polycentric urban region.[2]

The intensity of the changes in Toronto may be remarkable, but over the last half century many cities around the developed world have experienced similar transformations. They, too, have grown dramatically in population and extent, spawned multiple centers, expanded their airports, added skyscrapers and expressways, deindustrialized, designated heritage districts, been invaded by the franchises of multinational corporations, replaced mostly homogeneous populations with more diverse ones, and become globally interconnected. The scale and character of these changes have posed considerable problems for description and interpretation because the shapes of cities and their landscapes and processes are very different from those that prevailed even half a century ago and in many ways are unprecedented. Indeed, the very word "city" has come to seem inadequate. Presciently sensing this, the French philosopher Henri Lefebvre argued in 1970

that "the term 'urban' is preferable to the word 'city,' which seems to designate a clearly defined object," and he suggested that an urban revolution,
somewhat in the manner of the industrial revolution, was under way and
was causing everything, no matter how remote or rural, to become subservient to urban needs and values. In a similar vein, the American planner
John Friedmann has been moved to declare that "the city is dead," by
which he apparently means that the traditional language used for cities as
single, clearly defined objects cannot be usefully applied to urban regions
such as the diffuse concentrations and unlikely juxtapositions of activities
that occur for hundreds of square miles around London, Los Angeles,
Tokyo, and Toronto, even though they have functions and elements that
are unquestionably urban.[3]

Aneurin Bevan, a firebrand Welsh politician much admired in the years
after World War II in the part of South Wales where I grew up, once declared
that "the student of politics must always be on guard against old words, for
the words persist when the reality behind them has changed." This is equally
sound advice, especially given Lefebvre's insight about an urban revolution,
for anyone writing about cities and decentralized urban regions in the early
twenty-first century. What I have found in my explorations of the Toronto
region is that it is not only the word "city" that poses difficulties but also
other familiar terms, such as community, suburb, downtown, neighborhood,
heritage, public space, greenbelt, sprawl, and density. The words seem familiar and obvious but turn out to be almost impossible to define clearly because
the realities behind them are either changing or are understood very differ-
ently by different people. In the case of Toronto these language problems are
compounded by the thorny local fact (discussed in the next chapter) that the
reality behind the name "Toronto" has itself repeatedly changed as political
boundaries have shifted, so it is often not clear just *where* someone is referring
to. Is Toronto the old Victorian city, the municipality as it has been legally
defined since 1998, the built-up region of more than six million people, or
something else? This is not just an academic matter. How Toronto is defined
relates to the way the urban area developed over the last two centuries, apparently determines what is considered good and bad about that development,
constantly informs urban and regional politics, influences planning, and
affects policies concerning Toronto's role on the North American and world
stages.[4]

In this book my aim is relatively straightforward. I want to create a
broad-stroke portrait of Toronto's built-up metropolitan region, one that

brings together many different aspects in order to give a sense of how its urban forms and landscapes have come to be as they are, what their distinctive qualities and values are, and particularly how they have undergone transformations over the last fifty years. This raises the question of how to provide an account of something as large and complex as an urban region, especially when definitions of Toronto are inconsistent and when familiar urban words don't necessarily correspond with the way things really are.

The conventional historical idea is that Toronto began at the place of its first settlement in the 1790s and that it has grown out from this seed to the current limits of the built-up area. This outward-looking perspective works well to explain the city's growth until about 1970 but becomes problematic thereafter as the region began to acquire an increasingly polycentric form. It has nevertheless been enormously influential as a lens through which the entire region has been seen and judged, perhaps for the simple reason that most of those who have had things to say about Toronto live and work in the old central part of the city. This is where the head offices of most of the major Canadian banks are located, as well as the University of Toronto, the headquarters of the Canadian Broadcasting Company, the provincial legislature, theaters, galleries, high-end restaurants, and compact residential neighborhoods of late Victorian houses served by streetcars and subways. Far beyond those neighborhoods, according to Jane Jacobs, who lived in one of them for over thirty years, "the city region of Toronto . . . simply peters out and halts on gently rolling land presenting no change in natural landscape." Before this happens, she saw what she once described as "Toronto's massive post-war suburbs," which are "quite as baffling physically and incoherent socially as their counterparts elsewhere, and fully as ecologically destructive." She could not have conveyed more clearly a centrist, outward-looking perspective of the urban region, one that finds it difficult to come to terms with almost everything new, and in which everything—density, urbanity, walkability, coherence—declines the farther it gets from the desirable parts of Toronto in the old city at its center.[5]

I have lived in older parts of Toronto, on and off, for about twenty of the last forty years. I know and appreciate its walkable streets, subways, and many other amenities. I think that its street patterns and urban forms have considerable potential as models for future urban development. But there are limits to how much it should be used as the standard by which to judge other parts of the region. Apart from anything else, only about 650,000 people in the urban region live in the old, streetcar parts of the city, while most of the other 5,500,000 or so live in newer suburbs (including me, because that is where I have lived, on and off, for the other twenty of the past forty years). In short, most of the inhabitants of the urban region of Toronto do not necessarily share Jane Jacobs's experiences of the old city. Their Toronto is an urban region linked by networks of roads, electronic messages, and social connections—some of them on the other side of the region and some, such as business acquaintances and the homes of grand-parents, on other continents. They live not in baffling suburbs but in tidy subdivisions in specific places with their own histories and names such as Maple, Oakville, Markham, and Pickering. They enjoy the freedom that comes with driving, and they appreciate the modern schools, affordable houses, arterial roads, plazas, generous parks, and diverse and energetic communities of young families. For them there is nothing incoherent about the suburbs. And while the old city of Toronto may be an interesting place to work, or exciting to visit to go to a ballgame, club, or show, it's also dirty, noisy, and congested, with homeless people panhandling or sleeping on the sidewalk, and it's not where most people would want to live.

The fact is that the postwar suburban parts of Toronto have been cre-ated through economic and social processes very different from those that made the old city, and they cannot be reasonably understood by looking out from the center. Nor, conversely, should the old city be approached solely from the edge looking in, even if that is how the majority of the population experiences it. What is needed is a critical approach that some-how incorporates elements of both views. Robert Bruegmann, in his book on urban sprawl in the United States, remarks sarcastically that "many observers have skipped . . . quickly over the painstaking process of analyzing the way urban regions actually work, so that they could get on with the more exalted business of telling everyone how urban regions should work." His primary method for avoiding this he describes simply as "going out and looking around." This may seem naive, but given the centrist biases of much urban research and a dearth of accounts of the newest parts of Toronto, this seems like a reasonable way to begin.[6]

I have always considered landscapes, by which I mean the way places look, including their buildings, streets, and assorted other visible things, as expressions of what a society actually does rather than what people say it is doing. Landscapes are, according to the geographer Peirce Lewis, a "clue to culture," and this means it is important to go out and try to look at every-thing, no matter how mundane or exceptional, how old or new, in an attempt to make sense of what is going on. Urban landscapes are products of huge investments of time, effort, and money, and almost every aspect of them—subdivisions, sidewalks, the width of the roads, parking lots, skyscrapers, shopping malls, utility poles—has been thought about and discussed before being implemented. In other words, they look as they do for good reasons, except perhaps for the ways all the parts have been put together. Landscapes are, however, surfaces that can hide as well as reveal; neat apartment buildings don't expose the poverty within, and expressways tell nothing about lost opportunity costs for public transit. So, in the same way that it is necessary to be aware of the limitations of familiar urban words, it is necessary to be alert to the possibility that landscapes can deceive. I have, therefore, combined going out and looking at Toronto's landscapes with information gleaned from the Canadian Census, planning reports, numerous websites, and various sources that offer possible insights.[7]

I have also drawn particularly on the ideas of two well-known Torontonians—Jane Jacobs and Marshall McLuhan. Neither of them was actually born here, but because this is true for about half the population this is hardly a strong objection. They did both live in Toronto for many decades, and initially I considered it a simple geographical courtesy to draw on the relevant ideas of two popular authorities in their respective fields who knew something of the city and the region because they lived there. In various ways their ideas have informed many aspects of this metropolitan portrait.

Jacobs is best known for her critique of modern city planning and praise of old inner-city neighborhoods such as those in Greenwich Village, which she described in *The Death and Life of Great American Cities*. In 1968 she moved from New York to a neighborhood in the Victorian part of Toronto and quickly became an active participant in the life of the city. She lived there until her death in 2006. Although the extent of her influence in changing the course of development in Toronto is debatable, she is unquestionably regarded as a local urban hero. A Jane Jacobs prize is awarded annually to a citizen who contributes to the city's life. In 2007 a Jane Jacobs Day was created on her birthday in early May, with free, guided tours called "Jane's Walks" through neighborhoods of the city that are based on her claim that to know a place "you've got to get out and walk." These have turned out to be enormously popular not just locally but also globally, and there are now Jane's Walks in about seventy cities around the world.[8]

I admire Jacobs's work, but I am not uncritical of it. In particular, I find her remarks about suburban parts of the Toronto region poorly observed and judgmental, perhaps because she did not drive and did not visit them much. More generally, I agree with Jim Lemon, a historical geographer who lived just a few streets from her, who claimed that she failed to grasp the importance of the idea of newness in North America, picked the wrong target in attacking planners (rather than developers, politicians, and those who sought only profits), and that her emphasis on private freedom ignored its significant environmental and social limitations. However, by almost all indications the qualities of central city life that Jacobs extolled are flourishing in the old part of Toronto and her ideas offer invaluable insights into why that is the case. Furthermore, her arguments that cities and urban regions are the engines of economies are very relevant for explaining the growth of Toronto, though both provincial and federal politicians in Canada seem inclined to ignore them.[9]

Like Jacobs, McLuhan lived near the center of the old city and did not drive. Unlike Jacobs, his primary interest was in media of communication rather than cities, though he commented on city planning, air travel, cars, and many aspects of modern society that are affected by shifts in communications technologies. Originally from the Canadian prairies, he came to Toronto in 1946, where he began to develop the notion that different media have had a profound effect in shaping culture. Perhaps his major insight was that writing (and by extension printing) fixes ideas and generates standardized laws and codes, whereas oral communications promote flexible social practices, and electronic media (he often referred to them as "electric" because the word "electronic" was not then in common use) constitute a return to an oral culture. He was a scholar of literature who did not much like electronic media, but he felt compelled to understand their diverse and profound effects, including the ways cities are made and experienced, although he thought that the depth of this change would not be immediately obvious because "we continue to think in the old fragmented space and time patterns of the pre-electric age."[10]

McLuhan formulated his ideas in the 1960s, long before the age of personal computers, mobile phones, and social media. Nevertheless, his ideas resonate now more than ever in a city that has a skyline dominated by a telecommunications tower and a street named McLuhan Way in his honor. And his ideas echo throughout an urban region that bristles with cell phone towers and satellite dishes and is electronically connected into a network of world cities. With great foresight, McLuhan suggested that margins and boundaries would effectively cease to exist in the electronic gossipy global village and that every city would become a suburb of every other city. In short, his arguments speak directly to Toronto's recent and current transformations.[11]

With Jacobs's and McLuhan's ideas in mind, I have gone out, looked at, and thought about the landscapes of as many parts of the Toronto region as I could. I have walked and cycled where appropriate, though the reality is that neither expressways nor arterial roads are sympathetic to pedestrians. Moreover, the huge scale of Toronto's built-up area means that the only way to explore most of it is by driving, and while it is presumably by driving that most people come to know something of the region, it must be noted that this raises two significant issues. The first has to do with what might be called an urban uncertainty principle: driving broadens the range of experiences at the expense of depth and detail, whereas walking reveals details at the expense of geographical scope. The second problem is one of illustration. Although photos and sketches can offer reasonably accurate ways of representing the experiences of pedestrians, and maps give a sense of the bigger picture, none of these can remotely convey the dynamic sense of driving for miles through unfolding urban regional landscapes, which is how they are actually experienced.

Toronto has been the setting for most of my life and I have come to know a number of its districts from the inside out. I have lived and worked both close to the city core and in the inner suburbs. I have commuted on foot, by bike, in buses, streetcars, and subways, and by driving on arterial roads and expressways. I have shopped in small stores on downtown main streets, in suburban malls, and in discount outlets and big-box discount stores. I currently live in a suburb built in the 1950s that has access to the subway and where I can walk or cycle to shops yet is within what Reyner Banham described in his book on Los Angeles as "handy, traffic-roaring distance" of a freeway and is in a part of the city where aircraft turn over-head to make their final approach into the international airport. The sounds and sights of a restless region in constant motion are as much a part of my everyday life as city streets and buildings. It is, I think, fair to claim that my experience of the Toronto metropolitan region is based nei-ther from the center looking out nor from the outside looking in. Instead I occupy a liminal position somewhere between the two. While this does not make my perspective objective, with my deliberate investigations of urban landscapes it should provide a foundation for a reasonably comprehensive account of the various transformations of Toronto—which have happened in the absence of grand dreams or plans, without an Olympic Games or World's Fair—and have turned it from what fifty years ago was an inward-looking, colonial British, rustbelt city, into one of the largest, densest, most culturally diverse, globally connected, still rapidly growing, sunbelt cities in North America.[12]

Chapter 2

Confused Identities

There's a local urban myth, probably based on a claim by the nineteenth-century Torontonian Henry Scadding, that "Toronto" is the indigenous name of the site where the present city began and that it means "place of meeting" or "gathering place." While this is a great story for the convention business, the consensus now is that Scadding was wrong and the name is actually a corruption of the Iroquois word "Tkaronto," which means "where there are trees standing in water," and that it originally referred to a fishing weir at the northern end of what is now called Lake Simcoe, about a hundred miles north of the current city center. In other words the name was borrowed from somewhere else. What seems to have happened is that seventeenth-century French fur traders, who were collecting beaver skins used to make hats that were then in fashion in Europe, adopted it as the name for the entire lake, and they referred to the canoe and portage route they used as a link to Lake Ontario as the Toronto Carrying Place. In due course a trading post called Fort Toronto was created at the southern end of the portage. One of my family's heirlooms is a copy of Salmon's *Geography*, published in London in 1785, which has a map of North America that shows both Lake Toronto and Toronto Fort located in Iroquois territory on the north side of Lake Ontario (Figure 2.1). It was basically accurate, but information moved slowly in the eighteenth century and in fact the Iroquois had retreated to the south of Lake Ontario a century earlier, and the fort had been burned down in 1759 by the original French owners because they didn't want it to fall into the hands of the English, who had defeated the French in Québec.[1]

Figure 2.1. A detail from Salmon's 1785 map of North America, showing Lake Toronto, Toronto Fort, and the site of what was then the long-abandoned Iroquois village of Tegaogen (now usually written Teiaiagon) in the western part of the present City of Toronto. The international boundary is shown incorrectly on the Canadian side of the Great Falls of Niagara instead of in the middle of the river.

The English arrived in the 1780s. Having lost the American War of Independence, they were anxious to establish a secure foundation for managing trade and settlement in Upper Canada, a territory that included everywhere west of Québec and north of the Great Lakes. The initial administrative capital was at what is now called Niagara-on-the-Lake, where the Niagara River flows into Lake Ontario (on the British side of the river opposite Fort Niagara on Salmon's map), but this was within cannon shot of America, so it was decided that the English should relocate to a site with a protected, defensible harbor on the north shore of the lake to the east of the former Fort Toronto, where there were no permanent settlements. However, a few Mississauga families had moved into this territory after the Iroquois had left, and in 1787 they were persuaded to sell a large part of it to the English for £1,700 and some assorted goods, a deal that was known as the Toronto Purchase. Like many such deals with Native Canadians, this one was flawed. The English thought they had made an outright purchase and the Mississaugas assumed they would keep sacred lands on the spit that formed the harbor and would get hunting and fishing rights in perpetuity, inconsistencies that led to a land claim for much of the area occupied by the current City of Toronto that was not resolved until 2010.[2]

In July 1793 John Graves Simcoe, who had been appointed by the English as lieutenant-governor of Upper Canada, his wife Elizabeth, and a detachment of Queen's Rangers, an army corps he had commanded during the American war, arrived from Niagara to establish the new capital of Upper Canada at Toronto. A flat, sandy area adjacent to the harbor was selected for the town site. Simcoe immediately ordered a survey for a grid of eight small square blocks as the layout for the new settlement, a single act that symbolically established the authority of English colonial civilization over the forest wilderness that covered much of Upper Canada and was the first manifestation of a rectangular survey that has framed almost all subsequent urban development throughout the region. In gathering provisions for his duties as lieutenant-governor, Simcoe had astutely purchased the two-room canvas house that Captain Cook had used on his last, ill-fated expedition across the Pacific, and this was the first dwelling in the new settlement.[3]

Three observations can be made about this founding moment of Toronto. The first is that its creation as a colonial provincial capital shows that globalization in some sense has been part of the city's identity from the outset. The second is that the second-hand tent and the grid survey demonstrated a principle of frugal practicality that has echoed through Toronto to the present day. The third has to do with Jane Jacobs's argument that, contrary to the conventional idea that cities followed the development of productive agriculture and surpluses, in fact cities came first. I have no opinion about whether this was the case in ancient China or Mesopotamia or Central America, but it was unquestionably what happened with Toronto. As had already happened in America west of the Appalachians with the founding of cities such as Pittsburgh and Cincinnati, settlement here began with the town and it took decades for the surrounding forest to be cut down, fields made, crops grown, mills built, and roads constructed to bring grain into town and to connect with other settlements.[4]

The borrowed name of Toronto for the new capital lasted precisely three weeks. When Simcoe received news that several months earlier Frederick,

Duke of York, the second son of King George III (the same Grand Old Duke who marched three thousand men to the top of the hill and down again), had won a military victory in Europe, he promptly renamed the brand-new settlement "York." I can find no record of this putative victory and assume it to have been minor. However, a key part of colonization is to give everywhere in the new territory familiar names and this practice provided Simcoe with all the reason he needed to call almost everything he encountered or created after English places or officials. Consistency with the new name of York ensured that Yorkshire in England was a particularly fruitful source: the two main rivers near York—the Humber and the Don— were named after Yorkshire rivers, and the area east of the town site was called Scarborough because the bluffs along the lakeshore reminded Eliza- beth of cliffs at the Yorkshire town of Scarborough. Lake Toronto was renamed Lake Simcoe in memory of his father; settlements at Barrie and Markham were named respectively after a British admiral and a friend who was archbishop of York in England. The first road out of York, which was carved northward through the forest and is still the spine of the city, was called Yonge Street (pronounced "young") in honor of the English secre- tary of war.

Simcoe suffered from poor health and in 1796 he returned with his family to England. He had founded Toronto/York, established directions for its future growth and for the agricultural settlement of the region, and renamed the local geography. He had also banned slavery, an act that was in due course to make Upper Canada the northern terminus of the Under- ground Railroad for slaves escaping from the American South. In the larger order of things he was probably not an exceptional colonial administrator, but his role as the founder of Toronto is celebrated in the heritage of the city, and a local public holiday in August is called Simcoe Day in his honor.

Over the next four decades York grew very slowly, much more slowly than American frontier towns such as Pittsburgh, which by the 1820s had already begun to develop industries and a sophisticated social and cultural life. York remained a tiny imperial outpost, derisively described by visitors as "muddy little York." In 1834, when the population had reached a little over five thousand, a proposal was made to incorporate the town as a city because it was thought this status would give it a measure of authority appropriate for the capital of Upper Canada. At the same time dissatisfac- tions emerged about the current name, perhaps because nobody much liked being a citizen of muddy York but officially because "York was common to many towns and places" and a capital city needed a name that would "avoid inconvenience and confusion." In a single stroke "York" became "Toronto" again and was incorporated as a city. The name York was not entirely abandoned. It was used in various forms for several townships and counties over the next hundred and fifty years, most of which have now disappeared because of government reorganizations, but it does endure in the names of a major university and of the regional municipality that lies to the north of the City of Toronto.[5]

The Old and the New City of Toronto

Cities are obvious when we are in them, but defining a city is remarkably elusive. Dictionaries offer stunningly unhelpful definitions, suggesting for instance that a city is "a large town." The one precise sense ought to be that of a city as a legally incorporated jurisdiction, such as the one Toronto became in 1834. In Ontario this is actually not useful because any municipality with a population greater than ten thousand can request to be incorporated as a city, and some municipalities that are mostly rural do so, because this is considered to confer status, while others that are manifestly urban and have large populations choose to remain towns because this implies a stronger sense of community. In *The Economy of Cities,* Jane Jacobs takes a different approach and offers a definition of a city as a settlement "that consistently generates its economic growth from its own local economy." However, she also suggests that in economic terms "metropolitan area" is the same as "city," though politically it means a city that has expanded beyond its boundaries. This not only is confusing but also doesn't concur with her more familiar idea that a city, as opposed to baffling planned suburbs, is wherever there are densely built-up, walkable neighborhoods with an ineffable quality she refers to as "organized complexity." Statistics Canada, the agency responsible for the Canadian Census, has recently given up the challenge of resolving all these confusions and even replaced references to "urban areas" with the term "population centres," albeit on the paradoxical grounds that this will "help users in the study of the Canadian urban-rural landscape and its issues."[6]

I adopt one straightforward clarification in this book to offer a way through this bog of definitions. I capitalize City, Region, and similar terms whenever they refer to a legally incorporated political entity, and I use city, region, and so on, without capital letters to refer to geographical areas, such as the built-up urban agglomeration. Even this approach is compromised, because over the last fifty years politicians and political bureaucrats in Ontario have repeatedly reorganized, renamed, and agglomerated political jurisdictions in and around the City of Toronto, purportedly to resolve problems associated with urban growth. Whatever the reason, the consequence is that there are two distinct meanings for the City of Toronto, depending on historical context. "Metropolitan area," which is a common way to describe the built-up area around American cities, is almost never used locally and is best avoided because until quite recently there was a Municipality of Metropolitan Toronto. In addition there are at least five commonly used interpretations of what is called the Toronto region or area. The consequence of all of this is that it is far from obvious what is meant when somebody refers simply to Toronto.

The *old* City of Toronto lasted from 1834 to 1998. At first its rectangular area was only a few blocks larger than the original site of the town of York. As its population grew, adjacent villages and townships were absorbed and by 1912 it had taken on the rough form of an inverted T, spreading along the shore of Lake Ontario with a tail reaching north along Yonge Street. Although there were some small later additions, it stabilized in this rough shape and by 1940 it was fully built up, with a population of about 670,000.

The old City of Toronto was surrounded by five mostly rural townships that with one exception preserved the legacy of Simcoe's naming strategy— they were York, East York, North York, the one Elizabeth had named Scarborough, and Etobicoke (pronounced Etobico), which is derived from a Mississauga Indian word meaning "where the alders grow" (Figure 2.2). After World War II residential and industrial development spread rapidly into these townships, and in 1953, in a proactive move to control regional urban growth, the Province of Ontario linked all six municipalities in a two-tier system of regional government officially called the Municipality of Metropolitan Toronto, almost always referred to as Metro Toronto, which was the first legally constituted metropolitan government in North America. One consequence was that there were now two political jurisdictions named Toronto—Metro and the old City. When I was a resident of the municipality of Scarborough, I could claim with complete legal consistency that I was from Toronto.

In this two-tier arrangement Metro was technically the primary authority because local plans needed Metro approval before they could be

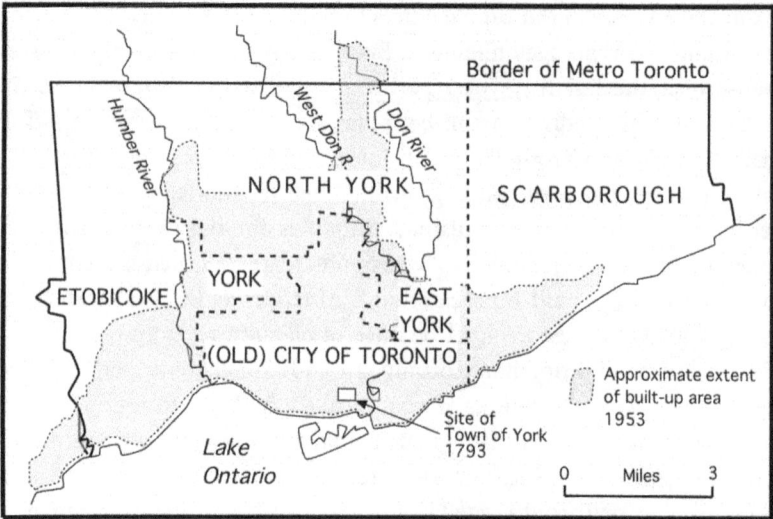

Figure 2.2. The old City of Toronto and Metropolitan Toronto, showing the approximate extent of the built-up area in 1953, the year Metro was created.

implemented; nevertheless at first there was no question that the old City of Toronto was the dominant partner. It had factories, offices, public transit, department stores and theaters, the wealth, the power, and most of the people. The five other municipalities were primarily dormitory communities of relatively low-density suburban housing surrounded by farmland. However, as their populations grew, the townships upgraded their official status, initially to boroughs, then (in all but one case) to cities. By the 1990s the City of North York had a population of more than six hundred thousand, almost equal to the old City of Toronto, and even though it was part of Metro it proudly branded itself as the sixth largest city in Canada.

All of this changed in 1998 when, against almost universal public opposition, the provincial government of Ontario, which has constitutional authority over local municipalities, abolished Metro and amalgamated its six lower municipalities into a single *new* City of Toronto with the same territorial boundaries that Metro had. Local councils and administrative departments were consolidated, internal boundaries erased, and the former municipalities ceased to have separate legal existences. The names of the former suburban municipalities are still popularly used even though they have little formal status, but the fact is that they were less than thirty years old at the time of amalgamation—too young for a deep sense of place to have emerged—and their loss was not deeply felt. Metro, which in its heyday had been a powerful force in shaping the city's development, had generated little sense of attachment and as far as I know nobody mourned its passing.

For the old City of Toronto the situation was very different. There the amalgamation represented an act of place elimination that stripped away power and identity from a city that had existed for one hundred and sixty years, a place that had heritage and historical depth. Margaret Atwood, Michael Ondaatje, and others have written novels about it; it was where the Maple Leafs in the dim mists of the past had won the Stanley Cup (actually 1967) and the Blue Jays had won the World Series (1992 and 1993); it was the Toronto where the International Film Festival had been founded; it was a city of galleries and skyscrapers, theaters and high-end restaurants, public squares, subways and streetcars, and busy main streets filled with pedestrians. From the perspective of most denizens of the old City, the *new* City of Toronto remains an egregious aberration. For them the intensely urban, transit-oriented old City, even though it no longer has a legal municipal identity, continues to be the essential Toronto, the vital heart of the urban region.[7]

It is, however, a small part of that region. In 2001 (the last year it was identified as a separate entity in the Canadian Census) the old City of Toronto had a population of about 675,000, not much changed since 1940. In 2011 the new City of Toronto/former Metro was fully built up with a population of about 2,600,000. This is, however, less than half the population of over 6,100,000 of the continuously built-up area of Toronto, which extends in a series of tentacles and patches around the western end of Lake Ontario and north along Yonge Street almost to Lake Simcoe. This area, which can be regarded as the geographical city or metropolitan area of Toronto, is part of several larger and commonly recognized greater Toronto regions, some of which extend across the border into the United States.

Greater Toronto and the Greater Golden Horseshoe

Toronto as an urban region is experienced as an everyday fact by legions of long-distance commuters, the people who shop at regional malls, delivery truck drivers, and parents of children on minor league hockey teams driving to far-flung ice rinks. The scale of this region may not be immediately obvious for those who live and work in the city center, but much of everyday life downtown, or indeed in any neighborhood or subdivision anywhere within it, is dependent on people and facilities that may be fifty or more miles away: the international airport, back offices processing bank accounts, universities and medical centers in nearby cities, casinos in Niagara Falls and north of Lake Simcoe, carrier hotels, nuclear power stations and sewage treatment plants on the lakeshore, and the distribution centers and intermodal facilities where most food and consumer goods arrive.

In the early 1970s as the built-up area expanded into mostly rural townships and counties surrounding Metro, the Ontario government reorganized them into four regional municipalities—Halton, Peel, York, and Durham. Like Metro, each of these contained several lower-tier cities and towns. In the 1980s these four regional municipalities, together with Metro Toronto, came to be known as the Greater Toronto Area, usually referred to as the GTA, and in 1996 a provincially appointed task force recommended that it should be constituted as another level of regional government, a sort of political region of Regions. This recommendation was firmly dismissed by the same provincial government that was to impose amalgamation on Toronto. Nonetheless, and in spite of the fact that the GTA has no formal political status, it seems to accord well with most people's sense of the geography of the region, and it continues to be widely referred to in academic papers and planning reports, by businesses and institutions, in radio and TV new programs, and on websites; one of the major local newspapers, the *Toronto Star*, devotes a daily section to it.[8]

Metropolitan areas in the Canadian Census are defined much as they are in the United States in terms of commuting patterns and other social and economic linkages to a central core area. This is probably how most people understand the GTA, but for obscure historical and political reasons, the City of Oshawa in the eastern half of Durham Region is regarded as a separate metropolitan area in the Canadian Census. This means that the GTA does not correspond to the Toronto Census Metropolitan Area (CMA), which is also often used in academic and other reports because of its demographic convenience but has about five hundred thousand fewer people than the GTA. As if this did not make things sufficiently confusing, the built-up area of Toronto and Hamilton, at the western end of Lake Ontario, began to merge about fifty years ago, and since then transportation planning has been based on what is now called the Greater Toronto and Hamilton Area (GTHA).[9]

Superimposed on all of these, and corresponding to none of the political boundaries, is the Greater Toronto Bioregion, an idea that came from a Federal Royal Commission (the Queen remains the nominal head of state in Canada) set up in 1988 to report on the environmental remediation of federal lands on the waterfront of the old City of Toronto. This commission was headed by David Crombie, a former mayor of the old City who had a strong environmental track record, and it adopted an ecosystem perspective that extended its scope to include the interlocking urban and ecological systems defined by the watersheds of rivers flowing through Toronto into Lake Ontario. These watersheds compose the Toronto bioregion, which is bounded by the limestone ridge of the Niagara Escarpment to the west and by the broad, hummocky band of the Oak Ridges Moraine to the north (Figure 2.3). Although there has not been a lot of subsequent discussion specifically about the Toronto bioregion, it clearly influenced the designation of the Escarpment and the Moraine as the key components of a greenbelt that will confine the future built-up area of Toronto.[10]

The greenbelt is associated with regional plans implemented by the provincial government since 2005 that are intended to direct future urban growth in an extensive area of south-central Ontario that includes Toronto, no matter how it is defined, and has been christened the Greater Golden Horseshoe. The Golden Horseshoe name has been used informally for sixty years to describe the Hamilton and Toronto conurbation around the western end of Lake Ontario. The Greater Golden Horseshoe is a considerable extension of this that stretches well over a hundred miles from beyond the General Motors automobile manufacturing city of Oshawa in the east; to Waterloo, where the Blackberry phone was conceived, in the west; and from Niagara Falls in the south to Lake Huron in the north (Figure 2.4). It includes at least twenty-five distinct urban centers linked by flows of goods, energy, information, and people, and it has redefined the Toronto urban region as an extensive polycentric network of urban centers.[11]

The Greater Golden Horseshoe has yet to enter regional awareness in the way that the GTA has done. However, the fact is that it corresponds closely with the area served by the GO Transit regional train and bus system that focuses on Toronto (GO stands for Government of Ontario), which provides rail services to Barrie, Waterloo, and in the summer to Niagara Falls, and bus services to Peterborough and Cambridge, and to that extent

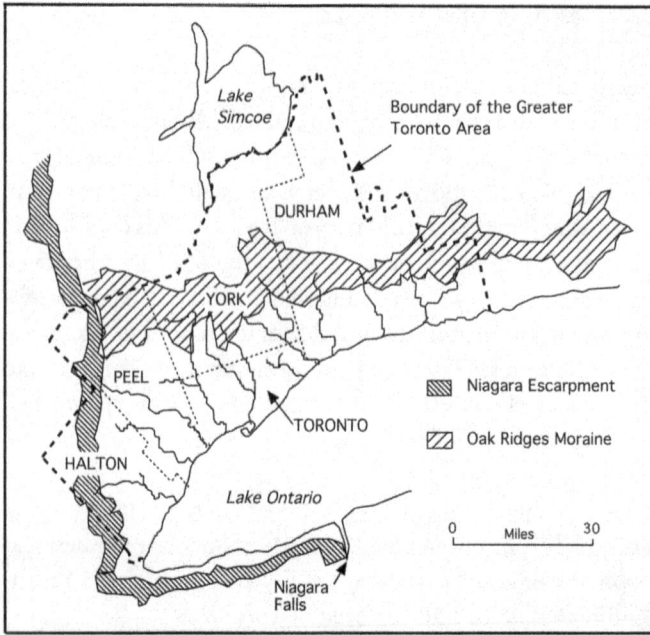

Figure 2.3. The Greater Toronto Bioregion is the area enclosed by and including the Niagara Escarpment and the Oak Ridges Moraine, two landform features that cut across the regional municipalities of Durham, York, Peel, and Halton and are where rivers that flow into Lake Ontario have their headwaters.

it has functional coherence. Furthermore, the Greater Golden Horseshoe is the province's preferred name for the extensive urban region around Toronto, and since the province has authority over municipalities and regional planning in Ontario the name is likely to endure.

Across the Border

As you leave Toronto's Pearson International Airport the first directional sign to a place rather than to an expressway is to Algonquin Park, a huge provincial park located 160 miles north on the Canadian Shield. Presumably this otherwise inexplicable bit of signage is for the benefit of international tourists whose intention is to bypass Toronto, whether it might be the City, the built-up area, or the Greater Golden Horseshoe, and head

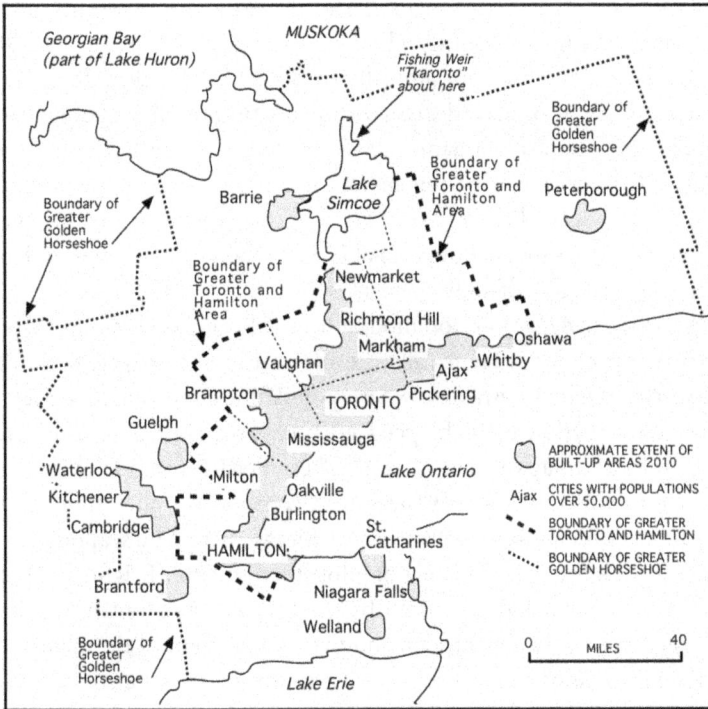

Figure 2.4. The Greater Golden Horseshoe. This map shows the Greater Toronto and Hamilton Area, built-up areas, and places with populations of more than fifty thousand.

directly to the closest bit of Canadian wilderness. In this they are only doing what thousands of Torontonians do almost every weekend in the summer as they commute back and forth to their cottages on the lakes of Muskoka, which is not considered part of the Greater Golden Horseshoe even though it has very close functional and emotional connections with the cities in it. While regional boundaries are useful for political and planning purposes, in most other respects they are permeable.

At its southern edge the Greater Golden Horseshoe stops at the U.S. border, which is hardly surprising for a Province of Ontario plan but is arbitrary from a functional perspective. The Regional Institute at the State University of New York at Buffalo has studied the permeability of the border by investigating such things as Canadian attendance at Buffalo Bills football games (about fifteen thousand), cars with Ontario license plates in the parking lot at Buffalo-Niagara International Airport (30 percent), and American memberships at country clubs in southern Ontario (up to 90 percent). In the other direction, almost half of the schoolteachers in the Niagara area of Ontario have degrees from institutions in western New York, the Bills play occasional games in Toronto, and the PBS channel in Buffalo gives Toronto equal billing in on-air announcements and fundraising campaigns. For these reasons the Regional Institute regards the Greater Golden Horseshoe as a binational U.S./Canadian urban region that includes Rochester and Buffalo.[12]

Even this extensive region is too modest for the Regional Planning Association, which promotes what it calls the megacities and megaregions of North America, in part to establish where populations and linkages might warrant the construction of high-speed rail networks similar to those in Europe, China, and Japan. The Great Lakes megaregion includes the Greater Golden Horseshoe as its easternmost component, plus the rest of southern Ontario, Pittsburgh, Detroit, and Chicago, with Minneapolis as a western outlier (Figure 2.5). This is not altogether fanciful. It is supported by indicators such as truck movements, Internet traffic, the number of daily flights between Toronto and Chicago, and the management of the environment and water quality of the Great Lakes. From the perspective of economic development, even this is insufficient. For instance, the Greater Toronto Marketing Association stresses the proximity of Toronto not only to Chicago but also to New York and the Northeast megaregion, and it claims that a population and potential market of over 135 million lies within one day's drive or a one-hour flight.[13]

Marshall McLuhan had already regarded this sort of spatial thinking as obsolete in the 1960s. Electronic communications, he wrote, "abolish the spatial dimension rather than enlarge it"; they involve an instantaneous implosion and interfusion of space rather than expansion from a center, an implosion in which margins and boundaries cease to matter. McLuhan may have overstated the abolition of space and borders, which obviously are still important when you drive from Toronto to Buffalo, but the idea that electronic communications have fundamentally changed the relationships between cities by speeding up the globalization of economic activities is now widely accepted. This is the basis for the notion of a network of "world cities," which act as the control centers of the global economy; this idea was formulated by the planner John Friedmann (before he claimed that cities are dead) and has now been widely substantiated. Since 2000 the

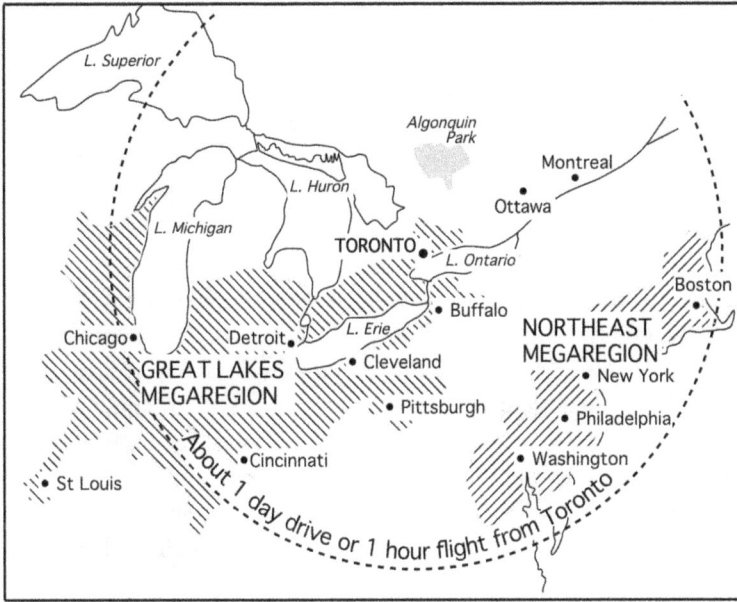

Figure 2.5. Toronto in the Great Lakes Megaregion. Variations of the one-day drive or one-hour flight circle are used by several economic development departments in the Toronto region to show the potential market within relatively easy reach. Source: Megaregions are based on maps from the Regional Planning Association at http://www.america2050.org/images/2050_Map_Megaregions2008_150.png.

Globalization and World Cities research group based in Britain has made four surveys to measure the intensity of linkages between world cities, which are ranked as Alpha, Beta, and Gamma. New York and London have always come out clearly on top as Alpha + + cities; Toronto has consistently been classified as an Alpha city and has never ranked lower than fifteenth out of more than three hundred cities analyzed, though it's not clear whether Toronto means the financial district, the new City, or some version of the urban region. Whatever the case, the evidence is that Toronto is actively engaged at a consistently high level in the global economy, and in that sense its region, like those of all world cities, reaches around the globe.[14]

The definition of an urban region of Toronto for the purpose of providing a metropolitan portrait is made unusually difficult by all these frequent changes and alternative interpretations. As far as I can tell, the name

"Toronto" in everyday speech, in newspaper articles, and on radio and TV usually has one of three different meanings: it can be the part of the city built before 1940, the new City, or the GTA, and you have to guess which one applies by the context. In planning and other official reports written before 1998 the City of Toronto meant the old City; since then it means the new City. In those same reports the Toronto region could be the Greater Toronto Area, the GTHA, or the CMA, and you have to read the fine print to be certain which one is correct. In this portrait of Toronto I am mostly interested in the urban forms, landscapes, and issues of the city region that reaches from Oshawa to Hamilton, and which includes the continuously built-up area of the new City of Toronto (with a 2011 population of 2.6 million) and the outer suburbs in Halton, Peel, York, Durham, and parts of Hamilton (2011 population, 3.5 million). The closest region to this that is defined by political boundaries is the Greater Toronto and Hamilton Area (2011 population, just under 6.6 million). In the background, especially for economic and planning purposes, is the Greater Golden Horseshoe (2011 population, 9.2 million), though its borders, like all regional borders, have to be considered as porous membranes through which ideas, people, and goods from across North America and around the world continually flow.

Chapter 3

Shaping the Old City

When Jane Jacobs's book *The Economy of Cities* was published in 1970 she had recently moved to Toronto and was living in a late Victorian neighborhood of streets lined with substantial brick and stone houses within easy walking distance of a busy commercial main street of small stores. In her book she argued that urban growth comes as cities replace imported goods by producing them locally, and when this happens streets and buildings like the ones where she then lived often have to be added in a rush to accommodate all the people who want to participate in the sudden economic prosperity. This offers a plausible explanation for Toronto's sudden expansion as an industrial city in the second half of the late nineteenth century but it doesn't explain why the streets are straight, the main streets in the old City are lined with shops packed closely together, and the houses are squeezed onto narrow, deep lots. In other words, it doesn't explain the shapes or urban forms of the older parts of Toronto. And it's not possible to understand the identity and current vitality of old Toronto without knowing something about how those urban forms came about.[1]

In 1970 Marshall McLuhan was living a mile north of Jacobs in an early twentieth-century Arts and Crafts house in a small development that had originally been intended as an idiosyncratic artists' colony quite distinct from the rest of Toronto. McLuhan is not normally regarded as an authority on cities, but he did have an ability to assimilate ideas from countless different sources and one he may have derived from contemporary writing in urban history was that the prevailing means of communication, which includes systems of transportation, directly influences what he called "urban structure" and offers an explanation for the shapes and patterns of city streets. From this perspective, the width of streets, whether they are straight or curved, whether building lots are shallow or deep, and whether buildings are low-rise or high-rise or made of brick, wood, stone, or metal and glass are matters always related in some way to the systems of communication and transportation that dominated at the time they were made. Buildings and the streetscapes they create are less resilient than street patterns, but it is not uncommon for them to stay virtually unchanged for many decades. In the old City of Toronto the layout of most of the streets dates from the grid survey that was made shortly after its founding two centuries ago, at a time when people traveled by foot, horse, canoe, or sailing ship. However, few buildings from that time remain and most of the existing streetscapes of the old City, both residential and commercial, were created between about 1870 and 1940, an era when streetcars were the standard means of transportation within the city.[2]

Rectangularity and a Little, Ill-built Town

In a broad continental context the founding of the Town of York in 1793 can be understood as the creation of one of what the urban historian Richard Wade refers to as "spearheads of the frontier . . . [towns] planted far in advance of the line of settlement." The grand idea of the frontier pushing relentlessly westward has never had much currency in Canada, and while one of York's roles was indeed to serve as the base for the settlement of the hundreds of square miles of forest that lay to the north, this was regarded as necessary not so much to push out the frontier as because of a lingering threat of a counterclaim to the territory by America. This threat meant that settlement needed to be achieved quickly and efficiently. The center of the British Empire was thousands of miles away in London, and in the days of sailing ships communications with York were infrequent, occurring perhaps no more than once a year. From our perspective of instant messages this seems scarcely conceivable, yet at the time it did not present a serious problem because the policies and practices for settlement had been clearly established in writing and these made possible a thoroughly businesslike British colonization of Upper Canada and the Toronto region. The process began with government agents making treaties of purchase with the indigenous peoples, who were fortunately peaceful and open to such arrangements; no private purchases were permitted. As soon as treaties had been signed, government surveyors moved in to make grid surveys and establish property boundaries that would ensure orderly settlement. These surveys, probably more than any other factor, are the foundation of the urban forms and landscapes of Toronto, not only the old City but also the entire region.[3]

Grid patterns have a history as long as that of cities themselves. McLuhan suggested that they are an expression of the linear rationality associated with written communications, not just because they both involve straight lines but also in the more subtle sense that writing, and especially print, makes possible accurate recordkeeping and all the other administrative procedures needed to impose neat order and demonstrate authority. The urban historian Lewis Mumford had an altogether more prosaic explanation. He maintained that the grid provided neat, abstract blocks for buying and selling, which are simplicity itself, so that a clerk without the slightest training could "plan" a metropolis with standard lots, standard blocks, and standard street widths. The gist is that when something has to be done in a hurry and without attention to local details and variations, nothing is as efficient as straight lines coupled with right angles. And this was how the old City of Toronto and its surrounding land was laid out.[4]

In 1793 the territory around the site of York had already been purchased, at least to the satisfaction of the colonizers, so one of the earliest orders of business after Simcoe arrived was to establish a base line for the survey of the region. This was made roughly parallel to the shore of Lake Ontario, along what was originally called Lot Street and is now Queen Street (royal designations are standard for major streets in British colonial towns). The alignment for Yonge Street, the road that would lead through the forest to Lake Huron and would serve as a major settlement route, was neatly perpendicular to the base line. With one deviation made because an easier route northward was determined shortly after the survey began, and which causes the entire survey north of Toronto to tilt eastward, the straight alignment was faithfully followed. Yonge Street originally ran through dense forest, and it was many years before it was much more than a rough trail, but it eventually became a main street and arterial road, and it is still the major east-west dividing line in the city in the sense that everywhere can be described as being either east or west of Yonge.[5]

The survey was systematically extended with various rectangles, large and small, that, like geographical fractals, have directed the patterns of settlement and urban development at every scale from concession blocks down to individual lots and the footprints of buildings (Figure 3.1). The

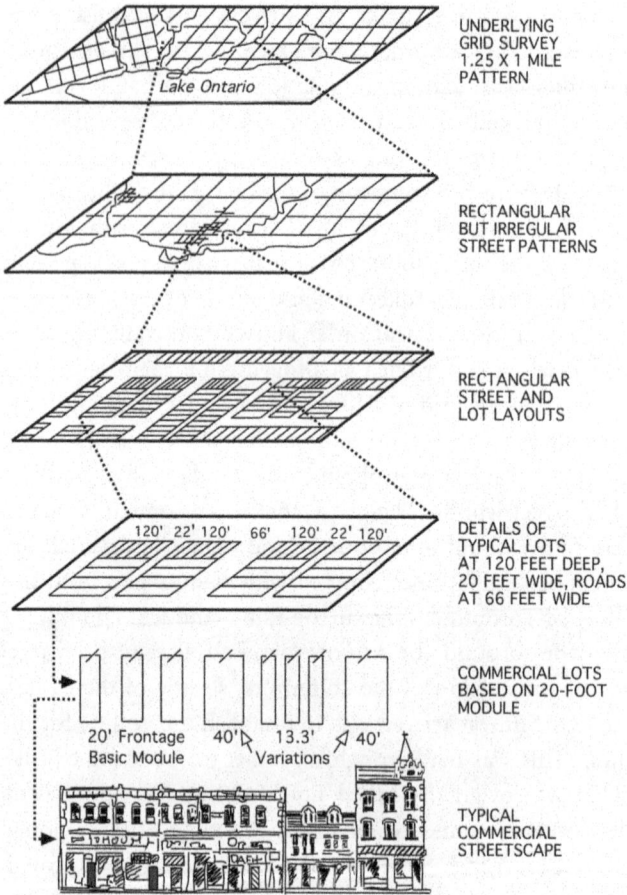

Figure 3.1. The grid survey and its impact on the details of Toronto's nineteenth-century urban form.

lines of the survey paid no attention to topography, running with uniform blithe disregard through marshes, across ravines, over steep hills, and straight into lakes. The basic measuring device was a chain of sixty-six feet, and this was used as the standard width for roads and streets. There were eighty chains to a mile, and the survey divided the land into concession blocks that were usually one hundred chains, or 1.25 miles, long and eighty chains wide that could be subdivided into lots, usually fifty chains by twenty chains or one hundred acres, which was judged to be sufficient for the size of a productive farm. Allowances for concession and side roads were provided around each concession block. In areas adjacent to the tiny settlement at York, sections of land were given to civil servants and others, in part to attract them to move to the isolated new capital of Upper Canada, and the dimensions of the blocks were smaller and less consistent. When those landowners subdivided the property they had been granted they didn't necessarily coordinate street alignments, so in some parts of old Toronto residential streets run mostly north-south, in others they run east-west, and streets don't always line up across the original concession roads. A few roads did follow trails or Indian paths laid out before the survey was completed, but otherwise there were scarcely any deviations from the fundamental principle of straightness until wealthy Torontonians started laying out picturesque subdivisions for themselves around the turn of the twentieth century. The urban landscapes of the Toronto region are above all rectangular: obtuse and acute angles are causes for confusion, and triangular buildings are regarded as oddities.

The natural environment of Toronto now seems quite tame—there are no mountains, wide rivers, deserts, and little likelihood of hurricanes or major earthquakes—but for the earliest settlers the forest posed a constant challenge to survival. As a condition of the land grant, each settler along Yonge Street had twelve months to clear five acres of trees, build a log cabin, and open up the section of the road in front of his property, all by hand. There were clouds of black flies and mosquitoes to contend with in spring, and sufficient food had to be grown in the short summers to last through the long, cold winters. Lives were spent getting nature to submit to human will in order to survive. Travel on uneven dirt roads was difficult, especially during the spring thaw when they were often impassable with mud. In the Town of York it took decades of hard work to push back the forest and to make streets, and unlike towns on the American urban frontier, which self-consciously based their architecture and plans on Philadelphia and New York, there were no national urban models to admire and follow. So it is hardly surprising that nobody seems to have been much concerned with urban design or planning or what the town looked like. Mary O'Brien visited in 1828 and in language that anticipated present-day accounts of sprawl she wrote that "the town of York . . . seems to be all suburb. The streets are laid out parallel and at right angles to each other, and are formed by low scattered houses. . . . The town is so scattered that I hardly know where the centre may be."[6]

Throughout most of the nineteenth century, when the main means of transportation in the city were walking or horse-drawn vehicles, even the best roads were unpaved and not easily traveled. It made obvious sense to keep everything compact, and the scattered dwellings were gradually replaced by rows of houses on residential lots that were mostly twenty or twenty-five feet wide and about one hundred and twenty feet deep. Along commercial streets, store frontages were based on a standard width of twenty feet, with larger stores taking double frontages. Many of these residential and commercial streetscapes remain, their basic forms scarcely changed since they were built in the last thirty years of the nineteenth century. They are the defining landscapes in the identity of old Toronto. In the former farmland beyond the borders of the old City, which were not subdivided until after about 1950, the only grid was that of the large-scale geometry formed by the grid of concession and side roads, and these have been widened and turned into a megagrid of arterial roads that is a defining characteristic of the newer urban forms and landscapes of the region.

In 1838, a decade after Mary O'Brien had visited the scattered little Town of York, another and perhaps more discerning visitor, Anna Jameson, who had traveled widely in Europe and was the estranged wife of the chief justice of Upper Canada, described Toronto, as it had by then been renamed, as "a little ill-built town on low land, at the bottom of frozen bay, with one very ugly church . . . like a fourth or fifth rate provincial town, with the pretensions of a capital city." In his commentary on the political situation in Upper Canada published in 1841, the American Donald McLeod was even more uncompromising in his criticisms. He wrote that Toronto is "a foul, loathsome, disgusting capital abounding in filthy lanes and alleys, muddy and unpaved streets, and as a whole presents a dreary and disagreeable aspect, both from its low situation and contemptible appearance of the buildings."[7]

Apparently, there then was a sudden turnaround. In 1842, just one year after McLeod's account was published, Charles Dickens spent two days in Toronto on his North American tour. While he disapproved of what he called the "rabid Toryism" of the colonial oligarchy, he found that "the town itself is full of life and motion, bustle, business and improvement. The streets are well paved and lighted with gas; the houses are large and good; the shops excellent." It's hard to know now whether Dickens or McLeod was the more accurate observer because, except for the patterns of streets and lots, there is very little left in Toronto of anything from before

1850—just a few isolated buildings. However, Dickens's positive impression may have had to do with the fact that in the intervening year gas lighting and some street paving had been installed, the first clear indications that Toronto was beginning to emerge from being a colonial backwater into an important center of commerce and industry in eastern North America and on the Great Lakes.[8]

Unplanned Growth

"It is . . . common," Jane Jacobs wrote in *The Economy of Cities*, "for small settlements that are selected arbitrarily as capitals to develop no other economic reasons for being. . . . Many provincial or state capitals are thoroughly inert towns or stagnated little cities." By all accounts, for the first fifty years of its history Toronto was a small, inert, stagnant little place. In the second half of the nineteenth century it grew into a major industrial city, in Canada second only to Montreal. There were no discoveries of natural resources to explain this, and in industrial terms Toronto's location is not exceptional, so the reason for the change must have been the one Jacobs proposed as a general explanation for urban growth—it came from within as local businesses began to find ways to produce goods that had previously been imported. In Toronto's case perhaps the previous isolation had also created a do-it-yourself habit of self-sufficiency, or it may have had something to do with a rapid influx of immigrants in the 1840s, many of them environmental refugees from the Irish potato famine. Whatever the reason, Toronto, which had struggled for years even to pave its few roads, suddenly began to adopt industrial innovations. Railways were chief among these, of course, but electronic communications came first.[9]

Samuel Morse demonstrated the practicality of the telegraph in 1844, with a line between Baltimore and Washington. Two years later the first telegraph company in Canada was formed in Toronto, and by early 1847 a line to Buffalo had been completed that linked into the network that would soon connect all the cities on the American eastern seaboard and then across the Atlantic. The telegraph was the first component in a global communications network, and the very first international agency was the International Telegraph Union, which formed in 1865 and established Morse code as the standard form of communication. The most obvious immediate effects of the telegraph were poles strung with wires running between cities

and festooning city streets. Its longer-term effects were more subtle. Mc-
Luhan argues that it meant that, for the first time, messages could be sent
faster than a physical messenger could deliver them. Apart from anything
else, this radically changed the ways news was reported. It led, for example,
to the first compelling descriptions of the blunders and horrors of war by
newspaper correspondents. It was also, he suggests, a medium that lent
powerful voices, such as that of Harriet Beecher Stowe, to the weak and
suffering, which created a "social hormone" that initiated changes in social
relationships that continue to this day. In the short term, however, the
telegraph was subordinated to railways, where it was quickly adopted as a
way to improve scheduling and signaling. As it turned out, railways and
streetcars, not the telegraph, would establish the shape and streetscapes of
the old City of Toronto.[10]

An indication of Toronto's growing industrial energy and import
replacement was the construction in 1853 of the first steam railway engine
to be built in Canada, proudly if unimaginatively named "the Toronto." A
railway line to Lake Simcoe had been completed the previous year, and this
was soon extended to Lake Huron, shortening to a few hours a trip that
had previously taken days along bumpy, rutted Yonge Street and creating
effective trade routes to settlements around the Great Lakes and eventually
in the Prairies. A second line was soon completed to Niagara Falls, where a
suspension bridge across the gorge, designed by John Roebling almost as a
prototype for his subsequent Brooklyn Bridge, was opened for trains in
1855. Since its founding Toronto had turned away from the United States
because of the perceived threat of republicanism, something that had been
made very real when American forces had sacked the tiny Town of York
during the War of 1812. The fact that the first telegraph line and the second
railway line out of Toronto both crossed into New York State constituted a
significant geographical reorientation away from goods shipped through
Montreal, and this was a clear manifestation that local attitudes toward
America had changed away from the former mistrust of republicanism to a
sense of shared economic destiny.[11]

Toronto soon became the center of a network of railway lines branching
across southern Ontario. Within a few years sugar and soy mills, grain
elevators, meatpacking plants, a multitude of small manufactories, and the
factory for Massey-Harris, which was one of the major producers of farm
equipment in the world, had been built on sites adjacent to railway lines.
Toronto prospered. The only other city in the region that grew much in the

last half of the nineteenth century was Hamilton, where the maintenance yards for the Great Western Railway were located, and growth there was a fraction of that in Toronto.

Economic growth led to rapid urban growth. This was facilitated by the introduction of horse-drawn omnibuses and streetcars. Previously everyone in the city had either walked to work or worked where they lived, but, as McLuhan notes, with the coming of streetcars in the 1850s and 1860s "towns developed housing that was no longer within sight of shop or factory." Home, shop, and workplace began to separate into distinct areas. Commercial and retail uses began to develop in continuous lines along the routes followed by streetcars because these carried potential customers who could easily get on and off a slow-moving, horse-drawn vehicle anywhere. The first shops were in converted houses, and the gables of some these can still be seen sticking up above and behind newer storefronts in the older parts of the city, but from the 1870s specialized two- and three-story commercial brick blocks were built, with apartments above and stores with frontages of twenty or forty feet each at street level. Many of these blocks remain, their forms essentially unchanged, and they remain critical to the vibrant main streets of the old City because they make possible a compact accommodation of a wide variety of small stores and restaurants. In residential streets rows of detached brick houses were built, mostly two and a half stories high, on narrow, deep lots, and in whatever international architectural style was in fashion at the time (Figure 3.2). In the 1880s a local variant of gothic revival known as bay and gable became especially popular. Many neighborhoods built in this distinctive Toronto style still stand in the old parts of the city, most of them gentrified but essentially unchanged on the outside, though the originally barren streets are now lined with avenues of mature maples and other trees.[12]

As commercial main streets and residential areas were extended, the downtown core of the city began to take shape. Two new banks and the stock exchange were established in the city center in the 1850s and 1860s, a form of import replacement that significantly reduced financial dependency on Montreal. The telegraph made it possible for administrative functions to separate from factories, and these relocated to office buildings that were close to the banks. Businessmen's clubs, an opera house, and theaters soon followed. Eaton's three-story department store opened in 1883 at the corner of Queen and Yonge, with state-of-the-art plate-glass display windows and electric lights. By 1885 the core of downtown Toronto had

Figure 3.2. Old City of Toronto streetscapes created in the 1880s and 1890s. Brick, bay and gable, and neo-gothic houses (top) are locally distinctive architectural forms. Queen Street West in Parkdale (bottom) is an example of a commercial main street created along a streetcar line in the 1880s that has scarcely changed since then.

effectively been established, and in spite of the fact that many of the original buildings have vanished as a result of fire or redevelopment, the narrow streets in and around the financial district still retain some of their late nineteenth-century character.

The growth and success of business was followed by growth in government. This was manifest in the construction of a new building for the provincial legislature in 1893 (outside which the statue of Queen Victoria, mentioned in Chapter 1, ruminates). This massive Romanesque structure was built in the middle of a great circular public open space called Queen's Park that is the only major deviation from the grid in the central city, and it terminates the view up a wide avenue, twice the width of other streets. Its façade has scarcely changed since it was built. Like many city and town halls in Ontario, it faces south toward the United States. Apparently not to be outdone, in 1899 the old City of Toronto built itself a scarcely less impressive, southward-facing Romanesque city hall with a splendid clock tower. In spite of a threat of demolition, this, too, has survived essentially unchanged.[13]

Industrial prosperity and urban growth came with costs as well as benefits. Near the heart of the city the first railway lines were put in along the lakefront, presumably because this was cheap and relatively easy. They effectively cut the city off from the lake, which had been critical in the choice of Toronto's location and hitherto essential for transportation. This separation of lake and city is a problem that rankles to this day, though streets now cross beneath the railway lines in ugly tunnels. To the east and west of downtown the railways and their adjacent strips of factories were superimposed at an angle across the grid of streets, creating a band of awkward intersections and triangular lots where many factory workers lived. Conditions in Toronto were never as bad as the slums of Manchester described by Friedrich Engels and the tenements of New York photographed by Jacob Riis, but much of the workers' housing was in cheap speculative developments, shoddy and grim, with poor water supplies and poorer sanitation. The factories have now closed and been demolished or renovated into lofts or high-tech facilities, but maps of low-income and disadvantaged areas in the City of Toronto still show a U-shaped band of deprivation that parallels railway lines constructed in the 1850s.

In the excitement of economic growth there was scant regard for natural environments. Creeks were buried in culverts or their valleys filled in and built over in order to cram in more houses and commercial blocks; sewage and waste from factories and houses was simply dumped into rivers and the lake and by 1870 was said to have accumulated in the harbor to a depth of two feet for at least three hundred feet out from the shore; fish from the lake, part of the staple diet of Torontonians earlier in the century, all but disappeared and the last salmon in the polluted Don River was caught in the 1870s. Almost all this pollution has now been cleaned up, though contaminants linger in the soil and the harbor. At the time all these seem to have been regarded more as signs of progress than as problems. The geographers Donald Kerr and Jacob Spelt claimed in their 1965 book *The Changing Face of Toronto* that in the industrial, late Victorian city there was an all-consuming commitment to economic growth coupled with deep indifference to planning and community services: "The City Fathers viewed all disbursements of public money as expenditures, as lost capital, and never as investments that might, in due time, yield returns." One indication of this was a reluctance to dedicate land to parks or public spaces. Apart from Queen's Park, the circle in which the provincial legislature building stands, the only substantial parks in the old City are on land that was given as bequests with the requirement that they not be built over, and the parks are embedded in the grid rather than as elements of an imaginative city plan. There are no grand, Olmsted-style parks here.[14]

In the context of the laissez-faire capitalism and arch utilitarianism that stood behind the making of late nineteenth-century Toronto, there were nevertheless two very significant local inventions whose effects were to echo globally through the following century. Sandford Fleming, the founder of the Royal Canadian Institute in Toronto (the oldest scientific society in Canada) and the surveyor and chief engineer for the Northern Railway, was the prime mover in creating standardized, international time zones based on the Greenwich meridian. Previously, every town in North America and Europe ran on its own time, probably set by the chimes of a clock such as the one on the Toronto city hall, which posed serious problems for railways in terms of missed connections and potential collisions. By 1929 international time zones, which are fundamental to modern economic globalization, had been accepted by all major nations. And in 1876 the commercial value of telephones was demonstrated by Alexander Graham Bell, who taught in Boston but lived with his family at Brantford near the western edge of what is now the Greater Golden Horseshoe, from where he made the first long-distance telephone call to the telegraph office in the small town of Paris, about seven miles to the west.[15]

It took a century before the urban impact of Bell's and Fleming's inventions, in concert with other forms of electronic communication, began to be revealed in the emergence of global city networks and polycentric city regions. In contrast, the impacts of railways and streetcars on late Victorian Toronto were clear and immediate. The railways made it possible for Toronto to become a prosperous industrial city even as they undermined its connection with Lake Ontario, and streetcars had created the pattern of linear retail streets and dense residential districts that is now locally regarded as the consummate model for good urban life. It is important to remember that these much-admired neighborhoods of the old City were the consequence of laissez-faire, speculative development that had filled in creeks and polluted the rivers and harbor in ways now scarcely imaginable. Writing in the 1960s, before Jane Jacobs's critique of modernist planning and her notions of organized complexity had effectively turned urban thinking on its head, Kerr and Spelt described those old neighborhoods as demonstrating "an appalling lack of governmental planning" that made no attempt to control land uses and lacked any vision of what Toronto might be like in the future.[16]

Streetcar Suburbs

In the 1890s Toronto's streetcars were electrified. This allowed them to travel farther and faster than their horse-drawn predecessors, and lines were soon extended several miles to the city limits. Commercial activity soon followed along the main streets where the streetcar lines ran. As the lines pushed outward, speculative residential suburbs were built, most of them using standard designs for houses that were smaller and less ornate than their bay and gable predecessors (Figure 3.3). The densities were still high, because this was before the days of widespread car ownership and the houses had no driveways or garages, although back laneways, which have recently been readopted as an element of new urbanist developments, did provide service access for delivering coal for furnaces.

At the ends of several of the electric streetcar lines were what have been called "unplanned suburbs." In the days before building codes and planning regulations, self-building was the least expensive way for families to obtain homes. Some bought relatively remote but inexpensive lots, then used savings from weekly wages to buy building materials with which they

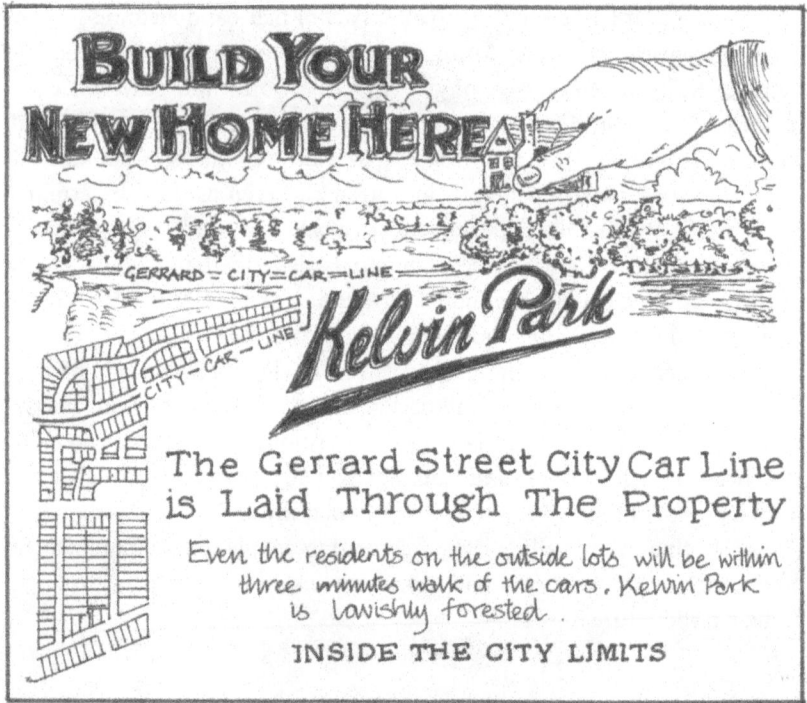

Figure 3.3. A 1912 advertisement for a streetcar suburb just inside Toronto's eastern city limits. The house in the hand is actually too grand for a typical streetcar house, many of which were one-and-a-half stories and semidetached. Source: Redrawn from the *Toronto Telegram*, October 25, 1912. I have abbreviated the original text, which verbosely extolled views of the lake and other amenities.

could slowly construct their own houses in their spare time. These un-planned suburbs were at first treeless shantytowns and though their streets followed the grid the houses had idiosyncratic and humble designs, with irregular setbacks and orientations. They are now incorporated into the fabric of the city and not easily noticed, but it is possible that as many as thirteen thousand self-built houses were constructed in Toronto between 1900 and 1914. At the other end of the economic spectrum and at about the same time, several self-consciously planned suburbs were laid out in a sort of picturesque grand manner with curving streets, large lots, and huge houses. Although these residences of the wealthy were contemporary with streetcar suburbs, they had little to do with streetcars and it is difficult to imagine their owners riding in anything except carriages, horse-drawn or horseless. They are conspicuously affluent, with stone and decorative details, ornate entrances, and intimations of English mansions and French chateaux. Forest Hill, one of these affluent suburbs that remained a separate municipality until its annexation by the old City in 1967, had a restrictive covenant that required any fake wood beams on the façades of houses to have axe marks so that they looked handhewn. It and the other areas of curvy streets in the old City, where many grand houses remain, are now among the most affluent parts of Toronto.[17]

By 1907 a few lines for radial streetcars (Toronto's name for inter-urbans) extended well beyond the city limits, running fifteen miles west and east of downtown and north along Yonge Street all the way to Lake Simcoe. These provided rapid, smooth travel along what were otherwise still mostly unpaved, bumpy roads that had sections where mud in spring was guaranteed to suck in a Model T. The radial lines generated some limited commercial and residential development along their routes, but they were the last grand gesture of an obsolescent technology. They began to lose money as the dirt roads were paved and automobile use increased, and by the mid-1930s they had all been closed down.

The growth of electric streetcar suburbs and commuting was paralleled by changes in downtown. A major fire in 1904 that destroyed several blocks in the city center made substantial reconstruction necessary, and the first modest office skyscrapers, an impressive new railway station (Union Station), and an adjacent railway hotel (the Royal York Hotel) were built in the following two decades and remain important landmarks. By the 1920s Bay Street in downtown had begun to acquire its current reputation as the symbolic financial heart of Canada; between the new railway station and Old City Hall, it was built up like a small-scale version of lower Manhattan, with twenty-story skyscrapers rising from the street line. In 1931, all these were overtopped by the Bank of Commerce Tower, a thirty-four-story Art Deco stretched temple that remained the tallest building not just in Toronto but in the British Commonwealth until the 1960s.

The End of the Streetcar Era

In the year the Bank of Commerce Building was completed, the population of the old City of Toronto reached 630,000. Apart from the affluent suburbs and the industrial zones next to the railway lines, it was above all a streetcar city—high density but low-rise, with single-family detached or semi-detached houses and some walk-up apartments, all within walking distance of a rectangular network of main streets where the streetcars ran as they zigzagged into and out of downtown. This urban form, in both its late nineteenth-century and early twentieth-century versions, has proven to be remarkably resilient and adaptable. Generations have come and gone, houses have been subdivided into apartments, then later converted back into single-family homes; they have been gentrified and renovated; rear laneways and front yards have been converted to accommodate off-street parking. Unlike most American cities, the streetcar system in Toronto was not dismantled in the 1950s, and most lines are still operating except for those replaced by subways. The old parts of the city still function in terms of transportation much as they originally did. But unlike the sleek new light-rail systems that have been introduced in Portland, Denver, and else-where, almost everything to do with Toronto's streetcars—overhead wires, unprotected stops in the middle of busy streets, even the sounds they make—has a patina of age. They remain a very distinctive feature of the old city, much celebrated, complained about, photographed, and painted.

Main streets along streetcar routes continue to be lined with small stores and restaurants. These have always provided excellent business opportunities for new immigrants and so they reveal the long history of Toronto's ethnic diversity—there are old Irish Orange Lodges, English fish and chip shops, Italian and Greek restaurants, Chinese and Vietnamese food stores with various goods spilling out onto sidewalks, Halal butchers, and Filipino corner stores. Some main streets look shabby; in affluent parts of the city they have been upgraded with trees and hanging baskets. Shabby or fancy, they are almost all busy with pedestrians, something that has moved Andrés Duany, a town planner based in Florida who is regarded as the dean of new urbanism and a great advocate of reviving street-grid patterns, to remark wistfully in his book *Suburban Nation* that Toronto has more street-oriented retailing than all the sunbelt cities combined.[18]

The cosmopolitan and vital character of old Toronto was not so evident in the 1920s and 1930s, when the streets were busy mostly with workers on their way to or from employment in factories or sweat shops, sometimes marching in support of unionization or lining up at soup kitchens during the Depression. Even for the middle classes, to whom Toronto might have seemed like a reasonably prosperous, business-oriented sort of place, this was the height of the inward-turned metropolis when streetcar suburbs must have been uneventful backdrops to life in what by most accounts was a very boring city. This was especially true on Sundays when everything closed and even the swings at children's playgrounds were locked. The documentary moviemaker Harry Rasky recalls the joy followed by deep disappointment of once finding an unlocked swing and then being apprehended by a policeman with the stern words "nobody swings on a Sunday." Frederick Grove, a novelist from the Canadian Prairies, wrote bluntly in 1939, "Toronto is hideous. . . . In a sensible world there would be no justification for a place like that." And Leopold Infeld, a European physicist who worked with Einstein and taught at the University of Toronto for a few years around 1940, offered what must be one of the most depressing criticisms of any city anywhere at any time: "It must be good to die in Toronto," he wrote. "The transition between life and death would be continuous, painless and scarcely noticeable." It had grown and changed enormously from the "little, ill-built town" Anna Jameson had written about almost exactly a century earlier, yet it still left visitors deeply underwhelmed. Once again things were about to change.[19]

In 1939, just before the onset of World War II, two important visitors contributed to a clear indication that Toronto's era as a city built and functioning around streetcars was coming to an end and that, rather as had happened a century before when the telegraph and railways had arrived, it was about to vault into another incarnation. During their royal tour of Canada, King George VI and Queen Elizabeth (the Queen Mother) officially opened the Queen Elizabeth Way. This limited-access, divided, long-distance highway was the first of its kind in North America. It ran, as had the first telegraph and one of the first railway lines, from Toronto to Niagara Falls, with a planned extension to Buffalo. It was innovative and fast, but its deeper significance was what it implied about future transportation and communications. Until then motor vehicles had used streets and roads that were originally created for horses and wagons and modified to accommodate streetcars. The Queen Elizabeth Way was for motor vehicles only. It anticipated a new type of urban form, one based on networks of highways intended specifically for cars, that would be constructed after World War II as Toronto expanded into an extensive metropolitan region.[20]

Chapter 4

The Ascendancy of Metropolitan Toronto

Canada's entry into World War II in 1939 had an immediate and lasting impact on the shape of the city and on life in Toronto as young men went into service overseas and women took over jobs in manufacturing. Because Toronto was safe from bombing raids the region became a center for producing weapons and munitions that were shipped to Britain by convoys. After 1945 some of the wartime facilities disappeared completely, such as a shipbuilding yard for minesweepers on Toronto's waterfront, and Camp X, a secret training center for spies and commandos near Oshawa that was a joint Canadian, British, and American initiative and is thought to have contributed to the James Bond stories because Ian Fleming spent some time there. Other facilities, however, were converted to peaceful uses and have left long shadows. A huge plant in the Township of Scarborough where the fuses used in shells and bombs were made was subsequently turned into an industrial and commercial district known as the Golden Mile. Further east, Ajax was created in 1941 as a new town for the employees of a nearby munitions factory, and it was named after a British naval ship that had been instrumental in an Allied naval victory in 1940 in the Battle of the River Plate. The factory is long gone, but Ajax is now a municipality in its own right and an urban center in the outer suburbs. The airport at Malton, established just before the war began on farmland several miles northwest of the borders of the old City, became a training center for pilots, and a factory adjacent to it was turned into a major production facility for Lancaster bombers. These events initiated its growth into the busiest international airport in Canada and what is by far the most extensive artificial feature in the geography of the Toronto region.

These were all quick responses to the urgencies of war. More carefully considered preparations for postwar development began in 1943, when the City Planning Board of Toronto, an advisory committee formed the previous year, produced a remarkable "Master Plan for the City of Toronto and Its Environs." This had no precedents. As the name implies, it covered both the old City and the urban region, and it is the only truly visionary and comprehensive large-scale plan for Toronto that has ever been created. It built on recent initiatives, such as the construction of the Queen Elizabeth Way and the industrial developments associated with the war, and projected expansions of these as ways to structure the future growth of the region. The most dramatic of these projections was of a dense regional network of "superhighways," roughly two miles apart and imposed on existing road patterns, several of them cutting right across the existing city into downtown. Streetcars were apparently regarded as obsolete, but routes for future subway lines, including some running down the medians of superhighways, were identified. Munitions plants were shown as future industrial districts. A slum area near downtown was to become a "model housing area" while large districts of late Victorian bay and gable houses were proposed for redevelopment, which implied urban renewal and more model housing. Approximate locations were shown for a dozen new suburban residential communities that would have populations between ten thousand and fifty thousand. Two greenbelts were suggested: an inner one with a parkway for recreational driving running through it that would link the two river valleys of the Don and Humber, which frame the central part of Toronto, and an outer one on the Oak Ridges Moraine well to the north of the old City.[1]

The 1943 plan had no official status, and there had been no local discussion of its unprecedented proposals that reached far beyond the boundaries and purview of the old City. In spite of this, the plan clearly influenced the course of development in and around Toronto for the next three decades. The model public housing area was implemented between 1949 and 1957 as a modernist social housing project. Several superhighways, including what was then seen as a northern bypass and is now Highway 401 (which runs from Montreal to Windsor and Detroit) were constructed. The parkway in the Don Valley was built as an expressway rather than a road for recreational driving. Two of the proposed subway lines were constructed (another is still under discussion as a possible relief line for downtown). And most of the proposed residential areas were built as dormitory suburbs within what was to become the Municipality of Metropolitan Toronto.

What seems to have happened is that the proposals in the 1943 plan caught the imagination of politicians and developers, were absorbed into political thought, then selectively introduced into official plans that did have legal status and were eventually implemented. This was facilitated by the fact that town planning became an international fashion in the years immediately after World War II, and many political jurisdictions around the world, including Ontario, passed planning legislation. In Toronto, as in many North American cities, there had been subdivision controls since early in the century, and general zoning of land use since the 1930s, but urban development had not been planned in the current sense of the term as a process to coordinate land uses and ensure the provision of adequate services in the public interest. The 1946 Ontario Planning Act changed that by giving municipalities the legal authority to direct development, manage land use, and prepare official plans.

It is debatable whether the introduction of urban land-use planning has been altogether positive. Jane Jacobs offered stinging criticisms in *The Death and Life of Great American Cities.* "City planning as a field has stagnated," she wrote. "It bustles but it does not advance"; it results in "desegregated sortings" of land uses that diminish the vitality of streets and create "dull, inert cities." For Jacobs the parts of cities made before 1940 in the absence of official plans are the ones that have the intricate texture and organized complexity she considered to be the hallmarks of urbanity. Of course, there is no way of knowing whether cities would have turned out better with less planning, or whether planning has prevented even worse changes that might have followed from the increasing use of cars and the emergence of large development corporations. What is clear is that urban landscapes in the Toronto region made after 1950 are different from those made before 1940, and both official planning and the increasing use of automobiles have been the context for all urban growth in the region since then.[2]

The first postwar subdivisions in Toronto were built in a rush to accommodate returning veterans, the baby boom, and rapid population growth. Except for the lack of streetcars and wider lots to accommodate driveways or carports, these were not unlike the streetcar suburbs put up thirty years previously, with unornamented small houses (more or less in the Levittown style, each about one thousand square feet with three bedrooms and one bathroom), and uniform setbacks on streets laid out in grid patterns. In the

Toronto region, and according to some accounts in all of Canada, this and all former types of suburban development were rendered obsolete by a single major project: the master planned development of Don Mills. This was effectively a new town, with a proposed population of 29,000 and employment for 4,500, on a greenfield site at the edge of the Don River Valley in the Township of North York, just north of the old City. The chief planner (and nephew of the developer) was Macklin Hancock, who had recently trained with the modernist planners and architects at Harvard, and in the plan for Don Mills he included many features then in international fashion. The most notable of these was probably the neighborhood unit, with its maze of curving residential streets intended to reduce through traffic and centered on an elementary school. In Don Mills four of these units are arranged around a giant cross that is formed by two old concession and side roads that were turned into arterials (Figure 4.1). Bungalows and small story-and-a-half houses line the curving local roads that feed into sinuous collectors, which in turn lead to these arterials. At the center, where the arterials cross, one corner was designated as a central shopping plaza surrounded by parking; the other three corners have clusters of three- and four-story apartment buildings—the first intimation of what would become a wave of suburban apartment building. The form of development in Don Mills bore no relationship whatsoever to the patterns of main streets and grids that characterize the old City.[3]

Except for modest renovations to individual houses and recent remodeling of the central shopping plaza, Don Mills has scarcely changed. It does, however, have signs identifying it as "Canada's First Planned Community" and a historical plaque in a parkette at the central intersection states: "An immediate critical and commercial success, Don Mills has been imitated in suburban development across Canada." Both claims can be challenged, but it was certainly the first large-scale residential project to be completed under Ontario's new planning legislation, and there is no question about its impact on suburban development around Toronto. Curvilinear neighborhood units arranged around a shopping plaza and an arterial crossroads were frequently imitated over the next three decades, though houses became gradually bigger, one- and then two-car garages were attached to them, and apartment buildings were turned on their end to create fourteen- and twenty-two-story slabs. Because of this Don Mills has been criticized as a precedent for suburban sprawl, but at the time it was celebrated as

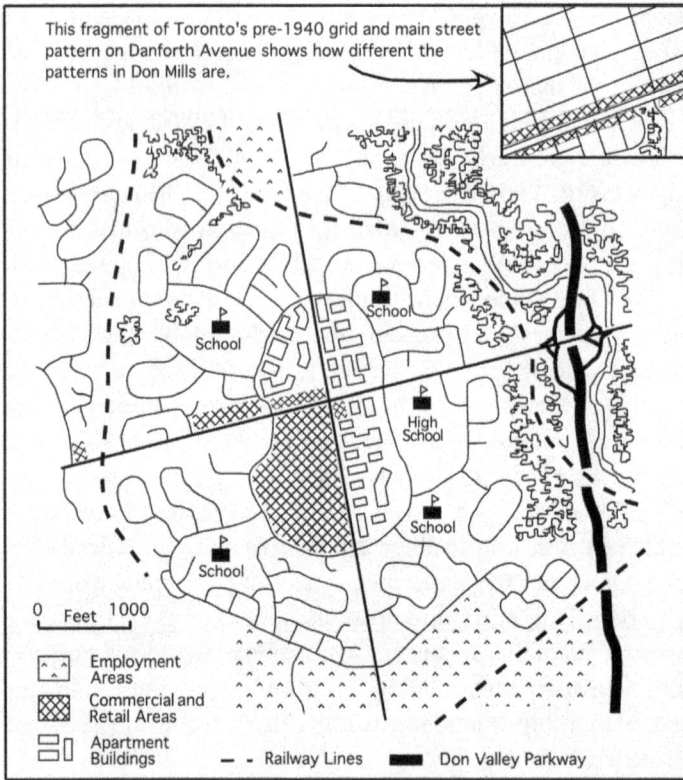

Figure 4.1. The layout of Don Mills, which was planned in 1952 and constructed between 1953 and 1965. Its curving streets, central plaza, and clusters of apartment buildings represented a radical change in urban form from the grid pattern with main streets, shown in the inset at the same scale, which was how most of the old City of Toronto was laid out before 1940.

a serious attempt "to create true communities" that were a great improvement over the "amorphous development" of nineteenth- and early twentieth-century Toronto.[4]

Utilitarian Metro

In the early 1950s, North York, where Don Mills is located, was one of twelve townships that surrounded the old City of Toronto, and because the old City was fully built up it was in these townships that the pressure for urban expansion associated with postwar population growth was occurring. In 1953 the Province of Ontario, in a remarkably innovative move, lumped all these townships and the old City together under the umbrella of Metropolitan Toronto. This new upper tier of government was responsible for all aspects of urban development in a territory that corresponded to the one shown in the 1943 Master Plan. Metro also coordinated tax assessments, water and sewage treatment, education and policing, and management of parks, arterial roads, and some expressways. While this took some responsibilities away from the old City of Toronto and the townships, these lower-tier municipalities continued to have jurisdiction over local roads, water supply, garbage collection, public health, and local schools. They also had political representatives on the Metro council, so they had input into whatever was decided at a regional scale.[5]

This two-tier system of local government was widely regarded in North America as an imaginative and effective way to regulate regional urban growth (though not in Vancouver, where the Greater Vancouver Regional District was deliberately crafted not to be a copy of Metro). In the Toronto region it represented the first time since about 1800, when the grid survey was being made, that there had been any serious attempt by any level of government to control anything to do with the city's large-scale development. In other words, Metro represented a profound reorientation in local city building, perhaps partly as a response to what was seen as the unprecedented scale of the challenges presented by projected growth in the 1950s, but also because it built on ideologies about the role of government that were implicit in the new planning legislation. While the two-tier system of government was not without tensions and inefficiencies, Metro was unquestionably a powerful force that effectively determined the patterns of Toronto's urban development until the 1970s, by which time most growth had moved beyond its boundaries. Metro continued to function in a more managerial capacity until 1998, when the Province blended it and the lower-tier municipalities into the single municipality of the new City of Toronto.[6]

Metro had a council made up of a selection of councilors who had been elected to the lower-tier municipalities and therefore served at two levels. It had no mayor, but, appropriately for business-minded Toronto, it did have an appointed chairman. The first was Frederick "Big Daddy" Gardiner, an imposing personality who left his mark on the city in the manner of a minor Robert Moses. Metro was large enough to raise bonds for major construction projects, and Gardiner used this financial clout to push successfully for expressway construction along several of the routes indicated in the 1943 plan, including a parkway down the Don Valley and an elevated expressway paralleling the railway lines close to the lakefront, which was named the Gardiner Expressway in his honor. He was not blind to the value of public transit, and he helped to preserve the streetcar network at a time when most American cities were dismantling theirs and also oversaw the initial construction of the subway system. Gardiner, who once declared that "the only symphony I understand is the one played on the cash register," ran Metro with a constant eye to engineering and financial efficiency. This view permeated the entire organization and there were few frills in anything it did: arterial roads were designed with lots of concrete, asphalt, and utilitarian fixtures to ensure maximum traffic flow and low-maintenance costs; parks, schools, bridges, water treatment facilities, and reservoirs under Metro's aegis all received similarly practical treatments.[7]

This utilitarian modernism was very apparent in the 1959 draft Metropolitan Toronto Official Plan, which grandly claimed to be the first official plan in North America for a large metropolitan area. The fact that this was not officially approved for several years didn't matter much because it was as much a statement of what Metro was already doing as it was a guide for the future. This plan addressed population growth, employment, housing (including public housing), transportation, water supply and waste disposal, schools, parks, and, last but by no means least, financial resources. "A balanced plan," it declared in a tone consistent with Gardiner's cash-register philosophy, "must . . . not only harmonize the physical components of development with one another and with the area's population and employment growth; it must also balance all the costs against incomes and expenditures." This frugal approach to managing the city was complemented by a sort of political egalitarianism; it was a difficult balancing act, but traffic, water, sewerage, low-rent housing, and employment opportunities were all planned so that the various lower-tier municipalities would grow at about the same rate.[8]

Metro officials were critical of previous postwar suburban developments that they considered had densities too low to support public transportation, so for new developments it proposed raising densities by including high-rise apartments in the housing mix. These were also favored for rental accommodation because they were the only form of rental building that

Figure 4.2. Sheppard Avenue near Kennedy Road in Scarborough. This inner suburban landscape was made under the direction of Metropolitan Toronto. Note the clusters of slab apartment buildings, drive-in plazas, and a 132-foot-wide arterial road.

was considered economically feasible or practical to finance under existing zoning regulations. Apartment towers were to be widely distributed in order to achieve "a judicious use mixture of different housing types." A map included with the 1959 plan showed that this was, in fact, already an established practice, with most apartments consisting of slabs of fourteen or twenty-two stories, sometimes standing alone but more commonly in clusters of four or more (Figure 4.2). In short, Metro Toronto deliberately orchestrated the mix of housing types and the widespread distribution of slab apartment buildings that remain strikingly distinctive features of the skyline of suburban Toronto, and they are a key reason why Toronto's suburban population densities are higher than those of most American cities and comparable to those of some European cities.[9]

The 1959 Plan also paid attention to the larger region, suggesting that urban growth should be concentrated in a broad band along the north shore of Lake Ontario between Oshawa and Hamilton and that it should not extend northward, where it would be difficult to provide water and sewerage services. Within this larger region the old City of Toronto, with its complete range of commercial and cultural functions, accessible by mass transit, should continue to be "the visually attractive symbol of the entire metropolitan area."[10]

Under Metro's guidance the suburbs rapidly spread outward, turning nineteenth-century concession roads into arterials, replacing old hamlets with neighborhood units and plazas, putting up high-rise apartments, and utterly remaking the landscape. If there were critics of the 1959 Plan and Metro's utilitarian approach to growth, they were substantially outweighed by enthusiastic supporters who regarded the new urban forms that were being made as a reason for civic pride and worthy of royal attention. When Queen Elizabeth II visited Canada in 1959 she was proudly taken to visit the brand-new Golden Mile Plaza on the site of the former wartime munitions plant in the Township of Scarborough. A decade later the author of *Boomtown*, a book of before-and-after aerial photos showing changes between 1949 and 1969, breathlessly though erroneously claimed that "Toronto is experiencing the most monumental expansion in the history of cities . . . [which is] triple the pace of New York, Chicago and Los Angeles." The basic ingredients of Boomtown were, he suggested, "the untamed optimism of its citizens, stable honest government, and good thoughtful planning."[11]

Well, perhaps. In the 1970s I lived for several years in a Metro-era subdivision in Scarborough and became familiar with long bus journeys along six-lane arterial roads lined with strip plazas and apartment blocks surrounded by grassy areas of indeterminate purpose. The planning that worked well from the perspective of developers and traffic engineers did not always seem so thoughtful when it had to be experienced directly on the long, windswept walk in the middle of winter to the local supermarket. Nevertheless, and perhaps in spite of that, in my townhouse complex and subdivision there was as much a sense of the "true communities" that Kerr and Spelt had previously glimpsed in Don Mills as I have found in any of the other six parts of Toronto where I have lived.

Modernizing the Heart of the City

The 1943 Master Plan for the Metropolitan Area had noted that a substantial area of the central city needed redevelopment. An additional report in 1944 identified *half* the housing in the old City of Toronto as "declining" because of high population densities, narrow streets, lots without driveways, and houses and schools that were regarded as "obsolete." The 1967 Official Plan for the old City of Toronto reaffirmed this concern, though it reduced the area considered to be in need of "improvement" to about a third of the city, including the central business district.[12]

For residential neighborhoods the fate of large-scale renewal was probably avoided only because Metro was committing most of its funds to building sewage treatment plants, expressways, and roads to keep pace with growth in the suburbs and couldn't afford the expropriations that would have been involved. In the financial district, however, private enterprise was perfectly capable of doing the renewal job without government assistance. In the 1960s entire blocks of old commercial streets and elegant buildings in what Metro had called "the visually attractive symbol of the entire metropolitan area" were razed to make way for the sleek black skyscrapers of the Toronto Dominion Centre, designed by Mies van der Rohe in the cloned modernist style he had already made famous in Chicago and New York. Other office towers soon followed. Few objected, because skyscrapers showed that Toronto was shaking off its Victorian ways, becoming modern, and competing with rival cities in North America.

The public sector was no less enthusiastic in its rush to catch up with the future. An expressionist New City Hall for Toronto, designed by the Finnish architect Viljo Revell and opened in 1965, has a pair of curved inward-looking towers, one for offices for Metro and one for offices for the old City of Toronto, that seem to embrace the council chamber (Figure 4.3). The pragmatically minded city fathers of Toronto had always eschewed anything as wasteful as public space, but times had changed and in front of New City Hall is a civic square, the first large public space to be created in the central city. As with the Toronto Dominion Centre, New City Hall and its square required the demolition of most of a city block, in this case displacing most of the small Chinatown that then existed in Toronto. If there were concerns about this they were outweighed by the sense that New City Hall symbolized Toronto's coming of age in the modern world.

In fact, the urban forms and landscapes of Toronto that were made between 1945 and 1970, both downtown and in the suburbs, were already an expression of modernist ideologies of function over form, out with the old, in with the new. They also reinforced the well-established dominance of the downtown core over the rest of the city and the region. In the 1960s the downtown had 25 percent of the employment and 65 percent of the office space in Metro, and it generated a huge daily pulse of commuting from the rapidly expanding suburbs, some of it on the new subways but much of it by car on the Don Valley Parkway and Gardiner Expressway. In

Figure 4.3. New City Hall, completed in 1965. One tower was intended for the old City of Toronto, with the taller tower for Metro, and the two shared the council chamber. This distinction has been lost in the amalgamated new City of Toronto. The water feature is used as a skating rink in winter. Part of the elevated walkway (intended as the first section of a system of pedestrian/vehicle separation) is visible on the right, leading to the podium. An outline of the clamshell towers has been adopted as the logo for the new City of Toronto.

the 1960s Metro ranked third in automobile ownership per capita in North America after Los Angeles and Detroit, with one vehicle per 2.9 persons, and traffic congestion downtown was a serious issue. An initial attempt to resolve this is apparent in the elevated walkways that surround the civic square in front of New City Hall—these were intended as the first stage of a system of midblock bridges for pedestrians, though their goal was not so much to benefit pedestrians as to reduce traffic slowdowns caused by pedestrians at crosswalks. As it happened, the idea of aboveground walkways in downtown was almost immediately abandoned in favor of pedestrian tunnels lined with stores, though the effect of getting as many pedestrians as possible off the streets to free them up for cars was the same. City planners subsequently came to regret this strategy because it reduced the liveliness of the streets, and in recent construction it has been somewhat mitigated by putting in at-grade, midblock walkways through buildings. However, retail tunnels have proved extremely popular with the developers of office towers because they constitute a sort of closed economy, generating revenue by providing easy opportunities for office workers to spend the money they have earned in the towers above in the linear mini-shopping malls below. The result is that the central part of the old City of Toronto now has a maze of pedestrian tunnels, officially known as the PATH, with more than 1,200 stores lining seventeen miles of shopping arcades and claimed to be the world's largest underground shopping complex. For all its extent and although it connects to six subway stations and Union railway station, it is for most intents and purposes a network of private spaces similar to those in suburban shopping malls, which, depending on your perspective, either undermines or supplements the public spaces of the streets above.[13]

Old City versus Urban Region

In their book *The Changing Face of Toronto* (1965), the geographers Don Kerr and Jacob Spelt were critical of the lack of planning that had allowed extensive speculation and the disorganized development in the late nineteenth and early twentieth centuries. In their opinion the old City of Toronto had been mostly concerned with the accumulation of wealth, and its citizens had "done little . . . to enrich the beauty of the city." In contrast, they praised Metro for the planning controls it was exercising and its imagination in directing suburban development. It is surprising that, in expressing these judgments, they did not mention two recently published and remarkable books about cities, Jacobs's *Death and Life of Great American Cities* and Jean Gottman's *Megalopolis*, that might have persuaded them to rethink their conclusions. These books expressed such different views and have had such a lasting influence that they have to be seen as marking a radical divergence in ways of thinking about cities, a divergence that is both professional and popular, and which deeply influences judgments about how cities should be developed, planned, and managed (Figure 4.4). To understand what has happened in and around Toronto since the 1960s, it is, I think, necessary to have some understanding of this split in urban understanding.[14]

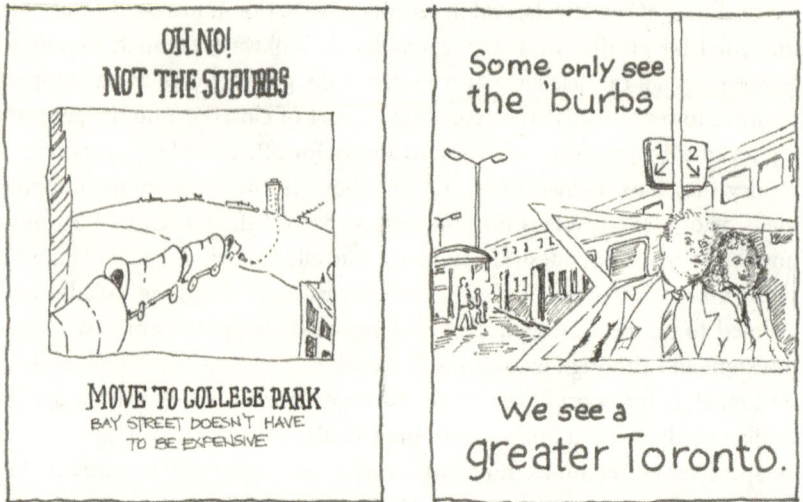

Figure 4.4. Two posters reflecting divergent views about cities in the context of Toronto. Redrawn from posters used in the early 2000s. "Oh No! Not the Suburbs" was an advertisement for a condominium at College and Bay Streets. "We see a Greater Toronto" was a promotion for the *Toronto Star* newspaper, which has a daily section devoted to the Greater Toronto Area.

With remarkable synchronicity, Lewis Mumford's *The City in History* was published in the same year as *Death and Life* and *Megalopolis*. Mumford's book is a masterful review of urban history from Mesopotamia to the mid-twentieth century, and it expresses well the idea that regardless of differences of opinion about what is good or bad in cities they are best understood as unified wholes. Mumford was a diehard advocate of garden cities and new towns as means of correcting the ills of industrial cities. Had he paid any attention to Toronto he would certainly have shared the opinions of Kerr and Spelt that Don Mills was an excellent way to correct past problems in the city's development.[15]

Jacobs could not have disagreed more. Her book is an attack on the "pseudoscience of city planning" and all the garden city, modernist, city beautiful principles it embraced. She thought these were producing the "fresh minted decadence of the new unurban urbanization" and the "suburbanized anti-city." She ridiculed Mumford's notion of an ideal garden city community by asking what people would do there—basket weaving and pottery? Instead she celebrated the type of city she had experienced in

Greenwich Village, the North End in Boston, and the core areas of Baltimore and Philadelphia, where there were high densities, diverse activities, and close-grained uses, and it was possible to engage safely with strangers because the streets were lively and there were always people around.[16]

If Jacobs used an urban microscope, Gottman's view was macroscopic. He looked at cities at the scale of the region, and what he saw were New York, Boston, Baltimore, Philadelphia, and Washington growing into the single, interconnected "urbanized area with a nebulous structure" that he called Megalopolis. In Megalopolis "the old distinctions of urban and rural do not apply" because there is "an almost continuous system of deeply interwoven urban, suburban and rural areas." This he understood as no threat to urbanity but as a differentiated, well-integrated, polynuclear urban system tied together by continually shifting flows of people and goods. It is a view of the world that bears a strong family resemblance to McLuhan's idea that cars and electronic media are decentralizing, pluralistic forces that "dissolve cities into sprawling aggregates."[17]

The ideas of Jacobs and Gottman are almost completely disconnected from one another. They seem to coexist in different urban universes, perhaps because each offers an accurate description of fundamentally different aspects of cities. Jacobs's observations and arguments offer excellent insights into the unplanned areas of the old City of Toronto. However, the reality is that this sort of urban form has not been built in North America since about 1940, when cars replaced streetcars as the preferred means of moving around; the most intense parts of it have not been built since the 1890s when horse-drawn streetcars disappeared. In short, Jacobs's arguments are a celebration of old urban forms and the need to protect them. If they are applied to newer, polycentric parts of cities, it makes everything appear defective, as, for example, when she declared bluntly of Toronto's newer suburbs: "Not to mince words, planners and their working colleagues did not know what they were doing."[18]

Urban forms have always reflected the social, economic, and technological forces in ascendancy at the times they were made. My sense is that planners did indeed know what they were doing—they were trying to find ways to make urban environments that worked for cars rather than streetcars, and they were responding to the shift in the forces that Gottman had identified when he wrote about "tidal currents of movement" that were creating "manifold concentrations and polynuclear structures." In other words, they were planning for current and future urban realities. Gottman's arguments were not intended to apply to the streetcar parts of cities and they offer no useful insights into how those parts function; they were instead the first substantial attempt to understand the characteristics of emerging polycentric urban forms and the ways cities have grown since the 1950s.[19]

What has happened in the Toronto region since the 1960s is that the old City has emerged from its inward-looking chrysalis and been transformed into a model of the good urban life, in part at least because of the application of ideas that have followed from the insights of Jane Jacobs. In contrast, the outer suburbs have grown as a differentiated, interconnected, polycentric mosaic that corresponds to the sorts of innovative forms that Gottman identified in Megalopolis. In effect, in Toronto's urban region two different types of urbanity now coexist.

Chapter 5

A Post-suburban Skyscraper City

The American social philosopher William Irwin Thompson suggested in 1971 that "Toronto is a city at the edge of American history. With its draft dodgers, deserters and émigré academics it is almost Tolkien's Rivendell." Well, not quite as dreamy perhaps, but it was certainly on the edge of what has been called "the urban crisis" of the 1960s that elsewhere was manifest in student demonstrations, race riots, freedom marches, and anti–Vietnam War protests. It was nevertheless caught up in relatively gentle ways in the currents of widespread social change that were contemporary with the urban crisis and which included protests about environmental destruction and loss of heritage, the rise of the women's movement, shifts in immigration patterns, and rapid deindustrialization as manufacturing jobs moved offshore or were lost to automation. Not all of these were entirely new, but it does seem that around 1970 so many of them happened or intensified at once that together they constitute a tipping point in the ways Toronto functioned with the result that in 1975 it was a very different place from the one it had been in 1965. There has been no going back.[1]

In the mid-1960s Toronto was an industrial and manufacturing city undergoing a modernist transformation at the hands of the urban power-house that was Metro, which was systematically implementing plans for the growth of the downtown core, suburban and industrial expansion, the creation of a network of expressways, and the renewal of old neighbor-hoods. By 1975 all those plans had been compromised or had run into dead ends: expressways had been stopped, old buildings and neighborhoods were being preserved rather than razed, deindustrialization was under way, new suburban centers were being built, and Metro had been surrounded by a set of new regional municipalities that eliminated any possibility of Metro's future suburban expansion.

Contesting Growth

This first intimation of this transformation occurred in 1967 in the heart of the old City with a public protest against a development proposal that would have demolished Old City Hall. This splendid Romanesque building was in good condition but had been made surplus to needs by the modernist New City Hall. It had hitherto been taken for granted that old buildings, no matter how grand, should be demolished to make way for new ones whenever the need arose. This time the protest forced the developer to back down; the building was saved and is now used as a municipal courthouse. In a broad context, saving Old City Hall was a small success in what was an emerging international movement to protect heritage; locally it contributed directly to the passage in 1975 of heritage legislation in Ontario that gave municipalities the power to designate and protect old properties for protection. Four decades later the value of built heritage is taken for granted and there are thousands of designated buildings and about forty-five heritage districts in the Toronto region.

The dust had hardly settled from the Old City Hall protest when a different challenge to modernist development arose. Metro's highway construction plans included the Spadina Expressway, which was an updated version of a superhighway that had been proposed in the 1943 Master Plan to run from the northwest into the heart of the city. Construction of the northernmost part had begun in the mid-1960s, and as the precise route for the southern end was being finalized it became clear that it would run through several well-established residential areas and then spill out onto local streets close to the University of Toronto. A powerful and vocal opposition consisting of professors, students, and residents called Stop Spadina quickly developed. It included Jane Jacobs, who had just moved to Toronto from New York and was fresh from a battle against the Lower Manhattan Expressway, and Marshall McLuhan, both of whom lived close to the proposed route. Metro stubbornly refused to back down, but in 1971 the provincial government, which has authority in such matters, overruled Metro and permanently stopped construction of the proposed expressway. The section already built remains as a stub (with a subway down the middle, as proposed in the 1943 plan), was renamed Allen Road, and ends aimlessly in midtown. All the other expressways that Metro had been planning were subsequently deleted from official plans.[2]

These two protests bred a generation of political activists. In 1972 a number of them were elected to what has been called a "reform council" in the old City of Toronto that immediately began to challenge entrenched practices of growth and renewal. Skyscraper construction in the financial district was then in full swing, and one of the council's first actions was to put the brakes on this by restricting development proposals for new buildings to a height of forty-five feet until a comprehensive plan for the central area had been prepared. When that plan was completed in 1975, it showed that downtown was reaching capacity in terms of the numbers of people taking transit to work and proposed a "deconcentration," or decentralization, strategy for future office employment. Metro planners immediately gave substance to this by identifying specific subcenters in the suburban townships of Scarborough, North York, and Etobicoke that could accommodate new offices. In fact, some of these subcenters already had large shopping malls and were being promoted by respective local municipalities as "suburban downtowns" that would have city halls, public squares, and transit connections, so it is not entirely clear who started decentralization. Regardless of who was responsible it constituted a radical shift in how the city and the urban region of Toronto would be shaped. Since the 1850s railways, streetcars, and then subways and expressways had fed from increasingly extensive suburbs into a single downtown core. From 1975 on Toronto would develop as a multicentered urban region.[3]

This reorientation from a monocentric city to a polycentric region was obscured at the time in part because the Province was dithering about a plan for what it called the "Toronto Centred Region" as a way to manage the urban growth that was spilling beyond Metro's borders. The main idea was the one that Metro had suggested in its 1959 draft Official Plan that urbanization should be restricted to a broad band next to Lake Ontario so that water and sewerage services could be easily connected to the lakefront. To this end the Toronto Centred Region plan proposed that a "parkway belt" act as a northern urban growth boundary, with the land beyond that forming an agricultural zone. However, the plan was never formalized and apart from the acquisition of some land for the parkway belt (which is now a major utility corridor with an expressway and power lines!), it was scuttled in the mid-1970s when the Province decided instead to fund construction of a six-foot-diameter sewer line, colloquially known as "the Big Pipe," that looped around the east side of Metro to link areas in the proposed agricultural zone to a huge new sewage treatment plant on the shore of Lake Ontario. It's a cliché that urban development follows plumbing, and this great plumbing decision made possible the northward expansion of the built-up area.[4]

The Big Pipe seems to have been related to a contemporary decision by the Province to fence in Metro as a municipality. Ever since Toronto's incorporation as a City in 1834, it had kept pace with apparently inexorable urban growth by the simple expedient of expanding its boundaries. For the old City this had been done by the annexation of adjacent municipalities, and the creation of Metropolitan Toronto was in some respects just a clever version of annexation as a way to manage growth. By 1970 Metro Toronto was mostly built up, and urbanization had begun to spill into adjacent townships. This time the Province, which holds all the cards with respect to local municipalities, decided not to extend political boundaries in a way that would create some sort of greater Metro. Instead, it reorganized the surrounding mix of townships and counties into the four regional munici-palities of Durham, York, Peel, and Halton, each with a two-tier governance structure similar to Metro's, and it was in these that the urban growth serviced by the Big Pipe would occur. The writing was on the wall. It would take a couple of decades for the remaining undeveloped areas in Metro Toronto to be built up, but Metro would no longer be able to expand indefinitely by annexation and conventional suburban growth. It was land-locked and henceforth would have to grow through redevelopment and intensification. By 1975 the modernist aspirations of Metro Toronto had been utterly thwarted and it had become a post-suburban city.[5]

Downtown Rises

The only part of the old City where modernist growth and redevelopment continued (after the short pause in the early 1970s when restrictions on tall buildings were in effect) was the financial district. There, the celebration of newness that had begun in the mid-1960s with the towers of the Toronto Dominion Bank and New City Hall was unabated. A flight of capital out of Montreal following the terrorist activities of the Front de Libération du Québec in the early 1970s helped to make Toronto the undisputed financial capital of Canada. Its symbolic heart is at the intersection of King and Bay Streets, around which the five major Canadian banks constructed towers of fifty or more stories that display their affluence and power in different ways: black metal and glass for the Toronto Dominion Bank, white Carrara marble for the Bank of Montreal, pink Finnish granite for Scotiabank, silver Canadian nickel cladding for the Canadian Imperial Bank of Commerce, and a film of real gold leaf (claimed to be excellent for reducing insolation) in the windows of the Royal Bank. Other financial institutions followed suit with slightly less pretentious towers. At street level it's hard not to be impressed by the sheer mass and glitz and to wonder how your own little bank balance makes all this possible. The reality is that in spite of their names and logos most of the downtown skyscrapers are owned by property investment companies and pension funds, so the bank towers do have an Oz quality to them as great brash statements that aren't quite what they seem to be.

The new skyscraper offices started a dramatic change in a downtown skyline that had not altered since the Art Deco Bank of Commerce tower had been finished in 1931 (Figure 5.1). This was accentuated by the completion of the CN Tower in 1975. For several decades this was the tallest freestanding structure in the world (technically it isn't a building) and it remains the preeminent emblem and landmark of the city, visible from almost everywhere up to thirty miles away, featured in countless logos for Toronto businesses, and repeatedly used in standard shots of the city on local television. Its stated purpose was to provide point-to-point microwave links, which at the time were the primary means of long-distance electronic communication, by reaching above reception shadows cast by the new skyscrapers in the downtown core. I am not aware that Marshall McLuhan bothered to comment on the CN Tower, even though its sheer scale seems to signify everything he claimed about the preeminent role of electronic communications in modern society; he would probably have warned against mistaking the apparatus for the impact of the medium and noted that its centralizing symbolism was exactly the opposite of the decentralizing effects of electronic media. In any case, the CN Tower was made obsolete by satellite communications almost as soon as it was built, though it remains a major tourist attraction and is still used for television and radio transmissions and other communications. Its role has been taken over by cell phone towers and satellite dishes, which are almost as widely dispersed as the messages they relay.[6]

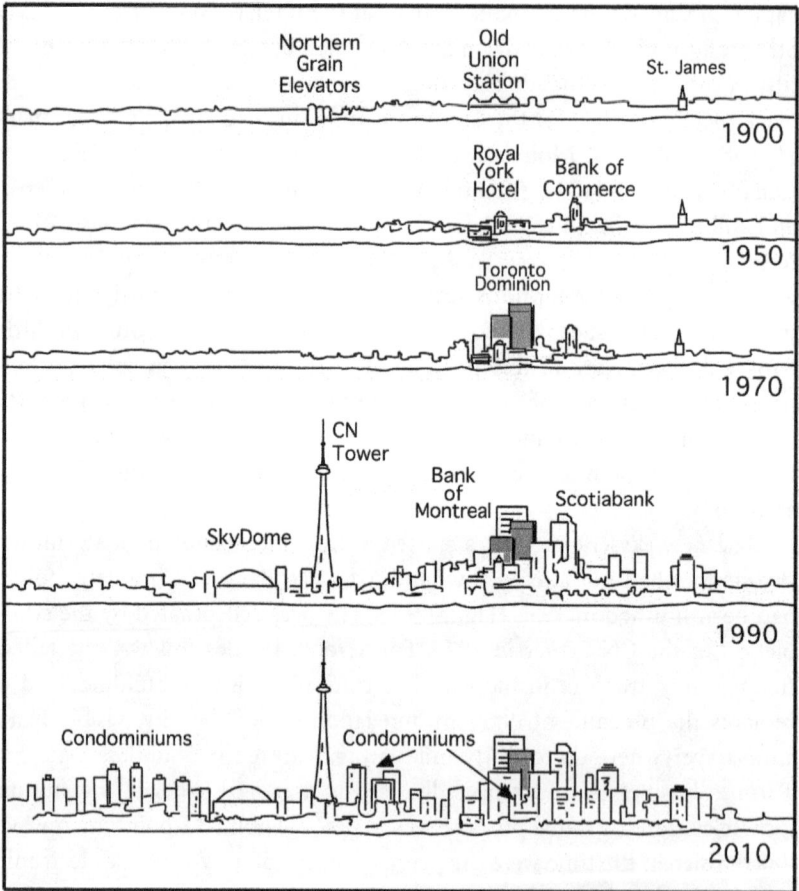

Figure 5.1. Changes in the skyline of downtown Toronto from 1900 to 2010.
St. James Cathedral was the tallest building from its construction in 1853 until the
1930s. Skyscraper offices and the CN Tower led to major changes between 1965
and 1990, but since then most of the new towers have been condominium
apartment buildings crowding along the lakefront and pushing westward. The
SkyDome, now called the Rogers Centre, is a baseball and football stadium.

The narrow, old streets of the central city where the new towers are
close to the street line have been turned into deep and often windy canyons
(Figure 5.2). Some of them function like large-scale versions of back alleys
that are lined with giant doors and ramps to below-grade parking and
service docks. Furthermore, the retail tunnels of the PATH have drawn

Figure 5.2. A street canyon in the heart of the financial district: King Street looking west from Bay Street. The black Toronto Dominion building is on the left, and the white Bank of Montreal building is on the right.

shoppers underground, so there are relatively few stores at the street level. In spite of all this, Toronto's financial district is not the sort of pedestrian-free zone that is sometimes found in other central cities, and there are small open spaces and plazas associated with most of the office towers that are packed with people in the summer when workers escape from their cubicles for lunch.

One simple reason there are people on downtown streets is because lots of them live nearby. Since the 1970s there have been concerted efforts to prevent the abandonment of Toronto's city center as a place to live, and these have been reinforced, especially since the early 1990s, by the necessity of intensification if the post-suburban City of Toronto is to compete with the regional municipalities of the outer suburbs for a share of regional population growth. One of the oldest and perhaps the most significant of these efforts is the mixed-ownership, mixed-income, social housing development of St. Lawrence Neighbourhood, situated on a former industrial

Figure 5.3. The St. Lawrence Neighbourhood. These co-op apartments (in the background) and townhouses are on street alignments extending those of the Town of York.

site a few hundred yards east of the financial district and adjacent to the original location of the Town of York. This project was initiated by the old City in the mid-1970s and was certainly influenced by many of Jane Jacobs's ideas about mixed housing on short blocks, eyes on the street, and a variety of land uses (Figure 5.3). Unlike previous renewal projects that had created superblocks with closed-off streets and high-rise apartments, St. Lawrence extends the original street patterns of York and consists of townhouses and some low-rise apartment buildings, with shops that front onto outside streets. The neighborhood now has a population of about thirty thousand, many of them families. Its principles for integrated social housing were widely used elsewhere in the old City until the early 1990s, when both the federal and provincial governments ended their financial support for public housing projects.

This did not, however, mean the end of residential development around the city center. The momentum for maintaining a residential population that had been established by social housing projects was transferred to private housing, especially condominiums. This began in earnest in the 1990s, when run-down commercial and deindustrialized areas close to the financial district, which were being used for low-intensity activities such as clubs and warehouses, were re-zoned to permit a range of uses, including residences. An initial flurry of loft conversions was followed by construction of condominiums in increasingly tall towers, the tallest of them now more than fifty stories tall. The condominium boom has lasted well over a decade. It has furthered the upward growth of the downtown skyline that began in the 1960s and then stretched it westward. Between 1976 and 2006, the various social housing and condominium developments increased the central city's population by seventy thousand within an area that extends about a mile in each direction from the financial district, and many of the new residents work in offices there to which they walk or cycle. In short, Toronto's city center has filled in rather than emptied out, and pedestrian street activity has intensified and the bike racks are often full.[7]

Retail developments and reinvestments have reinforced this. The most notable of these is the Eaton Centre, the project that initially threatened demolition of Old City Hall. Following the protest it was modified into a block-long galleria shopping mall that left the old building and a nineteenth-century church untouched. Completed in 1977, and still one of the largest malls in Canada, the Eaton Centre is a suburban phenomenon in the heart of downtown except for the fact that, instead of being surrounded by a parking lot, it has direct connections to two subway stations and the retail tunnels of the PATH. Like all malls, it is a private space that both turns its back to and sucks life from nearby streets. In part to counter this effect, and more generally to contribute to the enhancement of downtown, in the early 2000s the City of Toronto carved out what purports to be a new public space called Dundas Square, just across Yonge Street from the Eaton Centre. Surrounded by pixel boards and giant advertising signs, this has been developed as Toronto's version of Times Square (Figure 5.4). It is well used for programmed events and it does seem to have reenergized this part of downtown. From another perspective, however, it is a privately managed space with its own security guards, where revenue is generated from charges for events and where political activities of any sort are discouraged. It's a pseudo-public space that is more like an extension of the shopping mall than of the public streets that open into it, and it is an overt symbol of the neoliberalism that is gradually infusing the entire urban region.

Figure 5.4. Dundas Square. Toronto's version of Times Square, this was carved out of the side of Yonge Street in downtown in the early 2000s.

City of Dispersed Skyscrapers

Outside its downtown core, Toronto doesn't seem much like a city of sky-scrapers, certainly not compared with New York or Chicago. While the downtown skyline is impressive, it is not especially distinctive except for the CN Tower. Yet according to Skyscraperpage.com, a website with a detailed database of skyscrapers that have twelve or more stories (135 feet) in cities around the world, the new City of Toronto has 1,900 skyscrapers, and by this measure it ranks second in the world to New York City (with 5,800) and well ahead of Tokyo, Shanghai, and Chicago, which have fewer than 1,200 each. Another website, Emporis.com, provides a slightly different perspective by giving points for the total number of floors, and it ranks Toronto fourteenth (behind Hong Kong, Shanghai, Guangzhou, Moscow, and others) and third in North America (behind New York and Chicago). Whichever measure is used, it is clear that Toronto is internationally remarkable for its number of high-rise buildings. However, this is not immediately obvious because so many of them are widely dispersed and appear as modest bumps in an otherwise predominantly low-rise horizontal skyline and because about half of the buildings are shorter than twenty stories. Roughly 80 percent of the skyscrapers are apartment buildings, a percentage that is increasing. The construction of high-rise offices came almost to a standstill in an economic recession that began in the early 1990s and since then only about twenty commercial and institutional buildings more than ten stories tall have been constructed anywhere in the City, compared with more than three hundred high-rise condominiums. So, strictly speaking, Toronto is not so much a skyscraper city as a city of dispersed high-rise apartments.[8]

The commitment to building apartment towers had a specific origin in 1958 at Flemingdon Park, a private residential development intended for middle-class residents in a suburban area adjacent to Don Mills that included several fourteen-story apartment slabs mixed with townhouses. It was designed by Macklin Hancock, the same planner who had been responsible for the layout of Don Mills and who was presumably versed in Bauhaus theories of planning because he had trained at Harvard with Walter Gropius and other modernists. Flemingdon Park demonstrated that building high-rise apartments as rentals could be profitable in Toronto. It was an eye-opener for Metro Toronto planners who were trying to find ways to include mixed housing types in suburban subdivisions, and they immediately adopted high-rise towers as a way to provide low-cost social housing. They also decided that distributing both social housing and private rental towers in loose groups of four or five should avoid some of the problems that accompany large concentrations of apartment towers, yet still generate densities high enough to support public transit. In short, the economics of high-rise construction worked well for both public and private sectors. The construction of high-rise apartment buildings in Metro took off and by 1970 there were already several hundred dispersed across the city. Private developers had pushed them up to thirty stories and grouped them in communities with names such as Crescent Town and St. James Town—towns in the city with their own community facilities such as gyms. Some high-rise apartment buildings are point blocks, but most are slabs shaped like giant cereal boxes on their side or on their end, made of concrete and brick, almost always with balconies, underground parking, and a small skirt of lawn of indeterminate purpose required to meet coverage requirements in zoning bylaws. Regardless of whether they were intended for private or public housing, their architecture is generally consistent with the utilitarian

Figure 5.5. Toronto's distinctively crenellated skyline of slab apartment blocks rising above single-family houses. This is the Bridlewood area in north Scarborough in 1978. The view has not changed much since.

aesthetics espoused by Metro. They created a crenellated skyline that is a defining feature of Toronto's suburban landscape (Figure 5.5).[9]

The economics of building high-rise rental accommodation ceased to be profitable in the early 1970s but the experience of living in apartment towers was already familiar to many Torontonians, and as private condominium ownership became an alternative to renting, condominium towers began to be built as a way to meet the continuing demand for housing. This began as a trickle and has since the 1990s turned into a flood that has peaked on deindustrialized lands near the financial district and along the central waterfront. Nevertheless, like their 1950s and 1960s predecessors, condominium towers are distributed across the whole city. A corridor along Yonge Street, for example, with its access to a subway, has been a particularly desirable location for both rental and condominium high-rises, as well as for office deconcentration, and it now contains a knobbly spine of skyscrapers that cuts like a volcanic intrusion all the way across the City of Toronto from its northern boundary to Lake Ontario (Figure 5.6).

Intensification and Reurbanization

The vertical eruption of construction energy in apartment buildings is almost the exact opposite to what has happened in the single-family

Figure 5.6. The high-rise spine of the City of Toronto along Yonge Street. The condominiums and office towers of the linear suburban downtown of North York are in the center of the photo, and downtown Toronto and Lake Ontario are in the distance. The skyline of single-family residential areas on either side of Yonge has scarcely changed since the 1950s.

residential areas that compose most of the city. Many late nineteenth-century neighborhoods that were regarded as declining in the 1960s, and narrowly avoided urban renewal, plus large sections of streetcar suburbs, have now been gentrified, and it seems unlikely that streetscapes in these old residential areas will change much more in the next hundred years than they have in the last hundred years. Indeed, in marked contrast to the extensive renewal plans of the 1960s, the 2006 Official Plan for the City of Toronto acknowledges the stability of existing low-rise residential areas, both in the old City and the inner suburbs, and protects them from significant modification either in density or in form. The intensification that has to happen if post-suburban Toronto is to increase its population is mostly to be concentrated along main streets, such as Yonge Street, and along commercial strips in the inner suburbs.

Close to downtown some main streets bear witness both to intensification and to the rise of the creative class. There are a new headquarters for the Canadian Broadcasting Corporation, a new opera house, and a new building for the Toronto International Film Festival. Toronto is not generally regarded as an architectural mecca, but there are a few examples of destination architecture: the Ontario Gallery of Art has been remodeled by Frank Gehry (who was born in Toronto); a new building at the nearby Ontario College of Art, designed by the British architect Bruce Allsop, looks like a gigantic shoebox raised on splayed stilts above older buildings; the otherwise beaux arts Royal Ontario Museum has been given an incongruous façade of gigantic black crystals by Daniel Libeskind. A little farther from the core, however, streetcars still rumble along main streets that are mostly lined by old two- and three-story commercial blocks. There has been some infilling and intensification almost everywhere, but it is mostly in scale with the older buildings. It is not the shape of the streets so much as the way they are used that has changed. Streets that in the 1960s were among the shabbiest in the city now have banners, street trees, boutiques, patio restaurants, and small galleries specializing in avant-garde art and design. In part this transformation has been effected by business improvement areas (BIAs), a concept invented in Toronto in 1970 and now widely adopted in cities around the world, where local businesses pay a voluntary tax that is used to make improvements to local streetscapes such as pedestrian-scale lighting, benches, hanging baskets, and street trees. There are seventy-three BIAs in the city, each one with street signs to inform shoppers whether they are in Bloor West Village (the first one), Greektown on the Danforth, Corso Italia, Uptown Yonge, the Fashion District, or wherever. "Everywhere is a district now," reflects Elaine Risley, the central character in Margaret Atwood's novel *Cat's Eye*, set in Toronto and written shortly after BIAs were introduced. "We never used to have districts."[10]

In the inner suburbs, those parts of Metro that were developed as relatively low-density suburbs in the 1950s, 1960s, and 1970s, the arterial roads and commercial strips are being slowly "reurbanized" and intensified. This involves bringing new developments up to the street line to increase densities by building on parking lots in order to make them look more like the main streets of the old City. Numerous townhouse and apartment projects constructed since 1980 front directly onto arterial roads. A similar approach has been applied to retail redevelopments, where the expansive parking lots of plazas built in the 1960s are gradually being filled in with commercial buildings close to the sidewalk and the parking behind. The results thus far are piecemeal because they can only be implemented incrementally as plazas and strip malls are redeveloped. However, reurbanization is a part of the broader long-term strategy of intensification that also involves the development of brownfield sites, the adaptive reuse of former industrial sites and increasing densities by building upward, all of which have to happen if the population of the post-suburban City of Toronto is to continue to grow.[11]

Suburban Downtowns

Intensification of the inner suburbs is nowhere more apparent than in suburban downtowns. When the populations of the suburban townships within Metro expanded rapidly in the 1960s and 1970s, most of them chose to be officially incorporated as cities, and as cities they needed civic centers and other facilities to reflect their new status. In Scarborough a regional shopping mall, suggestively called the Scarborough Town Centre, was opened in 1971 next to Highway 401, conveniently at the geographical center of the municipality; the developers astutely offered a piece of their property to the municipality, and two years later the Teflon-coated, sparkling white Scarborough Civic Centre and its adjacent public square were officially opened by the Queen. Three years later Metro's office deconcentration strategy identified Scarborough's new mall and civic facilities as the core of a multipurpose suburban center for business, culture, and government. Several office blocks, including a federal office building, were subsequently constructed and a rapid-transit link to the subway system added. By 1985 the City of Scarborough was planning its downtown as "a dynamic urban core" for eight thousand residents and four thousand jobs.[12]

In the atrium of Scarborough Civic Centre, an installation of twenty-one small metal tetrahedrons curves from floor to ceiling to represent Scarborough's progress into the twenty-first century. The municipality didn't quite make it that far; when it was legally dissolved in the amalgamation that created the new City of Toronto in 1998, the futuristic Civic Centre lost its main reason for being, though it still houses branch municipal offices of the new City and hosts community meetings. The demise of local government has not, however, impeded the subsequent construction of several condominium towers, nor the renovation and expansion of the Town Centre mall, and Scarborough's suburban downtown is now a major development node in regional plans for the Greater Golden Horseshoe.

Downtown North York is more impressive. It is strategically located along a section of Yonge Street where there are still some two-story blocks that were built when radial streetcars ran there in the early twentieth century. Its expansion as a suburban downtown began in the early 1970s with the extension of the major north-south subway line and its identification as a subcenter in the office deconcentration strategy. A thirty-story complex of offices, apartments, and retail stores was built above one of the subway stations, and this was followed by federal government offices, a new city hall for North York, a large theater that hosts Broadway and other shows on tour, an aquatics center, about a dozen office towers (some with retail arcades), and fifty high-rise condominium buildings, many with streetfront retailing, all strung out along the line of Yonge Street (see Figure 5.6). Many residents have Chinese, Korean, Russian, or Persian backgrounds, and there are numerous small restaurants and a wide variety of shops that cater to them. As in Scarborough, the former city hall is little more than a shell, but in every other respect Downtown North York is a node of intense development that looks, functions, and feels in many ways like the busy downtown of a major city.

An Unintended Model of Urban Sustainability

By 2011, the new City of Toronto, formerly Metro, had effectively been a post-suburban city for thirty-five years, closed in by surrounding regional municipalities. If population growth is essential for urban prosperity, then post-suburbanization makes intensification essential. Both the old City and the inner suburbs have experimented with various forms of this, including social housing projects such as St. Lawrence Neighbourhood, the deregulation of zoning to allow housing on former industrial land, reurbanization, and suburban downtowns. In addition, the local habit of building skyscraper apartments has created an urban culture familiar with high-density, high-rise living that has facilitated intensification by the construction of

Table 5.1. Changes in Population and Number of Occupied Dwellings in the City of Toronto and the Greater Toronto and Hamilton Area, 2001–2011

	2001	2011	Change	%
City of Toronto population	2,481,494	2,615,060	133,566	5.4
City of Toronto total dwellings	943,080	1,047,887	104,807	11.0
Rest of GTHA population	3,090,600	3,959,080	868,480	28.1
Rest of GTHA dwellings	1,024,080	1,323,047	298,967	29.2

Sources: Statistics Canada, Census 2001; Statistics Canada, Census 2011; and City of Toronto, *Census Backgrounder*, 2011.

condominium towers. There is, in other words, ample evidence of redevelopment and infill that should have engendered substantial population growth. However, there was still land in Metro for conventional suburban growth in subdivisions until about 2000, so it is only since then that the effectiveness of intensification can be gauged.

The results are mixed. In the central city St. Lawrence and the condominium towers have probably now added perhaps about 85,000 people since 1970, yet there is evidence that about 80 percent of those have moved from a previous dwelling less than three miles away. In the City of Toronto as a whole the population increased by almost 134,000 between 2001 and 2011, a 5.4 percent increase. However, the number of dwellings increased by 11 percent in that period (Table 5.1). In other words much of the construction activity in the City seems to have been a response to household fragmentation and population redistribution. In comparison in the same period in the rest of the Greater Toronto and Hamilton Area, that is, in the outer suburbs, population and the number of dwellings increased at about the same rate of about 28 percent. In short, the indications are that while redevelopment, intensification, and reurbanization are contributing to the ongoing renewal of the streetscapes of the City of Toronto, and are making possible a modest increase in population, they are not proving effective in keeping pace with regional growth.[13]

Whether this matters except symbolically is another question. The indications are that although the City of Toronto can no longer expand through conventional suburban growth, it has nevertheless flourished. Since the city was enclosed by regional municipalities in 1975 its streets have become increasingly vibrant and many streetscapes have been renewed, the populations in the central area and suburban downtowns have grown, the financial district has come to play a significant role in the network of world cities, and the skyline has never stopped moving upward. In other words slow population growth relative to the rest of the region does not appear to be a major problem. This suggests that it is probably not a worthwhile goal to try to keep pace with the outer suburbs, most of which have ample space for suburban expansion for at least the next two decades and will outgrow the City of Toronto, no matter how much it intensifies. Instead it would make sense for the City of Toronto to accept that it is now post-suburban and to aim to become a model of urban sustainability essentially without growth by protecting those aspects that work well and by developing innovative strategies for renewal and continuing change.

Chapter 6

Diversity in the Outer Suburbs

The part of the urban region outside the City of Toronto is often referred to locally as "the 905," the telephone area code that distinguishes it from the 416 area code of the City. Because the 905 has mostly been built up since the 1970s it is also common to regard everything there as "the outer suburbs," a useful name that implies that while this recently developed area is an extension of the inner suburbs it is nevertheless different from them. The *Toronto Star* newspaper tested this assumption in 2010 in a survey of 1,345 residents to assess differences in daily life between the old city and the outer suburbs. I have no idea how rigorous the survey was, but the result, perhaps to the surprise of the editors, was that there are scarcely any differences in how well residents know their neighbors or whether they find it hard to walk around their neighborhoods. As a result there was no real story and the article based on the survey was titled "416 and 905: We're More Alike than We Think," a not unimportant conclusion in spite of the nonstory because it undermines prejudices about the supposed social incoherence of new suburbs.[1]

In terms of urban forms and landscapes, however, there are very obvious differences. Many aspects of the outer suburbs—such as districts of huge distribution centers, intermodal facilities, the international airport, networks of six-lane arterial roads, intensification along transit corridors, and their sheer extent across many different municipalities, each of which has its own identity—have no clear precedents in older urban forms and there is no well-established language to describe them (Figure 6.1). This combination of scale, an unfamiliarity because of newness, multiple histories, and a lack of suitable language makes it tempting to resort to generalizations about sprawl and low-density development. I have not found these

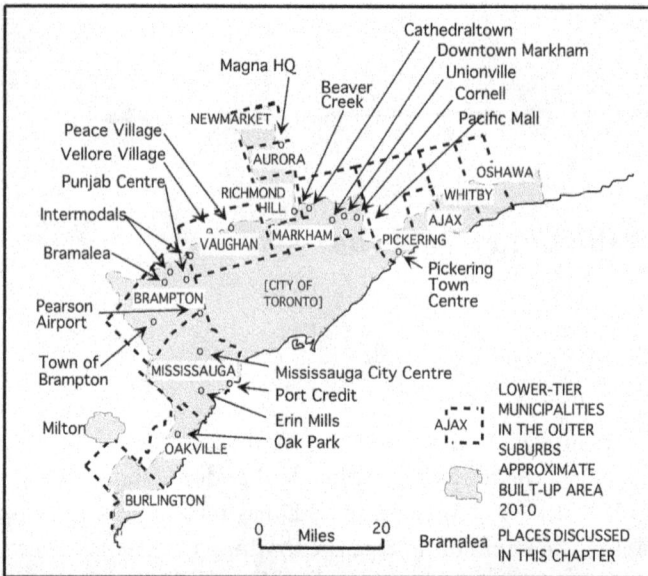

Figure 6.1. Toronto's outer suburbs.

sorts of generalizations helpful. Instead, I have followed the sensible general advice that Jane Jacobs offered at the beginning of *The Death and Life of Great American Cities*. "The way to get at what is going on in the seemingly mysterious and perverse behavior of cities," she wrote, "is . . . to look closely, and with as little previous expectation as possible, at the most ordinary scenes and events, and attempt to see what they mean." Accordingly I have driven, walked around, and looked closely at many of Toronto's outer suburbs to try to get some sense of what is going on. This straightforward approach has generated a wealth of observations, which I have organized by borrowing some basic notions from landscape ecology, a discipline that studies human impacts on ecosystems at a regional scale and that has been used specifically to investigate urban regions.[2]

Landscape ecologists employ a relatively straightforward conceptual framework that begins with an account of a background "matrix" that sets preconditions for ecosystems (for instance, climate, topography, and geology). Within that matrix different ecological "patches" or habitats, such as forests, farmland, and wetlands, are then determined, and the green corridors used by migrating animals and other species are identified. The complexity in landscape ecology lies in identifying the patterns of ecological patches, measuring flows along corridors, assessing permeability at the edges of patches and corridors, and determining the scale and nature of the disruptions to all of these that are caused by human activities. It may be possible to push the analogies with landscape ecology further, but my intention is simply to borrow the ideas of matrix, patches, corridors, and edges as ways to organize a description of Toronto's outer suburbs. I have added the notion of centers, because it soon became clear to me that, although centers may not be important in ecological processes, they are crucial in the urban structure of the outer suburbs. First, however, it is necessary to set aside the idea of sprawl, which is too often used as a simplistic description and judgment of recent suburban development, and obscures most of what is actually happening in the newest urban landscapes.

Not Sprawl

"The forces that automatically pumped highways and motor cars and real estate developers into the open country," the urban historian Lewis Mumford wrote in 1961, slipping effortlessly into the sort of hyperbolic prose that seems to be a common response to recently developed bits of cities, no matter when they were made, "have produced the formless urban exudation . . . an anti-city . . . a formless mass of thinly spread semi-urban tissue." Because he was presumably writing about developments of the 1950s, these urban exudations were by current standards rather modest. In Toronto they would have amounted to the first parts of what are now the inner suburbs, a mere fraction of the built-up area that now stretches from Oshawa to Hamilton along the north shore of Lake Ontario and which has reduced some recent local urban observers to Mumford-like despair. John Sewell, a former mayor of the old City of Toronto, laments in his book, which is subtitled *Understanding Toronto's Sprawl*, that "One can only sadly conclude that the culture of sprawl has established the upper hand and is now the unquestioned dominant force in the Greater Toronto Area. The battle to maintain the urban values that had found expression in the older city and protection in the Metro structure has apparently been lost."[3]

The opinion that recent urban development is anti–city sprawl is not universally shared. Jean Gottman, in a remark that might have been directed at Mumford and Sewell, noted that "modern urban sprawl" has for a long time been "condemned on moral grounds" and "is viewed by many as a threat to progress . . . a sickness, a cancer." In contrast, what he found in Megalopolis was "on average, the richest, best educated, best housed and best serviced group in the world"—hardly evidence of some massive urban failure. And what he saw was not undifferentiated semi-urban tissue but developments with "many contrasts, paradoxes and apparently contradictory trends." The geographer Peirce Lewis likewise thinks that sprawl is a misleading word, one which implies that recent urban expansion is "some kind of unfortunate cosmetic eruption, rather like a bad case of pimples" that cities might grow out of, except that "it is not temporary, and it is not cosmetic and it will not go away." More recently Robert Fishman, a historian of suburbs, clearly sides with Gottman and Lewis when he declares that "the new city at the periphery" needs to be approached not as a degeneration of urban values but as a "revolutionary system of urban complexity and order without traditional urban concentration."[4]

A common and apparently straightforward definition of sprawl is that it occurs when the area of urbanized land increases faster than the population, and densities therefore decline. Evidence that this is what is happening around Toronto is contradictory and confusing. A report made in 2002 for the City of Toronto on density changes in the Greater Toronto Area concluded that between 1992 and 1999 there had actually been intensification rather than sprawl; population had increased by 21 percent and land consumed by only 13 percent. This unexpected conclusion has been challenged in a more recent and precise investigation of urban growth in Toronto, Vancouver, and Calgary by the planning consultants Zack Taylor and Myron Burchfield. Using satellite images for 1990 and 2000, and Census population data for 1991 and 2001, they determined that in low-density Calgary the urban land area grew almost 20 percent more than its population needed, whereas in Vancouver the population increased 8 percent faster than the built-up area and was intensifying; Toronto was in between with the built-up area increasing 9 percent faster than the population. However, these numbers embody a couple of statistical conundrums. First of all, Toronto has a substantially higher population density than Vancouver, so Vancouver, which is widely admired for its progressive planning and development practices, has more potential for intensification and is presumably trying to catch up (Table 6.1). Secondly and more specifically, Taylor and Burchfield also provide detailed data for three zones in Toronto's built-up area—the core pre-1950 zone, the 1950–70 older suburbs, and

Table 6.1. A Comparison of Areas and Population Densities for Twelve
Metropolitan Areas

	Mayors: Land area (square miles)	Demographia: Land area (square miles)	Mayors: Density per square mile	Demographia: Density per square mile
Mexico City	800	790	21,750	24,600
London	627	627	13,200	13,700
Stockholm	200	146	7,000	8,800
Toronto	**639**	**883**	**6,800**	**7,000**
Copenhagen	315	175	4,800	6,700
Los Angeles	1,668	2,432	7,100	6,100
Vancouver	432	444	4,200	4,800
New York	3,352	4,495	5,300	4,600
Calgary	272	272	3,200	4,100
Portland	474	524	3,300	3,600
Chicago	2,122	2,647	3,900	3,400
Phoenix	799	1,265	3,600	3,200

Sources: Selected from *City Mayors Foundation* 2012 at http://www.citymayors.com and
Demographia 2012 at http://www.demographia.com/, both of which list several hundred cities.
Data from *City Mayors* have been converted from metric measurements.
Note: The 2011 Census indicates a density of 7,590 per square mile for the "population
center" (i.e., the built-up area) of Toronto, 4,800 per square mile for Vancouver, and 4,000
for Calgary.

the post-1970 newer suburbs—and these data indicate that between 1990 and 2000 the area of the newer suburbs grew only 3 percent more than the population, the old suburbs intensified slightly, and the built-up area in the pre-1950 core of the old City actually increased by 1 percent more than the population (presumably as brownfield sites were rehabilitated). In other words, some "sprawl" had occurred in the dense urban core of the city. What I take from these odd and inconsistent outcomes is that measurements of sprawl are similar to the attempts of late nineteenth-century physicists to measure the ether—it's probably the wrong way of looking at things.[5]

There may, however, be some limited validity in Sewell's claim that "Toronto's sprawl is twice as dense—or half as sprawling—as development around comparable American cities." I know of no figures specifically for the density of sprawl, but it is possible to make some rough comparisons of the overall densities of different urban areas, though caution is needed because the areas of different cities are defined in different ways—they might be political jurisdictions, census metropolitan areas, or built-up areas. Demographia and CityMayors are two websites that both try to correct for these sorts of inconsistencies, yet even so, as the figures in Table 6.1 show, their measurements show considerable variations. However, they do agree to the extent that either Toronto or Los Angeles (in spite of its low-density reputation) is the most densely populated metropolitan area in North America, with about half the density of London and Paris, and also that they are both considerably denser than Vancouver and also New York, presumably because Manhattan constitutes only a small part of New York's urban area. Toronto's overall density appears to be almost twice that of Chicago and Phoenix, and also of Portland, Oregon, a city widely admired for its urban growth boundaries and other progressive planning policies, and perhaps this also applies to what is regarded as sprawl.[6]

A Matrix of Green Corridors and Arterial Roads

The urban forms of Toronto's outer suburbs are structured by two linear networks, one of them associated with natural features and the other with the original grid survey. The landforms of the urban region consist mostly of more or less level plains of clay, sand, and glacial till, and once the forest on them had been cleared they posed few challenges to urban growth except for the steep-sided valleys carved by rivers making their way south from the Oak Ridges Moraine to Lake Ontario. Those valleys are protected from development, largely as a consequence of a hurricane in 1954, the only major one in recent history, which caused serious floods throughout the region, especially in the Humber Valley, and destroyed numerous buildings and killed eighty-one people. This disaster prompted the creation in 1957 of the Toronto and Region Conservation Authority, an agency responsible for managing the watersheds of all rivers that flow through the City of Toronto, watersheds that extend north to include parts of the Moraine. It has ensured that new urban developments do not bury watercourses in culverts and has prohibited all construction on valley sides and in flood-plains. In the City of Toronto the consequence is that the major river valleys, which once had many buildings, have been turned into a system of ravines with attractive linear parks, walking and cycling trails, playing fields, and wooded valley sides. It was too late to protect smaller creeks in the old

City of Toronto, which were almost all buried in the nineteenth century, but in the outer suburbs both small creeks and larger valleys have been protected from development and now form an extensive network of green corridors. These measures have contributed to a substantial improvement in water quality, and salmon, which completely died off in the 1870s because of pollution, have been successfully reintroduced to the rivers.[7]

Superimposed on these green corridors is a network of arterial roads that is the successor to the grid of concession and side roads created in the early nineteenth century. This carves the landscape of the outer suburbs into a giant quilt that effectively forces development into rectangular patches. It is tempting to see the arterials, many of them with four or more lanes of traffic, as channels that divide and separate. There is some truth to this, particularly at the local level. The urban geographer André Sorensen offers a different perspective. He describes the megagrid around Toronto as "a robust and comprehensive system," because it promotes block-by-block urbanization, buffering blocks from one another, yet also allows easy travel along the arterials. In this latter respect what Reyner Banham wrote of Los Angeles can appropriately be extended to the outer suburbs of Toronto: "The private car and the public freeway together provide an ideal . . . version of democratic urban transportation: door to door movement on demand at high average speeds over a large area." Unlike a radial system of roads that gives preeminence to a focal center, this network of arterial highways is spatially democratic because it makes all locations more or less equally accessible.[8]

Diverse Residential Landscapes

Between 1971 and 2011 the population of Toronto's outer suburbs grew by almost three million people, systematically filling in the spaces between the green and arterial corridors with differentiated patches of houses, shops, and employment districts. The first large-scale development projects, such as Bramalea in Brampton, borrowed heavily from contemporary practices within the borders of Metro. Bramalea, which is about twenty-five miles northwest of downtown Toronto, was planned in the 1960s as an independent satellite city with a population of seventy thousand, a central shopping mall, and a large industrial district for employment. Small creeks and

Figure 6.2. Bramalea in spring, with a section of a green corridor in the foreground. The center, with a shopping mall, the offices of the regional municipality of Peel, and a bus transit station, is located in the gap between the apartment towers.

watercourses were protected as a system of parks snaking through residential areas. The Metro practice of providing a range of dwelling types was adopted, so in addition to neighborhoods of townhouses and detached houses on curving streets, Bramalea has twenty-five high-rise apartment blocks arranged in clusters around the town center (Figure 6.2).[9]

More recent residential developments in the outer suburbs have not followed the Metro model as faithfully, though the standard practice has been to build them using the sorts of comprehensive planning principles employed in Bramalea, with neighborhood units, a mixture of housing types, parks, schools, provisions for retailing, and open spaces along protected greenways. While no other individual projects have been on the scale of Bramalea, master planned communities of several thousand dwellings are common. These have names such as the Vales of Castlemore or Milliken Mills, often derived from a local place, and adopt an architectural theme using a prescribed palette of styles, materials, and colors to establish a distinctive visual identity. Most houses are two stories in height and have brick or sometimes fake stone cladding over wood frames, and most have

Figure 6.3. A street of two-story brick houses in the outer suburbs. Yellow Brick Road is in Brampton and was built in the 1990s. Finding more or less unique names for streets in rapidly growing urban areas apparently presents a challenge.

two-car garages (Figure 6.3). Architectural styles are loosely Victorian, Georgian, or Colonial. There are about 510 apartment towers—the older ones rental and the newer ones condominiums—plus another 20 office towers distributed throughout the outer suburbs, though only in Bramalea and Mississauga do the clusters rival the scale of those found in the City of Toronto. Remarkably if the outer suburbs were a single city, by the ranking of Skyscraperpage.com for high-rises it would come fourteenth in the world, just below Los Angeles and above Sao Paulo. Many subdivisions also include townhouses or row houses, often squeezed onto small lots with tiny backyards, and these provide some of the least expensive family housing in the Toronto region—indeed, a three-bedroom townhouse in the outer suburbs can cost less than a studio condominium in downtown Toronto.[10]

The residential areas of the outer suburbs generally belie what Jane Jacobs once referred to as "the suburban sprawl called York [the regional municipality north of the City of Toronto] . . . with many gated, expensive housing tracts." There are a few areas of large, expensive houses with three-car garages on wide lots, but these are the exception rather than the rule, and some of them are integrated into subdivisions with a mix of housing types. Apart from some exurban developments on the Oak Ridges Moraine, I know of only a handful of gated communities in York Region or anywhere else in the outer suburbs. One of those, Swan Lake, is a retirement community of small houses and low-rise apartments adjacent to a repurposed former flooded gravel pit (the lake), with private roads substantially narrower than the municipality requires for public roads, so it is almost a model of what compact sustainable suburban development should look like.[11]

Almost half a million dwellings were constructed in Toronto's outer suburbs between 1991 and 2011, and because the same developers and construction firms operate throughout the region it is not surprising that in spite of attempts to give subdivisions distinct identities many of them do look similar. It is probably fair to say that they are more diversified by the people who live in them than by their architecture. In all but one of the fourteen outer suburban municipalities more than 20 percent of the population are immigrants; in seven of them, more than 20 percent are visible minorities; both Markham and Mississauga have higher proportions of immigrants and visible minorities than the City of Toronto (Table 6.2). In most outer suburban communities, different ethnic groups are mixed together, but there are several ethnoburbs, where particular groups of recent immigrants are so concentrated that English is a minority language. The most pronounced of these are in Brampton, which is predominantly South Asian, and Markham, where much of the population has come from Hong Kong and China.

Houses in the outer suburbs give few indications of this ethnic diversity, though it is sometimes apparent in retail centers. Pacific Mall in the Town of Markham promotes itself as "the Largest Chinese Indoor Mall in North America," is filled with glass-walled cubicles for more than three hundred shops selling clothes, electronics, and traditional medicines, and includes Heritage Town, essentially the food court, which is designed to look like an old Chinese street market. Next to it is Market Village, originally an outdoor mall designed and built in about 1990 to look like a Disneyfied small Ontario town at a time when most of the local population was white and Anglo-Saxon. It was not very successful, and as the surrounding area developed and became increasingly Chinese it was enclosed by the simple expedient of putting on a flat metal roof at about cornice height; its fake Victorian buildings now house noodle shops, numerous Chinese restaurants and food stores, an abacus training center, and stalls selling red bean ice cream. The Great Punjab Business Centre at Malton in the City of

Table 6.2. Immigrants in Outer Suburban Municipalities

	Municipality	Population (2011)	Population density per square mile (2011)	Population (2006)	Visible minorities (% of 2006 population)	Immigrants (% of 2006 population)
West	Mississauga	713,000	6,300	668,000	49	52
West	Brampton	524,000	5,100	433,000	57	48
West	Oakville	182,000	3,400	165,000	19	31
West	Burlington	176,000	2,400	164,000	10	23
West	Milton	84,000	6,900	54,000	17	25
North	Markham	302,000	3,700	261,000	66	51
North	Richmond Hill	186,000	4,800	164,000	45	52
North	Vaughan	288,000	2,700	239,000	27	45
North	Aurora	53,000	2,800	48,000	13	23
North	Newmarket	80,000	5,300	74,000	15	22
East	Pickering	89,000	980	88,000	30	30
East	Ajax	110,000	4,200	90,000	36	31
East	Whitby	122,000	2,200	111,000	18	21
East	Oshawa	150,000	2,700	142,000	8	16
	City of Toronto	2,615,000	10,800	2,503,000	47	50

Sources: Statistics Canada, Census 2006; Statistics Canada, Census 2011.
Notes: For each compass direction, the municipalities are arranged by distance from the City of Toronto to show that percentages of both immigrants and visible minorities decline toward the edges of the built-up area. The population density for Milton is for the "population center" or built-up area (the only one available in the 2011 Census); for all others it is for the municipality, which in most outer suburbs includes substantial agricultural and other green spaces. The density for Pickering is low because the municipality includes undeveloped sites for a new airport and a new town. Data for visible minorities and immigrants for 2011 are not yet available.

Brampton is a commercial and industrial project with about two hundred units, within easy walking distance of a Sikh temple and Khalsa community school. The City of Vaughan, which lies between Markham and Brampton, has a more established immigrant population, but a large new Jewish community campus and numerous banqueting halls and signs for imported Italian goods make it clear that this is part of a wedge of Italian and Jewish communities that extends from the heart of the old City to the farthest fringes of the urban region. More generally, restaurants and food stores in older strip plazas throughout the outer suburbs reveal the cultural origins of the local community.

In spite of these pockets of diversity, most patches of retailing in the outer suburbs are standardized. Many are the work of Smart Centres, a Toronto-based developer of midsized retail plazas, which for some incomprehensible reason has a small sculpture of a family of penguins carrying shopping bags at the main road entrance to each of its projects. Otherwise most plazas have a familiar mix of franchises and chains, and their layout and appearance are similar to new plazas in other cities across Canada and North America. Except for the standard palettes of franchises and big boxes such as IKEA, Walmart, and Home Depot, outer suburban retail architecture usually involves brick cladding and decorative elements that seem to be vaguely Italianate or possibly Georgian. The indeterminate bland designs belie the variety of populations that they serve and are simultaneously belied by the diversity of their customers and the employees who work in them.

Faith-based Subdivisions and New Urbanism

Ethnic diversity is, however, very apparent in religious buildings such as mosques, Catholic churches, gurdwaras, Chinese Baptist churches, Hindu temples, and synagogues, which are often the most architecturally striking elements of outer suburban landscapes. It seems to be a not uncommon practice, perhaps to avoid potential NIMBYism, for temples or churches to be built on greenfield sites beyond the edge of the built-up area, and this allows a faith-based community to grow around each religious structure as the city expands. The Avraham Josef Synagogue in Vaughan, which claims to be one of the largest Modern Orthodox synagogues in North America, was built in the 1980s as the anchor for a Jewish residential development. About seven miles farther north, the Baitul Islam Mosque was surrounded by farmland when it was built in the 1990s; subsequent discussions between religious leaders and municipal planners led to the development of the surrounding neighborhood as the Ahmadiyya "Peace Village," with streets named for famous members of the sect and houses that provide separate living rooms for men and women (Figure 6.4). A couple of miles away, a 1,100-seat Catholic church is the focal point of the primarily Italian subdivision of Vellore Village. When the Slovak Catholic Cathedral of the Transfiguration was consecrated by Pope John Paul in 1984 it stood alone in a field several miles north of the built-up area of Markham; by 2010 the city

Figure 6.4. A faith-based subdivision and ethnoburb in Vaughan in York Region. The Baitul Islam Mosque is the center of a Muslim neighborhood called Peace Village.

had reached it, and it is now the central feature of a new urbanist development appropriately called Cathedraltown that has streets of Georgian-style row houses and a piazza with fountains.

Cathedraltown is one of a number of new urbanist projects in Toronto's outer suburbs. Andrés Duany, the Florida-based planner who is one of the foremost proponents of this movement that aims to create compact new developments by drawing inspiration from old urban forms, has been a frequent visitor. New urbanism has gained remarkable traction in the Town of Markham, perhaps more than anywhere else in North America, and about 150,000 people there have been said to live in new-urbanist-influenced projects. Until about 1990 new residential developments in Markham were unremarkable though it had acquired a reputation as a place for high-tech industries, including one of the North American hubs for IBM. In an effort to establish a stronger identity for itself, in the early 1990s Markham hired Duany as a consultant both to provide general advice about new urbanism and specifically to develop concept plans for the master-planned development of Cornell, which is expected to have a final population of thirty thousand. There are elaborate design guidelines for

Figure 6.5. A cross section of a new urbanist development under construction in Oakville in the 1990s. The houses have a short setback from the street, tiny backyards, garages (some with mother-in-law apartments above), and rear laneways.

Cornell, the spirit of which was captured perfectly in a promotional poster that shows Duany shaking hands with the main developer, Larry Law, under the phrase "I have seen the future and it is the past." Cornell is roughly modeled on the streetcar suburbs of old Toronto without the streetcars, so there are a loose grid of streets (no culs-de-sac or loops), houses that are close to the street line, garages in rear laneways (some with mother-in-law suites above them), small parks in each neighborhood, and a main street that is lined with small stores and services. Much of the architecture is a sort of Victorian revival with front porches that are intended to promote people watching.[12]

Similar new urbanist design principles have been incorporated into other residential developments in Markham, including Cathedraltown, and for a number of other projects in other municipalities. Most, including Cornell, are currently incomplete and until they are finished it is difficult to judge how much they will promote pedestrian activity, which is one of their primary goals, though there are indications that population densities are higher than in adjacent, more conventional residential areas. They certainly have the appearance of squeezing houses onto small lots with tiny backyards (Figure 6.5). There is, however, a concern that they do not provide many employment opportunities, and because most residents drive to work they are, for all their innovations, still automobile commuter developments rather than radical contributions to an overall compact city form. Regardless of that it is clear that new urbanist developments now constitute a viable alternative choice for those who choose not to live in the more conventional sorts of residential subdivisions that prevail in Toronto's outer suburbs, and they could well be paving the way for the sort of overall residential intensification that is now being implemented throughout the Greater Golden Horseshoe.

Industrial and Employment Districts

Seen from an aircraft making its final approach to the airport, the industrial and commercial areas of the outer suburbs are easily identified by their rectangular patchworks of large brown rooftops and parking areas that, by comparison with houses and tree-lined streets, seem to be both barren and Brobdingnagian in scale (Figure 6.6). They cover thousands of acres, have been developed by corporations specializing in business and industrial parks, and provide over half the jobs in the Toronto region. At ground level these employment districts seem far less crowded than they do from the air—indeed they have a spacious, minimalist, mysterious quality. Spacious because roads have to be wide enough to accommodate semi trailers and most buildings are set back behind wide boulevards. Minimalist because many buildings are big, functional, undecorated, low-rise sheds (not more than one industrial story tall, the height that can be reached by a forklift truck), that are made of low-cost, low-maintenance materials, with long windowless walls. Mysterious because there is rarely an indication of what happens inside them. Clearly money is being made. Goods are brought in, sorted, and stored before being shipped out to retailers; pharmaceuticals are manufactured; DNA is sliced and spliced; electronic equipment assembled; data processed. But most industrial buildings are the architectural equivalents of modern electrical appliances—they have flat surfaces, clean lines, and are opaque.[13]

In spite of their architectural opacity, it is possible to deduce from names and signs that these patches of employment have a wide variety of activities. For example, Beaver Creek in Richmond Hill, which occupies a square-mile patch at the intersection of two expressways, has the Canadian

Figure 6.6. An industrial area near Pearson Airport: a treeless flatland of large gray and brown rectangles surrounded by trailers on standby.

head offices of Levi-Strauss, Compugen, and Suzuki; dozens of low buildings divided into units are variously occupied by accountants, lawyers, and companies manufacturing or repairing high-tech products; there are several fitness and health clubs; a couple of small office towers; a facility for recycling electronics; restaurants, fast-food places, and pubs to feed all the workers; two hotels; and the town hall for the Town of Richmond Hill. The population in this part of the region is primarily Chinese, and there is also a studio for Fairchild TV, which broadcasts in Cantonese, as well as several tutorial schools for Chinese students, and a plaza called Times Square entirely occupied by Chinese businesses.

Of all the outer suburban employment districts, the ones surrounding Pearson Airport are remarkable both for their sheer extent and for their role in transshipment. Here there are convention centers and hotels, a business park with the Canadian head offices of more than thirty major corporations, and industrial plants making a range of things to keep aircraft functioning, such as guidance systems and in-flight meals. On the grounds of the airport there are three cargo terminals (completely separate from the passenger terminals). A few miles to the west are two of the largest inter-modal facilities in Canada, where containers arrive by rail from the West Coast and are offloaded onto trucks. Many buildings are surrounded by trailers parked nose to tail and inches apart, with rows of trucks waiting to tow them and to keep the distribution centers and stores of the region supplied with stuff. This huge industrial patch, almost ten miles wide, func-tions as a gigantic portal where goods arrive and leave the Toronto region by air or rail or truck; where products are gathered, sorted, stored, and distributed; and where almost nobody lives. No less than the financial dis-trict in the core of the city, this is where Toronto makes contact with the global economy, though in a material rather than a virtual way.

Distinctive Suburban Centers—Old and New

The airport, employment districts such as Beaver Creek, and shopping malls are important focal points of activity in the outer suburbs, attracting thousands of people and vehicles every day. But each of these areas is rela-tively one-dimensional, serving a single primary function such as travel, transshipment, or shopping. In contrast, an *urban center* is multifunc-tional—it combines residential, retail, employment, and institutional activi-ties, and it serves a symbolic function as a focus for local identity. Toronto's outer suburbs are articulated by about thirty distinct urban centers. A few are entirely new but most are based on small towns that have been enve-loped by the continuously built-up area and are now protected and pro-moted as core areas that can articulate urban development.

Some old centers take advantage of their distinctive history, location, or architectural heritage to create what might be called an enhanced identity. For instance, Port Credit on the shore of Lake Ontario at the mouth of the Credit River was once a small industrial town with a large starch factory serviced by a small port. The former starch factory between the main street and the lakeshore has been replaced by a compact townhouse development that includes a small park where the history of the site is recounted, and the old industrial port has been turned into a marina that is the main base for the recent revival of sport salmon fishing in Lake Ontario. Unionville in the Town of Markham is remarkable in the region because it has a main street that curves (in order to avoid a steep-sided creek), and this picturesque characteristic has been used to promote what is described on its website as a "beautiful, European style Historic Village." Port Credit, Unionville, and most other old small centers in the outer suburbs have adopted urban design practices that follow provincial guidelines for redeveloping main streets, including pedestrian-scale streetlights, sidewalks and crosswalks of interlocking pavers, attractive street furniture, restricted parking, and traffic-calming measures. Together with heritage protection of old buildings and districts, these have helped small towns in the outer suburbs survive the considerable challenges presented by drive-to plazas and standardized big-box retailing.[14]

On an altogether larger scale the former small town of Brampton is being redeveloped as the heart of the current City of Brampton. Like most old centers in the outer suburbs, it first grew up in the nineteenth century to serve the needs of surrounding farms, but it also developed several successful nurseries for cultivating flowers. In 1961 Brampton had a population of 18,500, not much larger than it had been half a century earlier, and it had retained its role as a place for the production of cut flowers. With the establishment of regional municipalities and local government reorganization in the 1970s the old town was stripped of its political identity and reduced to little more than an old district in the more extensive new City of Brampton, which also included the new town of Bramalea but at the time was otherwise largely rural. The City of Brampton is now almost completely built up with a population of about 525,000, and it is the ninth largest municipality in Canada. About half of that population comprises immigrants and members of visible minority groups, especially from South Asia. However, Brampton has chosen to shape its identity around its old roots, brands itself as "Flower City" (even though nurseries are now a very minor part of its economic base, which includes automobile assembly and one of the major intermodals), and is redeveloping the former small town with its main streets, late Victorian residential areas, pleasant park and elegant old churches, as the core of that identity. Jane Jacobs, who rarely wrote about trips she had made in the region outside the old City of Toronto, visited Brampton in the 1990s and found it attractive, though she seems to have been most impressed with the scale of import replacement that was under way in the new industrial areas. The old town is now the location of the City of Brampton's updated city hall, and it has several high-rise apartments, a GO commuter train station, and the new Rose Theatre set in a pedestrian plaza. Further enhancements to create pedestrian-friendly and transit-oriented neighborhoods in and around the "historic downtown" are planned.[15]

The revitalization of downtown Brampton, like the smaller-scale enhancements of Unionville and most of the thirty other old centers in the outer suburbs, demonstrates that these have become critical for local and municipal identities and that communities are willing to go to considerable lengths and expense to preserve them and make them successful. Where there were no old towns that could serve as foci for new growth, multifunctional new centers have been and are being created. These could be considered edge cities, though that name fails to do justice to them because these are the planned centers of independent municipalities rather than commercially developed concentrations of offices and retailing on the margins of existing cities. Bramalea is one of these new centers, with a regional shopping mall, recreational facilities, and the municipal offices for the Regional Municipality of Peel. Pickering Town Centre dates from the early 1970s and although it was planned around a shopping mall it now has Pickering City Hall, a major recreational center, office buildings, a bus transit station, high-density townhouses and apartment buildings, and a pedestrian bridge connection across Highway 401 to the GO commuter rail station, which is inconveniently located on the other side of the expressway.[16]

The newest centers in the outer suburbs reflect changes in design philosophies that are less dependent on shopping malls. The City of Vaughan has plans for what it refers to as a "metropolitan centre," which will "offer all amenities of urban lifestyle including business offices, residences, entertainment and cultural facilities, pedestrian shopping areas and urban squares." Although at present the site is a mixture of grassy open spaces and big-box stores, renderings show future street scenes reminiscent of the Champs-Élysées. While this is obviously fanciful, the proposed metropolitan center will be the terminus of the first extension of the subway outside the City of Toronto (currently under construction) and this will be the stimulus for high-density development. The Town of Markham is constructing a new downtown that will serve as "a community-wide focus for cultural, entertainment and institutional activities." It reflects Markham's enthusiastic adoption of new urbanism and already has several Georgian-style streets of

Figure 6.7. The skyline of downtown Mississauga.

townhouses and midrise apartments, with parking below ground. A commercial street and piazza, yet to be built, will be lined with stores and pedestrianized except for the right-of-way for the bus rapid-transit system that already serves major corridors in York Region.

Markham, Pickering, and all the other centers in the outer suburbs, whether old or new, pale in comparison with downtown Mississauga. When several villages and townships were amalgamated in 1968 to create the new municipality of Mississauga, the area was mostly rural, although speculators anticipating urban growth had already acquired large tracts of land. Mississauga now has a population of 750,000, which makes it the sixth largest city in Canada (larger than Winnipeg), and this status is reflected in a dramatic high-rise skyline that dominates the western outer suburbs (Figure 6.7). Early conceptual plans proposed a broad structure of land uses that responded to the matrix provided by the grid of concession roads, with a finer grid around the proposed urban center that would be left partly open and gradually filled in as demand for more intense development grew. In other words, it would grow in toward the center rather than out from it as old cities had. The initial major development in the center was a regional shopping mall (called Square One, perhaps because it was in the first square of the grid of the master plan), located next to a future expressway. A civic building for the new municipality was soon completed on adjacent land. At first both buildings were surrounded by farmland, but in the 1970s and early 1980s development accelerated, and a number of apartment and office towers were constructed. Wide roads, generous spaces around the towers, and a huge parking lot for the mall initially made for a windy, rather vacuous, quintessentially edge-city landscape. Then in the late 1980s a new city hall and civic square were built in a postmodern design that attracted considerable international attention. Unusually for the time, these were built to the street line, and this promoted a more pedestrian-oriented approach for subsequent developments in the rest of downtown Mississauga that has been progressively implemented with the construction of a central library, a multipurpose arts center, and office and apartment buildings built at the street line. Two dramatic condominium towers, completed in 2011 and spiraling up more than fifty stories in sensuous curves, have been nicknamed the Marilyn Monroe buildings and are among the tallest apartment buildings in Canada.

Mississauga's city center is the second-largest urban node in the Toronto region; when it is seen from the departure lounges of Pearson Airport its high-rise skyline rivals that of the more distant downtown Toronto. Close-up, however, and in spite of the urban design guidelines, it has a divided personality. It has been suggested that the idea of the Mississauga city center came from a developer who effectively used a series of public/private partnerships "to shore up an urban landscape" with public buildings. The actual story is probably more complicated than that, though it is the case that much of downtown Mississauga is currently owned by a single pension fund (OMERS—the Ontario Municipal Employees Retirement System) that is certainly interested in ensuring a sound return on investment. Regardless of motives and ownership, the city center is compromised by two six-lane arterial roads that cut through it and by indeterminate open spaces around several of the buildings; parts of the parking lot surrounding the mall have been built on but it is still immense and has signs ominously forbidding the "distribution of literature" to remind everyone that it is a private space. There is, in fact, much that does not correspond to the scale and form that might reasonably be expected of a city center.[17]

There is a plan to change this. *Downtown 21: Creating an Urban Place in the Heart of Mississauga*, approved in 2011, proposes measures to transform the current landscape into "a vibrant, character-rich, pedestrian oriented core." Parking structures will be built around the Square One Shopping Mall, and surplus grade-level parking is to be redeveloped as a series of small blocks formed by a tight grid of streets that is already mapped out in the pattern of the lanes of the parking lot; some streets will be narrowed, and dedicated lanes for transit and bicycles will be installed on the arterial roads. All new buildings will be close to the street line and will be scaled or stepped back in ways that should encourage pedestrian activity. These may seem like unrealistic goals, not least because similar claims have been made about previous plans and never implemented, yet even with all its current flaws and indeterminate open spaces it is clear that Mississauga City Centre is already the vital core of a city that is less than fifty years old. There are people on the streets and frequent events in the civic square and the arts center. The Marilyn Monroe towers have street frontages with cafés and shops, and a new campus of a community college close to the Civic Centre has helped to promote pedestrian activity. It may take several decades before the city center is really transformed into "an urban place," as *Downtown 21* envisages, but there is no doubt that significant changes are under way.[18]

Intensification Corridors

One of those changes is the installation of light rapid transit. Downtown Mississauga, Brampton, and Port Credit are key nodes in a transportation corridor along Hurontario Street, an old settlement road that runs, as its name suggests, from Lake Ontario to Lake Huron. At present this is a wide arterial road with narrower sections where it passes through old urban centers. The intention, in concert with *Downtown 21* for Mississauga and the redevelopment plan for Brampton, is to turn Hurontario into an intensification corridor by installing a light rapid-transit system on a dedicated right-of-way and by implementing urban design strategies to promote pedestrian-friendly forms of associated residential, retail, and commercial development. The idea is that Hurontario will become a series of destinations rather than an arterial through route.[19]

In 2012 the Hurontario intensification corridor is in advanced stages of design and public discussion. In York Region the process of creating transportation corridors linking urban nodes is well advanced and based on a bus rapid-transit system called Viva that has been operating since 2005 and seems to be loosely modeled on the innovative approaches used in Curitiba in Brazil and Bogotá in Colombia. Rapid transit is not a popular travel option in the outer suburbs—the Canadian Census indicates about 15 percent of all journeys to work there are by transit, walking, or biking, compared with 45 percent in the City of Toronto. The Viva system is a serious attempt to increase this percentage. Buses are GPS monitored, with waiting times electronically displayed at stops; they provide free wireless Internet, and they connect with GO rail stations and also the subway system in the City of Toronto. Thus far, the buses have shared roads with other vehicles, but the construction of dedicated bus-only lanes (called "rapid-ways") is in process (see Figure 9.3).

The long-term planning aim in York Region is to have high-density, transit-oriented development along the Viva corridors, particularly along Highway 7 and Yonge Street. Renderings show them lined with shops and outdoor cafés, which is probably unrealistic given the width of the arterials. Nevertheless, sections of the Viva corridor on Highway 7 in Markham and Richmond Hill already have remarkable levels of intensification with a mixture of offices, employment districts, retail stores, and clusters of high-rise condominiums. Viva is an integral component of the "Centres and Corridors Strategy" in York Region, which is intended to link nodes of more intense development, such as those at downtown Markham and Vaughan Metropolitan Centre, and to reinforce the compact development associated with new urbanist communities. Where the main east-west and north-south Viva routes intersect in Richmond Hill, and also connect with a GO rail line, there are plans for a regional growth center, including a very high-density residential community that has been designed by the American new urbanist planner Peter Calthorpe.[20]

These intensification corridors are, in effect, attempting to change a key part of the matrix of the outer suburbs. To be successful they will have to undo some of the divisiveness currently created by arterial roads, which separate the patches of the outer suburbs even as they provide the means for connecting them. These arterials tend to function like little expressways, many of them 132 feet wide with six lanes of moving traffic, lined with commercial strips or with blank walls shielding the backyards of houses in

Figure 6.8. The edge of Toronto's built-up area is almost everywhere neatly defined by a precise but temporary urban growth boundary. This photograph shows the boundary as it was in 2006 at the northwest corner of Brampton at Chingacousy Road and Sandalwood Parkway. The modified grid pattern in this subdivision indicates a shift away from curvilinear street patterns.

subdivisions that are turned away from them. The hope is that rapid transit can maintain the connectivity yet reduce the separation, and that eventually intensification corridors will take on some of the characteristics and qualities of old main streets, though if current developments are an indication, they will be more spacious, at a larger scale, and somewhat less textured than streets in the old City.

The Edge

The development edge or urban boundary of the continuously built-up area is where the city abuts the countryside. In the Toronto region this is almost everywhere very clear, often a straight line with fields on one side and subdivisions either completed or under construction on the other side (Figure 6.8). The planning consultants Zack Taylor and Myron Burchfield found that 85 percent of new development between 1991 and 2001 was within two kilometers of the 1990 perimeter of the built-up area with almost none of the leapfrogging that is common around many U.S. cities. Richard White, a planning historian who has investigated post-1945 growth in the Toronto region, attributes the reasons for this to policies established in the 1950s by Metro, which created "a rather unusual set of subregional boundaries, expanded as land supply becomes tight," that have led to "a remarkably contiguous suburban carpet." Whatever the origin, these practices have resulted in a precise edge to the urban area of the outer suburbs, though the alignments of streets that lead directly toward fields indicate that this edge is temporary.[21]

Beyond the Outer Suburbs

Beyond the development edge is exurbia. In the Toronto region this takes two forms. The first is a band of more or less flat farmland, with a few small towns and villages, some with their own small new suburbs. Most of this band is a zone for the expansion of the city. Much of it has already been approved for development.

Farther away are the Niagara Escarpment and the Oak Ridges Moraine, key aspects of the matrix of the urban region and the territories of exurbia proper. These have hilly landscapes that in an otherwise mostly flat region are a major attraction for those who have money and opportunity. They are also ideal for golf courses and horse farms; in York Region alone there are more than one hundred golf courses, and a population of more than eighteen thousand horses on several hundred horse farms. In the 1950s and 1960s the Escarpment and the Moraine became popular locations for those who wanted to live a semirural dream in a grand house, with a few acres and a horse or two. This exurban pioneering was followed by the construction of exurban estates, many of them tucked away behind trees and difficult to see from the highway; a few are gated, and most have ultra-low densities because the houses have their own wells and septic tanks. The acme of exurbanization in the region may be the headquarters of the Magna Corporation, a major international supplier of automobile parts. The headquarters building in Aurora is designed to look like a French chateau that with trucks coming and going could well be a set for a James Bond movie; behind it, screened from public roads and visible to outsiders only on

Google Earth, are a gated golf-course community, a stables, and a track for training racehorses.[22]

As a functional region defined by regular daily and weekly patterns of movement, Toronto extends well past the Oak Ridges Moraine into the Greater Golden Horseshoe. The city of Barrie—an old town on Lake Simcoe about twenty-five miles north of the edge of the outer suburbs—is well within commuting range of Toronto (and vice versa—a former neighbor of mine commuted from Toronto to Barrie every day) and has been adding subdivisions and commercial strips for several decades. Northwest of Barrie, Blue Mountain Village near the town of Collingwood on Georgian Bay has been made into a four-season resort by the company that developed Whistler in British Columbia, mainly to take advantage of the best downhill skiing in southern Ontario (it's not dramatic—a mere 720-foot drop but still the best in the region). Blue Mountain Village is within day-trip range of Toronto. So are the casinos at Niagara Falls and at Casino Rama north of Lake Simcoe, to which privately operated buses run several times a day from numerous locations in the city and the outer suburbs. There may be a neat edge to the built-up area, but the functioning city reaches far beyond that into the rest of the Greater Golden Horseshoe.

Sprawling Fragmentation or Coherent Diversity?

The patches, centers, and corridors of the outer suburbs have many varied expressions that occur in patterns, which, given their scale, are probably most easily grasped from the air. The view in Figure 6.9 of an area near the old town of Brampton is reasonably representative. It shows several different landscape patches—residential, recreational, and industrial, and several different types of corridors—a greenway following a tributary of Etobicoke Creek, an expressway paralleled by an electrical transmission line, and an arterial road. The arterial is Hurontario Street, which in this section is part of the proposed intensification corridor associated with light rapid transit.

One reaction to this view would be that it shows quintessential sprawl, the fragmentation of low-density patches separated by corridors, wasted space around the interchange and beside the expressway: urban bits pulled apart rather than pulled together. An alternative response is that it shows well-ordered residential developments designed to protect watercourses and prevent through traffic, and it includes a range of housing options that are

Figure 6.9. The patches and patterns of Toronto's outer suburbs at Highway 407 and Hurontario Street, looking north, in 2008. At the bottom of the photo, barely visible, a corridor with power lines parallels Highway 407. The arterial corridor is Hurontario. In the foreground, two subdivisions of single-family houses with five apartment towers surround a district plaza. In the middle distance, the darker area is the old Town of Brampton, with streets lined with mature trees; the green corridor on the far left is a tributary of Etobicoke Creek; on the far right is a golf course; the treeless area above it in the middle distance is the industrial district of Bramalea.

conveniently close to a large employment district, are organized around schools, and have easy access to networks of expressways and arterials that makes it easy to get from place to place. There is some justification for both reactions. Fragmentation is, indeed, a shortcoming of the outer suburbs. Patches of activity are separated by greenways, arterial roads, expressways and transmission lines, most of which are difficult to cross. On the other hand, those patches have been shaped to protect environmentally sensitive areas, and the fact is that the expressways and transmission lines serve the entire region including the old city. Perhaps some of the fragmentation will be mitigated by intensification along transit corridors such as Hurontario Street, but it seems unlikely that there is a way to reconcile these two opinions that reflect the divergence of urban perspectives that emerged fifty years ago in the different urban views expressed by Jacobs and Gottman. What is apparent is that the streetscapes and urban forms of the outer suburbs can never mimic those of old Toronto because the means of transportation, development fashions, and social circumstances have all changed.[23]

What this means is that even for those inclined to see fragmentation rather than coherence Toronto's outer suburbs should not be criticized as some sort of degeneration from the assumed ideal of the old central city. It is not enough to dismiss them as some anti-urban exudation, as Mumford might have done, nor to claim that their planning has resulted in a formless suburban anti-city, as Jacobs expressed it. Instead they have to be seen as constituting a different type of city that has to be assessed on its own terms, an extended city of diverse landscapes and land uses, of ethnoburbs and new urbanist projects, of green corridors, distinctive old towns that are being refurbished, and new centers that are emerging as the focal points of still young municipalities. Of course, there are warts and problems: road allowances are almost all wider then they need to be, and too many shops are in large standardized plazas mostly well beyond walking distance of where people live. On the other hand, remarkable energy and imagination are being invested in the development of innovative types of urban form, rapid transit, and intensification. The regions of Halton, Peel, York, and Durham, and the municipalities and urban centers within them, have now effectively cut any umbilical cord that may once have tied them to the City of Toronto. They are creating their own urban landscapes, identities, and aspirations and have become distinctive participants in the networks of an extensive, multicentered urban region.[24]

Chapter 7

Polycentricity

Maps that show the ever-expanding built-up area of Toronto imply that the old core of the city is an energy source, a kernel from which it has grown inexorably outward. This might once have been the case, but it is an old truth. According to the geographer Peirce Lewis, the nuclear city that has grown from a single core is a "pre-automotive urban form," a form that was held together by the powerful magnetism of a center where rail and other transportation lines converged, and it is a form that was irreversibly changed by the invention of cars. Monocentric cities, he suggested with dramatic flourish, effectively lost their reason for being when the millionth Model T rolled off the line in 1915. Because the shapes of cities change slowly, it took decades for this urban existential crisis to become apparent, but when Lewis looked around in 1980 he saw a world permeated by mobility, in which "the residential subdivisions, the shopping centers, the industrial parks seemed to float in space; seen together they resemble a galaxy of stars and plants, held together by mutual gravitational attraction, but with large empty spaces between clusters." He called this unbounded mix of urban bits and pieces that reach into the smallest towns and most remote villages, "the galactic metropolis."[1]

The galactic metropolis is metropolitan not in the sense of a built-up area but in the sense that both information and much of the cultural and social complexity previously concentrated in large metropolises are now available almost everywhere. With networks of highways, satellite transmissions, and now the Internet, Amazon, and UPS, exotic goods can be delivered as easily and as cheaply, to use Lewis's example, to Miles City, Montana, as to Manhattan. The galactic metropolis is the geographical manifestation of the urban revolution, the huge cultural change in which virtually everything everywhere has come to be permeated with urban processes and values. It involves a sort of spatial democracy, an equalization of places made possible by networks of communication—highways, cars, electrical distribution grids, telephones, radio and television, and fiber optic cable for the Internet. Unlike railways that fed into grand terminals in the heart of cities, such as Union Station in Toronto, which reinforced centrality, these networks facilitate the distribution of goods and services and thus undermine centrality. This has become increasingly pronounced. The urban authority of downtowns that once dominated suburbs, and of central cities that once commanded extensive hinterlands, has been undermined.[2]

This does not mean that existing cities are about to vanish. What it does mean is that urban energy and activities have come to be widely distributed across many centers as metropolitan areas have expanded. Fifty years ago James Vance noted this "loosening of urban structure" and he saw it as being associated with the dispersal of former central area activities into "urban realms," more or less self-contained areas surrounding a formerly monocentric city. It is tempting to look at former lower-tier municipalities in the inner suburbs and existing ones in the outer suburbs of the Toronto urban region as distinct urban realms, an illusion they would like to maintain through branding (such as Brampton as "the rose city") and recreational and social programs because it reinforces their citizens' sense of belonging. In fact their boundaries are for most purposes virtually invisible and utterly permeable. Rather than consisting of more or less discrete urban realms, the Toronto region is better understood as "an evolving urban form that challenges conventional wisdom on how cities are organized." There are old villages, small towns and city centers, new urban centers, employment districts, golf courses, three major airports, half a dozen intermodal facilities, about a dozen regional shopping malls, each with its own constantly shifting sphere of influence and all interconnected by networks of expressways, arterial roads, delivery systems, intensification corridors, cell phone towers, fiber optic cable, and other types of infrastructure that, as McLuhan had it, "create centers everywhere." He suggested that electronic media are the key to understanding this multilayered, overlapping polycentricity, but in the Toronto region there appear to be many overlapping causes, and the trigger seems to have been planned decentralization.[3]

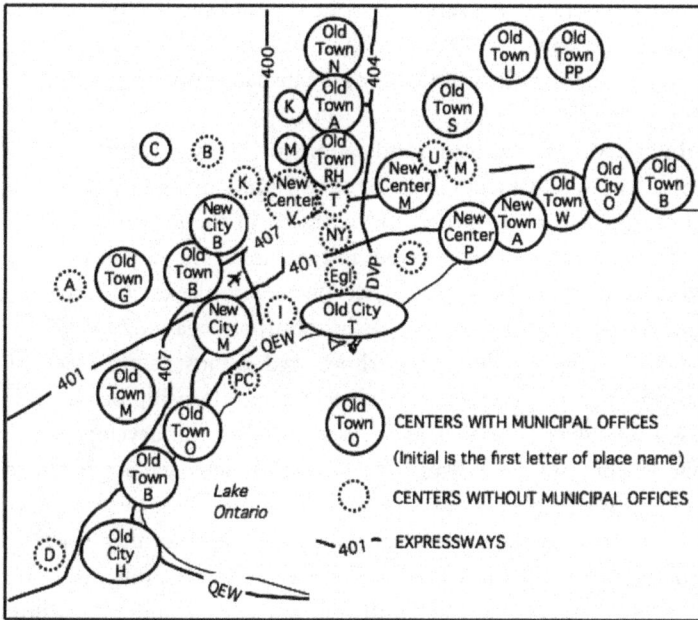

Figure 7.1. Urban centers in the Greater Toronto and Hamilton Area. The distinction between "Town" and "City" is based on the municipality's official name. Some centers, such as Newmarket and Oakville, have offices of both upper- and lower-tier municipalities. The circles are representative and not scaled to population.

Deconcentrated Concentration

Within the City of Toronto there are, in addition to the downtown core, at least five major urban centers. Outside the City, but within the conurbation of the Greater Toronto and Hamilton Area, there are more than twenty distinct downtowns that serve as centers of municipalities (Figure 7.1). The detailed forms of these vary considerably, but most have some combination of a town or city hall, federal office buildings, commercial offices, hotels, retail stores, high-density residential developments, and transit stations. And in the more extensive region of the Greater Golden Horseshoe there are a dozen more cities. Altogether there are about forty distinct urban centers, though these range enormously in scale from downtown Mississauga with its apartment and office towers, huge regional shopping mall, and massive civic center which serves a population of 713,000, to King City, which in spite of its name is little more than a village where a few units in a strip plaza are the municipal offices for an exurban municipality that has a population of 20,000.[4]

Until about 1960 there were no indications that this polycentric urban pattern would emerge. Almost all major urban functions—hospitals, universities, government, shops—were concentrated in the downtown of the old City of Toronto and to a lesser extent in Hamilton. The first intimations of future decentralization came in the late 1960s with the establishment of new universities and community colleges in suburban areas and the smaller cities of the Greater Golden Horseshoe, and almost simultaneously (though, as far I can tell, there was absolutely no relationship between the two processes and they are nowhere juxtaposed) with the development of several regional shopping malls, such as those in Mississauga, Scarborough, and Pickering, located next to expressways. Together these seem to have established the idea of spreading resources around, and since then the polycentric structure of the Toronto region has been self-consciously planned, with many of the centers associated with shopping malls and almost none with new college campuses. This process began with the office deconcentration policies of the old City and Metro in the mid-1970s, which were subsequently entrenched in the 1981 Metroplan for Metro Toronto that aimed "to create a multi-centred urban structure, with each centre multifunctional, compact and pedestrian oriented." At about the same time municipalities in the outer suburbs that had been created by local government reorganization began to establish their new identities by building civic buildings and town halls. More recently this multicenteredness has been reinforced by the 2006 Growth Plan for the Greater Golden Horseshoe (discussed in Chapter 9), which has the explicit aim of building "compact, vibrant and complete communities" in twenty-five widely distributed "urban growth centres."[5]

This all seems clear enough at a broad scale, and each of the places identified in Figure 7.1 does have its own identity as a multifunctional center. However, complexities in the practice of polycentricity begin to emerge when things are looked at in more detail. The Official Plan for York Region, for example, identifies the four provincial urban growth centers in its territory, plus a number of additional local centers that are described as "concentrations of residential, human services, commercial and office activities," which will play a supporting role to the regional ones, plus historic centers (the downtowns of old small towns), several healthcare centers, and employment centers such as Beaver Creek. That's five different types of center. In the Town of Newmarket four of them occur within a mile of each other. At the scale of the Greater Golden Horseshoe this becomes even more complicated. There are, for example, a dozen major healthcare centers, most of which are parts of subregional networks of several hospitals that are not located in urban growth centers. There are fourteen university campuses linked by specialized computer networks, and several of those are networked with community colleges, which in turn have their own networks of several campuses. There are also regional shopping malls that are not part of urban growth centers, probably about twenty historic downtown centers, and Pearson Airport and other major employment centers.[6]

A comprehensive view of polycentricity has to recognize all these sorts of centers that attract and generate flows of people, ideas, goods, and traffic. From this perspective the Toronto region is characterized by what the eminent urbanist Peter Hall has called "deconcentrated concentration." Activities that were once focused in cities and towns, and above all in the downtown of the old City of Toronto, are now widely distributed across the region in various types of centers that are interconnected by many different superimposed networks.[7]

The Declining Role of Downtown Toronto

In his book *The 100 Mile City*, which offers an innovative account of the unprecedented patterns and functions of extensive urban regions that have emerged since 1970, Deyan Sudjic suggests that even though an old urban core may have been where urban growth began, in every other respect, "it is just another piece on the board, a counter that has the same weight as all the others." In the Toronto region this isn't quite right, because the old urban core of Toronto, while it may no longer be the only piece on the board, is still clearly the largest and most powerful piece. It continues to play a crucial role because it has deeper history than all the other centers, because it is where financial services are concentrated, because it offers high-quality entertainment and cultural amenities, and because it provides most of the social housing and comprehensive social services in the region. Furthermore, the old City is the only urban area with densities that can support mass transit and that has many neighborhoods with the street-oriented, fine-textured urban environments that Jane Jacobs celebrated. For cultural and creative activities it is not merely regionally important but is the third most significant center of English theater in the world. It is also where the major galleries and museums are located and where the major professional sports teams have their facilities. And, for better or for worse, it is where the provincial legislature is located. In short, the downtown core of Toronto has provincial, national, and international prominence, and it exerts a strong gravitational pull within the galactic city of southern Ontario.[8]

Nevertheless, there is no question that this pull has weakened as jobs, services, and residents have dispersed throughout the urban region. Buckminster Fuller, the former futurist and inventor, saw this coming as early as 1968 when he was privately commissioned to undertake a conceptual study of the future of Toronto. In his report he wrote that the central city was no longer the sole focus of urban life and that the automobile had taken away goods, services, and people to what he called the "outer belt," where the orientation to highways and mobility had created a new type of focus. About forty years later, in what it refers to as a territorial review of Toronto, the Organisation for Economic Co-operation and Development (OECD) took it for granted that Toronto's urban economy now functions at the scale of the polycentric region. And the importance of this assumption has been locally stressed in a report about Toronto titled "Breaking Boundaries: Time to Think and Act like a Region," prepared by Civic Action, a powerful advocacy and research group that addresses a wide range of economic, cultural, and social issues that spill across municipal boundaries and political hierarchies. The reports of the OECD and Civic Action are primarily concerned with economic development but they lend support to a view about regional planning that is embodied in the provincial Growth Plan for the Greater Golden Horseshoe, which scarcely mentions Toronto except to note briefly that the downtown office core will continue to be the primary center for international finance and commerce.[9]

Networks of Infrastructure

Manuel Castells, who is especially interested in the global geography of communications and its impact on cities, claims that the significance of networks lies in the fact that they are dynamic, open structures and are able to expand, incorporate additional nodes, and adapt to change. In this respect, the expansion of the networks of the humblest of infrastructures—water and sewer lines—played a critical role in the post-1970 growth of Toronto's outer suburbs when the six-foot-diameter "Big Pipe" sewers and equally large water supply lines made possible urban growth in York Region, Mississauga, and Brampton by connecting them to Lake Ontario and freeing them from dependence on limited groundwater sources. Buried networks of pipes are easily ignored, the various pumping stations and other surface structures are anonymous and utilitarian, and even the huge sewage treatment plants on the shore of Lake Ontario (more than half a dozen of them serve greater Toronto) are out of the way, largely hidden from view behind berms and fences. These networks of pipes cannot be said to have created the polycentric region, but they certainly made possible the growth of the outer suburbs that resulted in the planned development of urban centers, such as those in Markham, Richmond Hill, Mississauga, and Brampton.[10]

Even when networks of infrastructure are very visible they often seem to go, if not exactly unseen, at least unremarked. Electrical transmission corridors with up to sixty overhead power lines slice across the urban landscape with equal disregard for the grid of arterial roads and greenways as they bring in energy from northern Ontario, Niagara Falls, and two nuclear-generating stations on the shore of Lake Ontario in the eastern part of the region. They feed into step-down transformers, some covering several acres, from which they branch into lesser capacity networks into neighborhoods, factories, offices, shops, and houses and disappear into every television, computer, and cell phone charger in the city. Fiber optic cable links Toronto with other cities through buried conduits, many of them running along railway rights-of-way, and surfaces in carrier hotels such as the one at 151 Front Street West. This plain brick, seven-story, former telegraph building, less than a hundred yards from both the Union railway station and the CN Tower in downtown Toronto, hosts TORIX (Toronto International Exchange), said to be Canada's premier telecommunications hub. From there the cable feeds out into the region in lines laid beneath streets, sometimes threaded through sewers, sometimes strung between poles, and so into individual houses, offices, coffeeshops, and computers, each of which, as McLuhan anticipated, constitutes its own center within the World Wide Web.[11]

Networks of electrical lines and fiber optic cable, and their nodal interchanges in transformers and carrier hotels, have very little direct impact on urban form. They seem to adapt to and disappear into whatever facilities are already available. They are also spatially egalitarian because, like water and sewage lines, they provide essentially the same services to all parts of the region, rich or poor, residential or commercial. Interchanges in transportation networks do, however, affect the shape of the city, particularly where several types of transportation intersect. Union Station in downtown Toronto, although it serves railway lines that run across the region, has functioned as a terminus and a point of entry to Toronto since the construction of the first station on the site in the 1850s. Indeed, the original station was a major impetus for the growth of the monocentric downtown of Toronto in the late nineteenth century. Its important role is reflected in the current building, a grand beaux arts structure with a soaring interior hall constructed in the 1920s that for decades was where almost all immigrants, tourists, and businessmen arrived. Union Station is what planners call an "anchor hub," a place that interconnects intercity VIA trains, GO commuter trains and buses, the subway network, and the PATH system of shop-lined pedestrian tunnels that link offices in the financial district. It is said to be the busiest transit facility in Canada, with about two hundred thousand passengers passing through it each weekday. Its continuing importance is sustained in no small part by the subway system in the City of Toronto, which is not a big or complicated network but still has just over a million riders a day making it either the third or fourth busiest subway system in North America (after New York, Mexico City, and, according to some data and not others, Montreal).[12]

Most immigrants, tourists, and businesspeople now arrive at Pearson International Airport, located mostly in Mississauga, where it meets the borders of Brampton and the City of Toronto. This is Canada's major airline hub; it had almost twenty million passengers passing through it in 2010. This is less than half the number of those who pass through Union Station each year, though at the airport they depart for and arrive from far more remote and exotic locations that are connected through a worldwide network of international airports. Perhaps it was this that Deyan Sudjic was thinking of when he suggested that international airports have a sense of being at the heart of things even though they are necessarily on the fringes of metropolitan areas. In another sense Pearson Airport is unquestionably a very important regional center and contributor to the processes of deconcentrated concentration because it is surrounded by an extensive node of employment that is the second largest in the region, providing jobs directly and indirectly for about 186,000 people.[13]

The Busiest Highway in North America

Sudjic, who has many provocative things to say about contemporary cities, has suggested that "in its new incarnation the diffuse, sprawling and endlessly mobile world metropolis is fundamentally different from the city as we have known it." For him the new species of city is not an accretion of streets and squares that can be comprehended by a pedestrian but is instead one that manifests its shape from the air or from cars. While a sense of the scale of the Toronto urban region can be grasped from the air, especially at night when lights seem to reach to the horizon in every direction, this is a detached view. To be fully appreciated, the galactic character of the patches and multiple centers of the region have to be experienced from its network of expressways.[14]

The importance of expressways in Toronto's metropolitan identity seems to have gone largely unacknowledged. Perhaps this has something to do with the fact that, unlike railways, expressways don't actually lead anywhere; they bypass downtowns, shopping malls, airports, cities. To get somewhere you have to take an exit ramp. In Toronto they seem to be regarded mostly as little more than commonplace, utilitarian, and unfortunate necessities to be driven on but not written about, except perhaps to complain about congestion or the way they undermine real urban life. They are indeed utilitarian. They display few flights of design fancy or decoration: most bridges are supported on sturdy squat columns, crash barriers are made of rusty ridged metal or mass-produced concrete slabs, and, apart from some Russian olive trees, there is almost no landscaping along them (though in fairness the climate and use of salt to keep surfaces ice-free in the winter are not friendly to lush roadside vegetation). The driving is fast, at least ten miles an hour above the speed limit. Vehicles often bunch together: it's mostly hurry-up and businesslike driving with always the possibility of unexpected slowdowns in spite of the efficient systems that handle accidents and breakdowns. There is little of the sense of swooping freedom and possibility that can make California's freeways so exciting.

Figure 7.2. Downtown Toronto from the Gardiner Expressway, looking west, at a quiet traffic moment. The towers to the left of the CN Tower are condominiums crowding the lakeshore; skyscraper offices in the financial district are in the center; the tower on the right is a condominium.

Nonetheless, each expressway that cuts across Toronto does have its own distinctive personality.

The Queen Elizabeth Way (QEW), built in 1939 and the first limited-access intercity freeway in North America, still has a few sections with its original ER lampposts (for Elizabeth Regina, the Queen Mother) or perhaps replicas of them—it's impossible to tell which as you pass at seventy miles an hour. The QEW originally ran through farmland and orchards but is now pressed on either side by a mixture of old industrial and new commercial buildings, and it is crowded with cars, trucks heading across the border, and buses going to the casino in Niagara Falls. Near downtown it morphs seamlessly into the Gardiner, an elevated expressway constructed in the 1950s that has been strongly criticized for cutting off the core of the city from the lake yet soars past condominiums and the CN Tower and offers dramatic views of skyscrapers in the financial district (Figure 7.2). As it turns north up the Don River Valley, the Gardiner becomes the Don Valley Parkway, also built in the 1950s, which snakes its way north under high bridges and past steep, forested valley sides, offering glimpses of Flemingdon Park and the industrial part of Don Mills. Towards the northernmost edge of the city it becomes Highway 404, built in the 1980s, which has one of the few high-occupancy vehicle lanes in the region, heads past glassy towers and electronic corporations, provides a glimpse of the new urbanist development of Cathedraltown, and then enters the countryside of the Oak Ridges Moraine.

Both Allen Road, the stub of the Spadina Expressway that was stopped after public protest, and Highway 409, leading to Pearson Airport, are spartan concrete channels. Highway 407ETR (which stands for electronic toll road, where license plates are photographed as you enter and leave and bills come in the mail) bypasses the City of Toronto to the north and west; it is new and sleek, still under construction at its eastern end, and seems more spacious than the others, possibly because space has been reserved for future widening. Highway 400 connects Toronto with Muskoka and Northern Ontario; coming south into Toronto it climbs over the Oak Ridges, abruptly crosses the urban edge where subdivisions surround the Baitul Islam Mosque (see Figure 6.4), passes the towering roller coasters and artificial mountain of Canada's Wonderland theme park, widens to six lanes in each direction, and, on a clear day, offers what is perhaps the most expansive albeit fleeting view over about half the Toronto conurbation—the CN Tower in the far distance, aircraft making their approach to land at Pearson—then turns and drops to join Highway 401.

Highway 401 is the main traffic artery, the aorta, of the Toronto region (Figure 7.3). It is the busiest expressway in North America, an unenviable distinction it shares on and off with the Santa Monica Expressway in Los Angeles. Officially called the MacDonald-Cartier Freeway (after two eminent nineteenth-century Canadian politicians), it connects Montreal to the U.S. border at Detroit. For much of that distance it runs through countryside and is a mere six lanes wide. As it approaches Toronto it swells into eight lanes, then splits into express and collector lanes, and later widens to ten, fourteen, sixteen, and, at its maximum, according to some claims, twenty lanes (this includes acceleration and deceleration lanes, so it's a bit of an exaggeration), eventually shrinking back to six lanes on the far side. The stretch that runs across Toronto from Pickering to Mississauga is said to be the world's longest stretch of freeway with ten lanes or more.[15]

There is no clear explanation for the 400 numbering of expressways in Ontario; the best guess is that it originated in the 1940s as a way to designate four-lane as opposed to two-lane highways. Highway 401 was built in the early 1950s as a four-lane bypass for the city in what was then mostly farmland, along the alignment of a "superhighway" indicated in the unofficial 1943 Master Plan for Toronto. As the city traffic increased, it was widened, collector lanes were added, it was widened again; parts are still

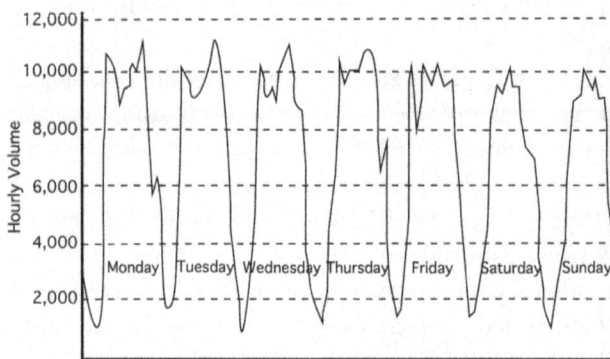

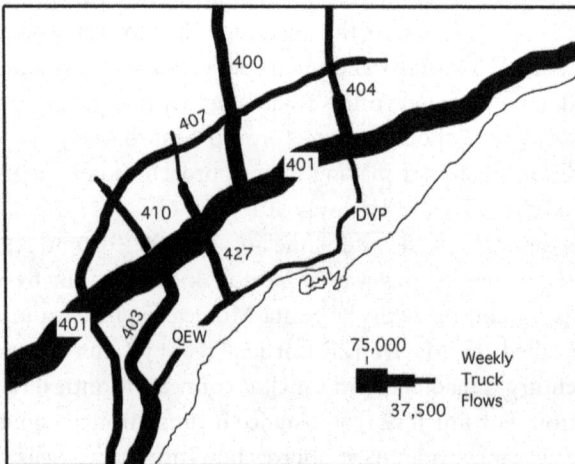

Figure 7.3. Highway 401, the traffic aorta of the Toronto region. The graph shows pulses in daily and weekly traffic flow at the highway's intersection with Weston Road, where the highway is at its widest. The map shows weekly flows of truck traffic. Top, redrawn from G. Nikolic, M. Chan, and R. Pringle, "Planning and Implementing a Full Closure of Highway 401 Express Lanes," paper prepared for the 2005 Annual Conference of the Transportation Association of Canada, Calgary, Alberta; bottom, redrawn from S. Sureshan, "Impact of Intercity Trucking on Urban Environment: Greater Toronto and Hamilton Area Case Study," paper prepared for the 2009 Annual Conference of the Transportation Association of Canada, Vancouver, British Columbia.

being widened. Tall metal sound barriers have been installed in sections where it runs through residential areas; elsewhere it rises above adjacent landscapes of industry, offers views of three regional shopping malls, passes four proposed urban growth centers, and skirts the southern edge of Pearson Airport. As it crosses Toronto it feeds into and is fed into by eight other expressways and about fifty arterial roads. Traffic flows along it in pulses like a gigantic diurnal heartbeat, with the relatively small peaks at rush hour sufficient to slow traffic to a crawl in each direction. At its busiest point near its intersection with Highway 400 the flows peak at about 437,000 vehicles per day. Some parts of it are always being repaired, repaved, widened, and adjusted, mostly by construction crews working at night, to deal with the abuse it suffers from huge volumes of traffic and from Toronto's climate, which swings from 35C and torrential thunderstorms in the summer to −20C temperatures and ice in the winter.[16]

To drive the 401 and the other expressways when traffic is moving freely with trailer trucks and delivery vans and cars is to be forcefully reminded that the Toronto region is in constant motion. Sudjic claims that freeways with their flows of vehicles define urban space as much as public squares, buildings, streets, and neighborhoods. It is, I think, impossible to understand completely the urban space of the region without driving and experiencing its various expressways, getting a sense of the rhythm of the traffic, encountering convoys of trucks that function as rolling warehouses, getting caught in and enduring traffic jams, and watching how the skylines of the landscapes and nodes of the city unfold as you pass them. Expressways provide the clearest experience of the extent of the polycentric city region with its many centers and mosaic of land-use patches, even though they lead directly to none of those centers or patches. The fact that the countless trucks and cars always on the move keep the region running has not escaped the attention of planners. Of the twenty-five urban growth centers identified in the Growth Plan for the Greater Golden Horseshoe only three are not within a mile or two of an expressway interchange.[17]

In spite of the importance of traffic flows for the polycentric urban region, all too often they seem to involve slow motion. It may well be the case, as Jane Jacobs once astutely noted, that although it is common to blame traffic congestion on progress and growth, it is not a new problem, just one that is persistently unsolved. Nevertheless, congestion around Toronto is getting worse as traffic volumes and vehicle ownership continue to grow faster than the population. An IBM survey made in 2010 of traffic congestion in twenty global cities uses a "commuter pain index" that combines delays in travel times with perceptions of the aggravation this causes. It ranked Toronto twelfth, well below Beijing and Mexico City, about the same as London and Paris, but worse than all the other North American cities in the survey, including New York and Los Angeles. A Toronto Board of Trade assessment of average daily commuting travel times in nineteen cities, also in 2010, again ranked Toronto as the worst in North America, with average commuting time at eighty minutes a day, compared to sixty-eight minutes in New York and fifty-six in Los Angeles. It should, however, be noted that these travel times in Toronto include commuting by both private cars and public transit. An analysis completed in 2005 for Statistics Canada found that while the average commuting time in Toronto was the longest in Canada, the commute by public transit was forty-one minutes longer than that by car alone, mainly because journeys by bus in the suburbs are so slow. Because 45 percent of all journeys to work in the City of Toronto are by transit, these slow journeys weigh heavily on the average. The blunt fact is that in spite of the traffic jams on the 401 and other expressways it is almost always faster to get somewhere by car than by bus or other forms of transit.[18]

Traffic congestion is nevertheless a serious economic concern. The OECD territorial analysis of Toronto published in 2010 emphasized its economic costs, especially for the sectors of the local economy dependent on rapid delivery, in terms of extra fuel, lost time, and environmental impacts. Similar concerns have been expressed in studies by Transport Canada and by Metrolinx, the provincial agency with responsibility for transportation planning in the region, both of which estimate the cost at several billion dollars annually. There's not a lot that can be done in terms of road widening, and there are no plans or financial resources for new expressways, so it appears that the regional network of expressways in and around Toronto will be maintained but not expanded. How this will play out is difficult to imagine. The hope appears to be that congestion will force people to use mass transit, yet cars offer the flexibility of door-to-door journeys in a polycentric urban region where most of the galactic urban form has been created in response to flexible travel, and cars will not be lightly abandoned in favor of buses.[19]

Visible Networks of Identity

Even though the use of public transit in the region is currently dwarfed by expressways and cars, it is above all the distinctive colors and equipment

Figure 7.4. The first Tim Horton's coffee and donut restaurant in East Hamilton: the origin of a Canadian fast-food phenomenon. There are now about five hundred Tim Horton's in the Toronto region.

associated with networks of public transit that give a visible identity to the region and its various parts. The green and white signs, buses, and double-decker commuter trains of the regional GO Transit system reach almost to the limits of the Greater Golden Horseshoe. They are probably the strongest single visual identifier of the Toronto region. The trains follow the nineteenth-century pattern and feed into Union Station in downtown Toronto, but GO bus routes follow expressways and arterial roads to connect the centers of the outer suburbs and exurbs. The visual identity of the region is further but less obviously reinforced by the stores and other retail chains that originated and are concentrated here. Easily the most prominent of these is a quintessential Canadian phenomenon of the last forty years, a hugely popular and inexpensive coffee, donut, and sandwich chain called Tim Horton's. Founded in 1964 by and named for a player on the Toronto Maple Leafs and Buffalo Sabres hockey teams, the chain has expanded from its first store in East Hamilton to about three thousand outlets across Canada, with more than five hundred of these concentrated in the Greater Toronto and Hamilton Area (Figure 7.4). Several other well-known Canadian food chains also began in Toronto. They include Second Cup, a fair-trade coffee competitor to Starbucks; Swiss Chalet barbecued chicken (which has no known connection with Switzerland); Harvey's

Hamburgers (named for another hockey player—Doug Harvey of the Montreal Canadiens); and Pizza Pizza (once so clearly identified with Toronto that a local myth in the days before strict border control was that immigration officials at Niagara Falls could confirm where people were from by asking them to recite Pizza Pizza's phone number). All now have branches across southern Ontario and in other provinces, but their greatest concentrations are in and around Toronto, and it is the combination of all of these and other familiar chains, plus the distinctive colors and equipment of public transit systems, that constitute the unheralded, taken-for-granted yet distinctive background to daily life in the Toronto region. I suspect it is the appearances of these stores and buses as much as anything else that give expatriate Torontonians the sense that they have returned home.[20]

Well, it's not quite this straightforward. Whenever you step into the outlet of a retail chain, regardless of whether its provenance is local like Tim Horton's, or remote such as Starbucks (about two hundred in the Toronto region) or Home Depot (about forty), you step out of the present place and into a node of a network that is defined by its standardized products and all the colors and other paraphernalia of branding. In this disconnection from local geography, franchise outlets correspond with the spaceless geographies of the Internet, cell phones, and other forms of electronic communications that can make anywhere its own center.

Everywhere Is Now a Center

"The medium is the message," Marshall McLuhan wrote in the preface to *Understanding Media*, "means, in terms of the electric age, that a totally new environment has been created." This environment, he suggested, is one in which electronic communications make everyone feel as though they are close neighbors in a global village and where emotions, feelings, and gossip are at least as important as reason and regulations. In the current context of Facebook and tweeting, it is hard to disagree with this. There are consequences for cities and understanding how they work. From McLuhan's perspective, much of the current form of cities—for instance, in Toronto the grid patterns of streets and the carefully controlled suburban expansions managed by Metro—can be seen as the outcome of systematic, rationalistic processes associated with the linearity of print media. McLuhan believed that the new environment of electronic communication makes this sort of approach obsolete. "Metropolitan space," he suggested, "is equally irrelevant for the telephone, the telegraph, the radio and the television. . . . Our electric extensions of ourselves simply by-pass space and time"; they "abolish the spatial dimension" and permit "any place to be a center."[21]

Howard Rheingold, an American who has written about the impact of electronic media, gives substance to these theoretical ideas when he observes how the nature of public spaces is changing as "more and more people on city streets and on public transportation spend time speaking to other people who are not physically co-present." He thinks that the impact of electronic technologies "will lead cities to change faster than a centralized urban planning structure will be able to understand, let alone develop policies for." Others have gone so far as to suggest that urban regions are now "post-polycentric." If everywhere, every household, every cell phone can be a center of communications, then the very idea of centers, whether in the sense of multipurpose urban nodes or anything else, ceases to matter much because cities have been turned into force fields where constant communication and motion prevail over urban forms.[22]

There is some physical evidence to support these claims. In addition to carrier hotels and buried networks of fiber optic cable, there are almost three thousand cell phone relays dispersed more or less uniformly throughout the Toronto region. Antennae rise on towers in new subdivisions and adjacent to expressways; they make bristly fringes on the cornices of high-rise apartments whose balconies are adorned with satellite dishes. There are maps of the phone towers in the Toronto region, and most cell phones and tablets have GPS, but neither the towers nor maps of the devices reveal anything insightful about the consequences of constant, instant communication with people who are not physically co-present. Unlike the effects of streetcars and motor vehicles, which were technologies that changed the shapes of streets and the built forms of cities, electronic communications pass through walls and disappear into buildings and leave the streetscapes of cities essentially unchanged. What they alter are relationships between people, and between people and places, and this profoundly affects the meanings of cities and the ways they function.[23]

Although some aspects of the Toronto region might be regarded as post-polycentric electronic fields, the straightforward geographical evidence of urban landscapes is that this is actually a region of many distinct urban centers linked by different types of networks, some visible and others hidden. Many of these centers originated in the nineteenth century, and though they have been much changed by incremental redevelopment and are now surrounded by the ever-expanding conurbation, some aspects of their old identities and distinctiveness have endured. They are remnants of a time when a different set of relationships between towns and their peripheries prevailed and the old City of Toronto was the economic, political, and cultural heart of the region. What all of this means is that there are now, in effect, three superimposed urban forms in the Toronto region—the mostly monocentric one focused on the core of the old City, a polycentric one with many overlapping networks, and an amorphous, still poorly understood, post-polycentric one. In other words, the urban region of Toronto is simultaneously centralized and decentralized, spread out and concentrated, networked and dispersed. In these respects it is a microcosm of the processes that are associated with globalization.

Chapter 8

Globally Connected and Locally Divided

Globalization is most often discussed as an economic phenomenon. This is a limited perspective. In Toronto for sure, and presumably everywhere, it is both economic and social. It involves flows of money and goods, and it involves flows of people. The fundamental process behind Toronto's expansion into a polycentric region has been population growth, which since 1981 has been somewhere between 84,000 and 134,000 people a year, depending on how the region is defined (Table 8.1). Almost all that growth has been the result of immigration from outside Canada. Of the 6.2 million people living in the Greater Toronto and Hamilton Area (GTHA) in 2006, 43 percent were foreign born. Before 1980 most immigrants came from Europe, but since then the great majority have arrived from the global South, especially Asian countries, with the result that the region is now intensely multicultural and ethnically diverse: 38 percent of the population in 2006 were people of color, and in some outer suburbs the proportion exceeded 50 percent.

Toronto would not have been so successful in attracting such large numbers of immigrants if the local economy had not been flourishing and providing jobs. And many of those opportunities were created directly and indirectly as the region was transformed from dependence on manufacturing to increasing participation in economic globalization. In other words, Toronto's population growth and multicultural character have been fueled by the region's increasingly important role as a player on the economic global stage, even as its global economic role has been boosted by high levels of immigration. The consequence is summarized neatly in a recent Price Waterhouse Coopers report that considers how trends in global competition could affect the future development of world cities: "Toronto is in

Table 8.1. Population Growth in Various Toronto Regions

	Old City of Toronto	New City of Toronto (Metro)	Census Metropolitan Area	Greater Toronto Area	Greater Toronto Hamilton Area	Greater Golden Horseshoe
1951	675,800	1,117,500	1,262,000			
1961	672,400	1,619,000	1,825,000	2,106,000		
1971	712,800	2,086,000	2,628,000	2,923,000		
1981	599,200	2,137,000	2,999,000	3,418,000	3,968,000	
1991	635,000	2,275,000	3,893,000	4,236,000	4,688,000	
2001	676,300	2,481,000	4,264,000	5,300,000	5,810,000	7,779,000
2011	amalgamated	2,615,000	5,584,000	6,054,000	6,574,000	8,693,000
Growth per year, 1991–2011		17,000	84,000	91,000	94,000	

Sources: Mostly Statistics Canada, Census, various years.
Note: By 1951, population had begun to spill from the old City into Metro, and by 1971 from Metro into the rest of the region.

many ways both a hub of McLuhan's global village in financial services, communications and creative and performing arts, and is, at the same time a village of the globe, with people from virtually every country of the world calling Toronto home."[1]

That's part of the story. Another consequence is that Toronto, like global cities elsewhere, is now caught up in the aggressive competitions of economic globalization that lead to an intensification of social inequalities. It has a reputation as a place that accommodates and integrates a large number of immigrants from diverse parts of the world, but in the City of Toronto there are indications that economic disadvantage is becoming concentrated among recent immigrants and visible minorities. This is less evident in the racially diverse outer suburbs where a sort of middle-income multiculturalism now appears to prevail.

Economic Globalization

Economies have long been global in the sense that they have involved trading goods around the world. One of the reasons Toronto was founded in the 1790s was to facilitate sending beaver furs (used for fashionable hats) and other resources to Europe. By the late twentieth century, world trade, with the help of rapid advances in electronic communications to keep track of everything, had intensified so much that the metaphor of globalization had effectively displaced the idea of the autonomous national economy. Evidence of this shift in thinking can be garnered indirectly from Kerr and Spelt's book *The Changing Face of Toronto*, written in the mid-1960s. An economic geographer and urban geographer, respectively, Kerr and Spelt were mostly interested in indications that Toronto was winning a long-running competition with Montreal to be the leading financial center in Canada; there is not one mention of global or international connections of any sort. The Toronto they described was a national and industrial city with a third of the jobs in manufacturing. By 2006 the proportion of manufacturing jobs had fallen to 12 percent, 11 percent of the jobs were in finance, and Toronto had become both the leading financial center in Canada and a major cog in the machinations of the global economy.[2]

In *The Economy of Cities*, written at a time when manufacturing was still ascendant though declining in importance, Jane Jacobs argued persuasively that cities, not nation-states, are the real engines of economies. Two leading authorities on global urban change, Manuel Castells and Peter Hall, have extended this insight by suggesting that cities and regions are critical agents of economic development because they are more flexible than nations in adapting to changing markets and technologies. In Canada both federal and provincial politicians have had great difficulty accepting these insights, presumably because they threaten their authority in establishing economic policies for their relevant constituencies. It is different in the business world. For instance, *Forbes* (which describes itself on its website as "the home page for business leaders") claims that: "For corporations, cities and their economies matter most, since picking the right city will be the key to prosperity in the future," and it laments the fact that most economic data are for nations, not for cities. An important consequence of these various perspectives is that Toronto's economic situation looks rather different depending on whether it is regarded from a global, North American, national, provincial, or regional perspective.[3]

Toronto in the Global Economy

Almost everything about economic globalization is profoundly positivistic—stated in numbers that are thought to reveal winners and losers in a

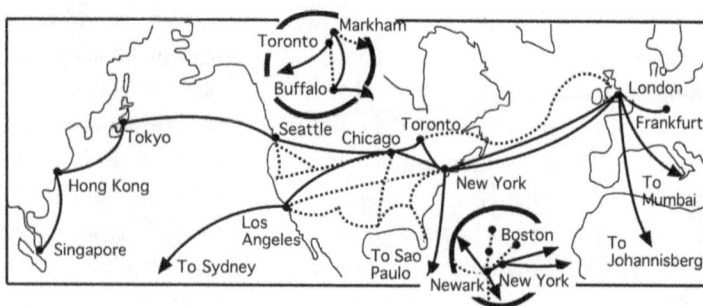

Figure 8.1. Hibernia Atlantic's Global Financial Network of fiber links Toronto with major world cities and demonstrates its connections to the global economy. Solid lines indicate connections having the greatest bandwidth. Redrawn and simplified from Hibernia Atlantic's website, 2011, at http://www.hiberniaatlantic.com.

great global competition. For cities these measurements are often presented as rankings of such things as economic potential, cost of living, quality of life, economic power, and gross value added per capita, rankings that are updated every year to show how individual cities are moving up or down the economic league table. Toronto has, to my knowledge, never been first within any of these tables, though it is sometimes second or third and rarely falls below twentieth. Most rankings are made by various agents of globalization, such as international accounting or consulting firms, which have a vested interest in the results, and they therefore have to be regarded with some degree of skepticism. However, the Globalization and World Cities project is an impartial academic attempt to classify several hundred different world cities by determining the strength of economic interactions among them. Four assessments made since 2000 have all shown New York and London at the top, with Hong Kong, Paris, and Chicago below them. Some cities have moved up and others down, but Toronto has always been ranked at about fourteenth, roughly comparable to Beijing, Milan, Los Angeles, Brussels, and Mumbai. Toronto is particularly well connected with New York and Chicago, so it is not surprising that there is a "global financial network" of fiber optic cable linking these three cities with London, Paris, and Frankfurt (Figure 8.1). These indicators of global status are supported by the fact that in terms of market capitalization the Toronto Stock Exchange ranks about eighth in the world and about fifteenth in the value of shares traded.[4]

Because rankings of world cities generally present Toronto in a favorable global economic light they are faithfully reported by local agencies, such as the Greater Toronto Marketing Alliance, that promote the region's economic development. However, a rather less positive conclusion was reached by the Organisation for Economic Co-operation and Development (OECD), which undertook a very thorough review of the Toronto region in 2010 and concluded that it had lagging productivity, below the mean for the metropolitan regions that the OECD monitors. This was attributed to a combination of poor infrastructure, especially regional transportation, and a lack of unified government. Competitiveness, it suggested, might be improved through better regional governance.[5]

There is some justification for this recommendation, but it also reveals clearly the ideological foundation for the various economic surveys and rankings. They are, in effect, report cards on the neoliberal processes of globalization that treat everything and everywhere as open for business. Neoliberalism is the set of ideas and practices that values the efficiency of private enterprise above everything else, and thus devalues social and environmental issues. This agenda has become pervasive. Julie-Anne Boudreau, Roger Keil, and Douglas Young, urban researchers at the City Institute at York University in Toronto, have argued forcefully that in Toronto neoliberalism now intersects with everyday life and has undermined the authority of local governments except for their role as brokers trying to attract the attention of global corporations. As one explicit example of this, the municipality of Ajax in the eastern part of the Toronto region proudly declares that it is ISO 9001–registered, meaning that it has a quality management system to ensure that it is providing good service for its "customers."[6]

The narrowness of neoliberalism becomes especially apparent in the security measures taken to protect G8 and G20 meetings, which serve as types of annual conferences for their strongest ideological advocates and are inevitably and symbiotically protested by those who do not benefit from globalization. When the G8 and G20 met in Toronto in the summer of 2010, the protests were described in the *Economist* as "relatively modest." This was not the view in Toronto, where they constituted a major disruption to the civil order. To ensure that demonstrations did not impinge on the political leaders and their retinues who were advancing their neoliberal agendas behind a specially installed security fence, large parts of the central city were temporarily turned into a police state, civil liberties were suspended, and temporary legislation was passed to permit arrest without reason. It was a sharp reminder that civil liberties are more easily taken away than they are achieved, not least when it is thought that they might impinge on the freedom of economic debate.[7]

Toronto in North America's Urban Economies

According to Boudreau, Keil, and Young one manifestation of neoliberalism in Toronto is the emergence of a "new urban geography" of airports, distribution centers, business parks, and industrial districts. They claim that, after Chicago and Los Angeles, the Toronto region has the third largest concentration of industrial floor space in North America. Indeed, in North America it is among the top five metropolitan areas for almost everything economic, which is consistent with the relative size of its population. In terms of employment, it is said to rank second for the automotive industry, second in food and beverages, third in financial services, third in film and media, third in information and communications technologies, third in design, and third in biotechnology. Its stock exchange is the third largest in North America. In short, the Toronto region is a major player in urban economies; in Canada it constitutes about 20 percent of the national economy. Furthermore, the range of these high rankings shows that the Toronto economy is "extraordinarily diverse," something that has given it resilience against economic downturns including both the decline of manufacturing industries and the post-2008 recession.[8]

Toronto's status in Canada and in the Province of Ontario is tied up with the Canadian constitution, which gives provinces exclusive control over municipalities. The federal government has only ad hoc and indirect mechanisms for providing funds for cities, even though some federal programs and policies (in Toronto, most notably those to do with immigration) do directly affect them. This constitutional allocation of authority has become increasingly problematic since about half the population of Canada currently lives in the six urban agglomerations of Vancouver, Calgary, Edmonton, Ottawa, Montreal, and Toronto. Indeed, the population of GTHA is not only larger than that of any other Canadian urban area, but also larger than any of the provinces except for Québec and Ontario. Yet it lacks the constitutional and political authority of a province, and neither it nor the municipalities within it have powers of taxation. Because any official recognition of this manifest imbalance could undermine federalism, Canadian federal governments, regardless of the party in power, have shown little enthusiasm for urban initiatives or reform.[9]

This imbalance is exaggerated within Ontario, where half the population of 12.8 million currently lives in the GTHA. In terms of voters, economic activity, tax revenue generated, and just about everything else, it poses a constant potential challenge to the provincial government of Ontario regardless of the province's constitutional authority. Toronto is an urban monster that consumes resources and attention and is remote from the concerns of mining towns and native communities in the north and the agricultural areas in the southwestern part of the province. With its diversified economy it continues to grow even as other cities in the province are afflicted with the rustbelt malaise of high unemployment and old manufacturing plants that are no longer competitive.[10]

I do not think it is too cynical to claim that as Toronto has burgeoned in the last fifty years, regardless of which political party has been in power, the province has consistently sought ways to keep it firmly in its constitutional place. It has, for instance, refused to allow the City of Toronto to use hotel or other local taxes as a source or revenue, and it has deflected attempts to create a super-metropolitan government such as the one proposed in the 1990s for the Greater Toronto Area. While the OECD, with its neoliberal perspective, regards various provincial initiatives for regional planning as commendable, from a local perspective it is significant that these are top-down plans that scarcely mention Toronto even though Toronto's growth is their main concern. It's hard not to conclude that a paradoxical form of blindness permeates the provincial government. The Ontario Legislature is ensconced in a massive sandstone building in Queen's Park in the heart of the old City, yet the politicians and mandarins apparently prefer to pretend that Toronto does not really exist.

Fragmented Regional Perspectives

In the context of this provincial blindness, the Toronto region has had to invent ways to promote itself in the global marketplace. The Greater Toronto Marketing Alliance was formed in 1998 in the vacuum that followed the decision not to make the Greater Toronto Area a formal level of metropolitan government. It is based on the recognition that, from the perspective of the global economy, Toronto has to be understood as an urban region and the Alliance's purpose is to project a single economic identity for that region in order to attract foreign direct investment. It is a public-private partnership with representatives from twenty-nine municipalities, provincial and federal governments, not-for-profit groups, and numerous businesses. It promotes the region as "Canada's number one business centre," which offers access to a market of 135 million people within five hundred miles of the city, in contrast to New York City, which can offer a mere seventy million within five hundred miles.[11]

Another, and more innovative, organization dedicated to the promotion of the region, and also a public-private partnership, is the Greater Toronto Civic Action Alliance (it was founded as the Toronto City Summit Alliance in 2002, changed its name in 2011, and is usually referred to simply as Civic Action). According to Boudreau, Keil, and Young, Civic Action "has all but established itself as an alternative form of government in the region in such strategic areas as immigrant settlement, economic development and urban sustainability." Its motivations come from frustration about the persistent unwillingness by federal and provincial politicians to acknowledge the recognition that cities are the engines of economies, as well as the ability of politicians to ignore the facts that Toronto generates at least 20 percent of Canada's GDP and is heavily subsidizing other parts of the country. Municipalities in Canada are hamstrung because they are under the constitutional authority of the provinces; alternative types of agencies are required to address the economic, social, and environmental issues of urban regions. Civic Action is an innovative coalition that involves thousands of community leaders drawn from business, education, government, labor, and not-for-profit sectors across the region. It has quickly evolved into an umbrella organization because it has generated and spun off many active and effective subsidiaries—including Greening Greater Toronto, the Toronto Region Immigrant Employment Council, Emerging Leaders Network, Luminato (a Toronto arts festival), and, from the particular perspective of economic development, the Toronto Region Research Alliance, which promotes research and research-intensive industries in a region that roughly corresponds to the Greater Golden Horseshoe. The clear understanding of Civic Action, shared by the Toronto Board of Trade and other economic lobby groups, is that in a global economic context it is above all the Toronto urban region that matters most, not Canada, not Ontario, and not the local municipalities within it.[12]

This hasn't stopped those local municipalities from blowing their own trumpets. In an ideal neoliberal world the Toronto region would compete in the global marketplace through the coordinated efforts of agencies like the Greater Toronto Marketing Alliance, and while local municipalities would compete among themselves within the region they would not have a direct presence on the global stage. It's already too late for that. There is a profusion of local development offices clamoring for the attention of potential global investors. Most have a map showing themselves at the center of a circle that embraces Chicago and New York, most offer a list of general reasons why they are the best place to choose, and all have a catchy brand slogan: York Region is Canada's Business Gateway, Markham has superb quality of place, Brampton has available land waiting, Waterloo is the Happiest City in Canada, and the City of Toronto is Canada's Corporate Capital and Gateway to North America and the Globe.[13]

It is not difficult to understand what is happening. Local municipalities have been infected with the restless competitiveness that characterizes almost everything to do with neoliberal capitalism. They are faced with the conflicting tasks of competing with each other to attract business investment, yet simultaneously cooperating with each other in a regional economic strategy. However, as the OECD Territorial Reviews and the numerous rankings by international agencies indicate, from the global perspective it is the region as a whole that competes with other urban regions in North America, Europe, and, increasingly, China and India, two nations that happen to be the native homes for two groups of immigrants that together make up one-fifth of the population of the GTHA.[14]

Social Globalization and Transnationalism

Leonie Sandercock is a professor of planning who is less interested in the sort of economic globalization that involves "urban political regimes rushing out to embrace global investors, terrified that their city/region will be left out and drop off all the relevant maps" than in the consequences of social globalization associated with the mass migrations of the last fifty years. The latter, she argues, have turned what were previously ethnically homogeneous cities into "mongrel" ones, a word she explicitly borrows from Salman Rushdie, who uses it as a term of both approbation and prov-ocation to raise questions about multiculturalism, diversity, and hybridity. Sandercock is dismayed by the gap between widely used, rationalist, one-model-fits-all approaches of modernist planning and the mongrel cities of the twenty-first century, where multiethnic populations have in many cases been "marginalized, displaced, oppressed or dominated." In contrast, she imagines "cosmopolis," a city where planning involves acceptance and respect for those who are culturally different, a city that continually prac-tices tolerance and responsiveness to difference, and a place where equality and social justice prevail.[15]

A claim frequently made by the media, politicians, and others promot-ing Toronto is that, according to a UN report, it is "the most multicultural city in the world." I am not sure that multiculturalism and diversity can be measured comparatively, and attempts to find the putative UN report have been unsuccessful, but this nice conceit does promote the view that Toronto is a mongrel city approaching Sandercock's ideal cosmopolis. The reality is not quite this rosy.

There is no question that Toronto is exceptional in North America and the developed world for the scale of its ethnic diversity. This is a recent development. Until about 1970 Toronto was a WASP city—white, Anglo-Saxon, and Protestant—because immigrants had mainly arrived from Brit-ain and Western Europe. When fertility in Canada began to drop in the 1960s, eventually falling below replacement levels, the federal government became concerned about economic and other consequences. To ensure a continuing population growth and labor supply, the federal government revised immigration policies by removing aspects in them that had been racially discriminating in favor of WASPs. In the 1970s Canada's doors were effectively opened to the whole world (Figure 8.2).

This policy change was part of an international shift to encourage migration from the global South to developed countries, a shift that has paralleled the globalization of economic activity. In Canada it has been remarkably concentrated in Toronto, perhaps because the Toronto region began to boom economically in the 1970s as financial businesses moved out of Montreal just at the time the change in immigration policy hap-pened. Since 1975 the core area of the Toronto region (the City of Toronto and the adjacent lower-tier municipalities—see Table 6.2) has consistently been the destination of choice for almost half of the two hundred thousand immigrants who enter Canada every year, with the consequence that in

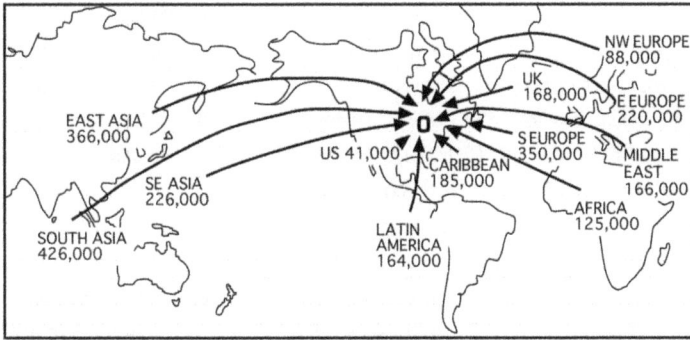

WHERE TORONTO'S IMMIGRANTS COME FROM (2006)

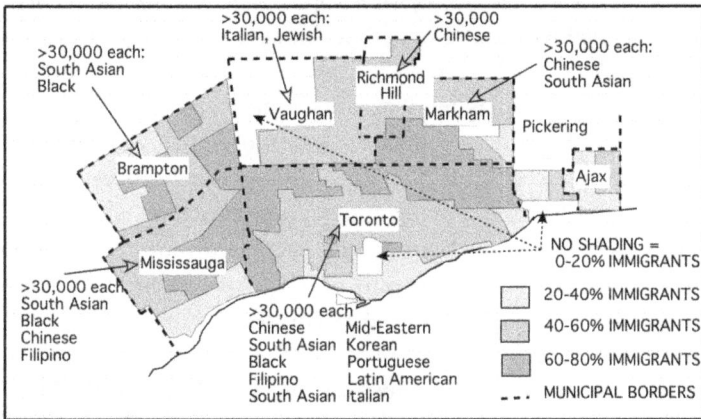

WHERE MOST OF THEM LIVE (2006)

Figure 8.2. Immigrants to the core of the Toronto region: where they came from and where they live. Sources: based on "Place of Birth for the Immigrant Population for Census Metropolitan Areas," Highlight Tables, 2006 Census, Statistics Canada; 2006 Community Profiles for Mississauga, Brampton, Vaughan, Richmond Hill, Markham, Pickering, Ajax and Toronto, 2006 Census, Statistics Canada.

2006 about 45 percent of the 5.1 million people in the Toronto Census Metropolitan Area (the CMA roughly corresponds to the core area) were foreign born, a proportion that had probably increased to almost 49 percent by 2011. According to the OECD, among all metropolitan areas in North America or Europe, Toronto has the highest level of foreign-born residents. Put another way, more than two million people have immigrated to the Toronto region in the last thirty years from countries where the prevailing racial background is not Caucasian. The Canadian Census has a category for visible minorities and in 2006 this category comprised 43 percent of the population of the Toronto CMA (probably close to 46 percent in 2011), with particularly large populations of South Asians (684,000), Chinese (486,000), blacks (352,000), Filipinos (172,000), Latin Americans (100,000), Southeast Asians (70,000), Arabs (55,000), West Asians (from Iran and Afghanistan; 75,000), and Koreans (55,000).[16]

It used to be that almost all immigrants to Toronto arrived by train at the great vaulted hall at Union Station in the heart of downtown. Most would find accommodation and employment somewhere in the old City, and many established small businesses there. Ethnic districts in old Toronto, most of them identified by street signs such as Little Italy, Portuguese Village, Chinatown, and so on, are testaments to this historical process. These are striking neighborhoods because most of them are intensely urban and seem to reflect qualities of original home countries and cultures, even though many of the immigrants have now moved to the suburbs and some actually commute to run their ethnic businesses and restaurants.

With continuing waves of immigrations, these processes and patterns of immigrant settlement have changed. New immigrants now arrive at the international airport and most go directly to live in apartments in the inner or outer suburbs where there are well-established ethnic communities. More than 60 percent of the population of the inner suburb of Scarborough belongs to a visible minority. It's much the same in North York. In the outer suburbs of Brampton (mostly South Asian) and Markham (mostly Chinese), the numbers are, respectively, 55 percent and 66 percent; both are ethnoburbs where much of daily life is conducted in another language and there are specialized shopping malls and community facilities. Overall, a quarter of the population in the Toronto region speaks a language other than English or French at home, a fact of considerable significance for elementary schools, where many of the children in kindergarten and first grade may have little or no English, and also for public institutions and local governments that have to be able to provide services in many languages. The Toronto Transit Commission recently had a campaign indicating that its employees spoke seventy languages.

Ethnic diversity is apparent everywhere in the urban landscape, most obviously in signs and stores along main streets and in plazas (Figure 8.3). *OECD Territorial Reviews: Toronto*, published in 2010, suggested that in 2003 there were more than sixty Chinese plazas in the region, a number I cannot confirm but does not seem unreasonable, though almost all the ones

Figure 8.3. Selling goods on the sidewalk in Chinatown on Spadina Avenue in the center of the City of Toronto.

with which I am familiar have Korean, Vietnamese, and other ethnic stores and restaurants as well as Chinese ones. There are clusters of Portuguese, Punjabi, Russian, Italian, Afghan, Italian, West Indian, Persian, Somali, Korean, Pakistani, African, Latin American, Lebanese, and Jewish shops and restaurants, but these too are invariably mixed together on main streets and within shopping plazas. Ethnic concentrations in the Toronto region are porous enclaves rather than areas of exclusion. This is evident on the streets of the old City in an everywhere mixture of peoples and cultures that is captured by the black poet Dionne Brand when she simply lists store names in one neighborhood: "Selam Restaurant, Jeonghysa Buddhist Temple, Oneda's Market, West Indian and Latin American Foods, Afro Sound, Lalibela Ethiopian Restaurant, Longo's Vegetable and Fruits, Astoria Athens Restaurant, Coffee Time, Star Falafel, Vince Gasparos Meats," and so on, names she refers to evocatively as "the ghosts of old cities." An equivalent list can be made for many of the 1950s and 1960s drive-in plazas of the inner suburbs where the small stores have been taken over by mixtures of newcomers similar to those in the old city, except that more stores there seem to be used for tiny churches and ethnically focused beauty spas.[17]

The infusion of people since 1970 from places other than Britain poses issues for understanding cultural heritage. Most heritage sites in the Toronto region tell a story about pioneers who pushed back the forest and managed to make comfortable lives for themselves in attractive houses, pioneers who were mostly British, a fact evident in the names of heritage museums—Campbell House (1822, the oldest remaining house from the Town of York), Montgomery's Inn (1830, built and run by an Irish settler), the Old Britannia Schoolhouse (1851, a fine example of a one-room schoolhouse), and so on. There is now a marked discontinuity between this pioneer heritage and the cultural backgrounds of about half the current population of the region. It is not uncommon in American cities for ethnic heritage to be preserved in museums and for significant sites to be restored to reflect the history of particular ethnic groups, but to the best of my knowledge this is not the case in Toronto, where ethnic heritage is celebrated and maintained primarily through special festivals such as Diwali and Nowruz; by online networks; in temples, mosques, and churches; and in community centers that provide opportunities for developing social and business connections. These celebrations and community centers are a clear local manifestation of the observation by the anthropologist Arjun Appadurai that "for every nation that exported significant numbers of its population as refugees, tourists, students, migrants, there is now a transnation which retains a special ideological link to its place of origin."[18]

Prior to the mid-twentieth century, communications, even by telephone, were not always easy, travel back home was difficult and expensive, and Canadian immigration policies promoted assimilation, so nationalism at a distance was soon attenuated into romanticized memories and an occasional trip back to the old country. In the last forty years this has changed dramatically because of relatively inexpensive air travel and electronic communications that allow diasporic transnational families to stay in constant contact. Overt signs of transnationalism can be seen in almost every ethnic plaza—money transfer services, imported CDs and DVDs, exotic foods, discounts on long-distance phone rates to countries in Asia, Africa, and Latin America. When Italy or Brazil wins the soccer World Cup, entire sections of Toronto are shut down for spontaneous celebrations. Less publicly obvious manifestations of transnationalism include individuals returning to India or Turkey to get married, and preschool children of recent immigrants in Toronto being sent to China or El Salvador to live with grandparents so that both parents can work full-time without incurring child-care costs.

Early in his career McLuhan wrote that "by pushing spatial communication to its limits we have today created a global melting pot of peoples and cultures which can only end by making of the world a single city." For Toronto at least, this was prescient because ethnically it now seems to be an urban fragment of that single city. This means that the distinctive local heritage derived mostly from Toronto's British-influenced history prior to 1940, and the diverse traditions associated with its many new transnational ethnic communities now coexist. The Sikh Heritage Centre on the fringes of Brampton is housed in a century-old farmhouse; the pioneer museum with its split-rail fences and log buildings in Markham is in the middle of a mostly Chinese community. David Lowenthal, a historical geographer and self-proclaimed heritage activist, believes that all heritage consists of a "jumbled, malleable amalgam" and in the multilayered ethnic communities of the Toronto region this certainly seems to be the case.[19]

Multiculturalism and Inequality

From a political perspective it is a significant question whether transnationalism undermines citizenship and a sense of belonging to a place. Can diversity and the recognition of minority rights, for instance, of religious beliefs and cultural practices, be respected without the acceptance of differentiated forms of citizenship, which could pose a risk of political fragmentation? Canada has a federal multiculturalism policy that aims to strike a balance between acknowledgment of ethnic differences and their connection to mainstream institutions and values. The Canadian political scientist Will Kymlicka argues that this balance requires "public reasonableness," in which the cultural traditions of both minority and dominant groups are adapted to one another. In Toronto, perhaps in part because of the sheer weight of immigrant numbers, there is considerable evidence of this sort of adaptation. It can be found, for example, in everything from play-by-play commentaries of National Hockey League games that are offered in Punjabi, to the range of social services offered by municipalities in a dozen or more languages, to the slowly growing participation of visible minorities in municipal, provincial, and federal politics.[20]

Multiculturalism could, however, be tested by growing inequalities, especially in the City of Toronto where poverty seems to be concentrated among recent immigrants and visible minorities. From an economic point of view, transnational diversity is an expression of a sort of globalization from below, which parallels and complements the globalization from above associated with multinational corporations and international transfers of capital. Toronto has a very positive reputation for its multiculturalism, and the OECD Territorial Reviews, for instance, states that it has historically excelled in the integration of newcomers. Numerous federal, provincial, and nongovernmental services provide assistance for immigrants. Nongovernmental organizations, such as the Toronto Region Immigration and Employment Council (a branch of Civic Action) and the Maytree Foundation, have well-regarded programs dedicated to finding ways to engage the skills of immigrants that should contribute to the enhancement of both personal and regional prosperity. While this might well be the case for some, and perhaps the majority of immigrants, there is also evidence that what is happening for many of them, especially in the City of Toronto, is not prosperity but persistent poverty.[21]

The expectation associated with economic globalization has been that the increased wealth it generates would come to be widely distributed, especially in world cities where control over global wealth is concentrated, and that everyone, whether native citizens or newcomers, would end up better off. In what seems to be an international failure of expectations, this does not seem to be happening; instead income disparities and levels of poverty are intensifying rather than diminishing in world cities. Toronto is no exception. On the streets outside the glitzy towers of the downtown financial district, where high-income professionals put together complex loans, handle mergers and acquisitions, and make the sorts of international financial transfers that help to drive the global economy, homeless people sleep above heating vents in the sidewalks. Those office towers are maintained by legions of cleaners and service workers, many of them immigrants holding two or three jobs paying low wages that have been steadily declining relative to the cost of living. A less obvious but no less significant form of inequality is revealed in the fact that while downtown office districts attract massive private investments for renewal of the buildings, the clusters of aging high-rise apartments in the old City and the inner suburbs, which are where many of the low-end service workers and immigrants in Toronto live, struggle to get financial support for renovations in order to maintain basic services.[22]

In the Toronto region low-income areas are concentrated particularly in a broad U-shaped band within the City, the alignment of which corresponds in part to the railways that were built in the mid-nineteenth century and whose negative impact on the urban landscape seems to have endured for 150 years. There are some low-income pockets in the outer suburbs, but the extent of these is relatively limited. High-income residential areas are found beside the spine of Yonge Street in the City of Toronto and in patches in the outer suburbs. Wealth should theoretically be trickling down and over from these wealthy areas to the poorer ones, which should therefore be shrinking in size. In Toronto, as in many other cities, this is not happening. On the contrary, indications are that disparities are increasing. This has been documented in a number of recent, carefully researched reports, the most telling of which is called *The Three Cities within Toronto*. This investigation by David Hulchanski and a team of colleagues at the Cities Centre of the University of Toronto uses Census data from 1971 to 2006 to trace changes in income levels and their geographical distribution, and it reveals a steady increase in income polarization across the so-called three cities (Figure 8.4). In City 1—the high-income areas mostly associated with affluent suburbs originally built in the early twentieth century adjacent to Yonge Street and near the Humber River Valley in the west end—income levels relative to the averages for the overall region have risen substantially since 1970 in comparison with the regional average. City 3 is a broad zone that includes most of the modest tract housing and apartment clusters of the inner suburbs, where already-low incomes have fallen relative to the average since 1970. In between is City 2, where incomes over the last four decades have stayed fairly close to the regional average. The key is that it is City 2, the middle-income one, that is shrinking, and the rich, who have individual incomes about three times those of the poorest group, are getting richer while the poor are getting poorer and the area that the poor occupy is getting larger. The proportion of middle-income neighborhoods has dropped from 66 percent in 1970 to 29 percent in 2005, while the proportion of low-income neighborhoods has increased from 19 percent to 53 percent. There is, in other words, a process of income polarization under way that is playing out in the geography of the city.[23]

In effect, poverty in Toronto has been suburbanized, at least to the extent that it is now focused in the inner suburbs of the City of Toronto. This would seem to follow, at least in part, from the public policy decisions

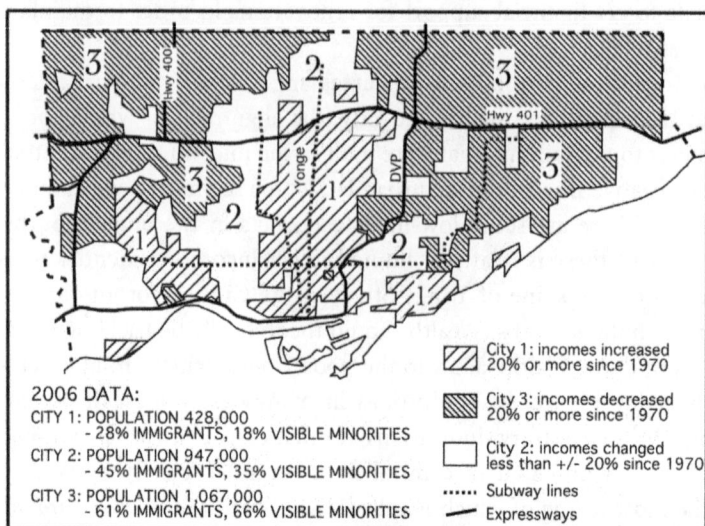

Figure 8.4. Income disparities and polarization in Toronto. This map shows the "three cities" within the City of Toronto as determined by changes in average individual income as a percentage of the Toronto CMA average 1970–2005. City 3 is expanding more rapidly than City 1, and City 2 is shrinking. Source: simplified, redrawn, and population data added from D. Hulchanski et al., *The Three Cities within Toronto: Income Polarization among Toronto's Neighbourhoods, 1970–2005*, Centre for Urban and Community Studies (now the Cities Centre), Research Bulletin No. 41, first published 2007, updated 2010, available at http://www.urban centre.utoronto.ca/redirects/3cities/Dec2010Report.html.

made by Metro in the 1960s about the location of public housing and low-rent apartments, but it is also the case that the inner suburbs are where there are high concentrations of recent immigrants and visible minorities. It is not a straightforward matter to extend the *Three Cities* analysis to the outer suburbs because these have been developed too recently to establish trends over four decades, and any comparisons in income levels would be between the current large cities and the small towns and rural areas that preceded them. But it is worth noting that there are clear pockets of low-income neighborhoods in Brampton, Mississauga, Richmond Hill, and Markham, outer municipalities where at least a quarter of the population consists of recent immigrants (see Figure 8.2). In these same municipalities there are also some manifestly wealthy neighborhoods, a fact that suggests that polarization and income inequalities similar to those in the City of Toronto are beginning to emerge in the outer suburbs.[24]

The *Three Cities* report complements and adds detail to a previous study titled "Poverty by Postal Code" that was conducted by the United Way in an attempt to assess poverty, as defined by low-income levels in the Canadian Census, at a regional scale. That study found a regional imbalance in the distribution of poverty, with 23 percent of the population of the City of Toronto in 2000 identified as low-income, whereas no municipality in the outer suburbs had levels greater than 13 percent. This regional imbalance has been politically recognized through "pooling costs," charges that the province imposes on municipalities in the outer suburbs to help pay for the social services provided by the City. The reasoning behind these is that many homeless and disadvantaged people from the outer suburbs drift into the City of Toronto where there are more hostels and social services. There are indications that this regional imbalance is declining because income disparities in those outer suburbs are also growing. For instance, the number of Census tracts with middle incomes in the outer suburbs dropped by almost 20 percent between 1971 and 2001. And although about 85 percent of visits to food banks in the region are still within the City of Toronto, since the recession in 2008 the most rapid increases in the use of food banks have been within the outer suburbs.[25]

The United Way's postal code analysis was particularly important because it indicated that the most intense poverty is concentrated in a relatively small number of areas in the City of Toronto. This observation led to a public/nonprofit partnership between the City of Toronto and United Way, which has involved a strategy of focusing funds for social services and reinvestment in thirteen priority areas, rather than distributing them throughout the City. With this focused support, the priority areas have emerged as centers of grass-roots initiatives that include community gardens, social support services, food banks, homework clubs, furniture exchanges, immigrant integration, and effective lobbying for such basic things as improvements to local bus services.[26]

While the strategy of priority areas appears to have been effective, it has not countered the very important concern in the context of Toronto's multiculturalism and diversity that poverty seems to be concentrating among recent immigrants and people of color. For example, the *Three Cities* analysis revealed that the population of wealthy City 1 is 82 percent white and 18 percent visible minorities, so it is a sort of wealthy white enclave. In City 3, the poor one, the population is 34 percent white and 66 percent visible minorities. The United Way study similarly identified the fact that the highest levels of poverty are found among visible minorities in inner suburban areas. A local lobby group, Colour of Poverty has taken head-on this matter of what it calls the "racialization of poverty." It has synthesized evidence from a wide range of reports, including a Children's Aid Society investigation of child poverty in Greater Toronto, which concluded that while one child in ten in European groups lived in a family with low income; for East Asians, it was one child in five; for South Asians, Caribbeans, and Latin Americans, one in four; for Arabs and West Asians, one in three; and for Africans, one in two. Other reports by different organizations, dealing for example with youth violence, high school dropout rates, food insecurity, and dependence on food banks, indicate similarly high levels of representation among people of color.[27]

A related concern is the lack of representation of visible minorities in positions of authority—as elected officials, on boards of corporations, and in the media. This disparity is being monitored by a branch of Civic Action called DiverseCity: The Greater Toronto Leadership Project. The current situation is that only 14 percent of the 3,256 leaders identified in the region are from visible minorities, compared with about 40 percent of the population. Leadership in the corporate sector is the least diverse, with only about 4 percent who are not white. The main role of DiverseCity is to lobby for "leaders who have a diversity of skills and experience that reflects the richness and complexity of our region." It has support from powerful leaders of all colors, and there are signs that the situation is improving, but there is a long way to go.[28]

It is apparent from these various reports that a concomitant result of the ethnic and racial diversity that has transformed Toronto into a village of the globe is increased income disparity, with poverty especially pronounced for new immigrants and visible minorities. It would be easy to jump to the conclusion that the trend is toward a concentration of those visible minority immigrants in ghettos of poverty, especially in the inner suburbs. This assumption has been examined carefully by two geographers, Alan Walks and Larry Bourne, and they concluded that in the City of Toronto there is no statistical evidence to suggest that this is actually the case. There are certainly some areas, Flemingdon Park and Regent Park, for example, where more than 80 percent of the population consists of relatively recent immigrants of color and income levels are among the lowest in the region, only one-third of the regional average. Yet there are also neighborhoods and subdivisions of single-family houses that suggest this is by no means the norm. Morningside Heights in the northeast corner of the

City of Toronto was built up in the late 1990s and first years of the twenty-first century with streets of detached brick houses (similar to those shown in Figure 6.3); its population of about twenty thousand is 94 percent visible minorities, about half South Asian but otherwise a mixture. In 2005 the median household income was 16 percent higher than the regional average. In those outer suburban municipalities—Markham, Richmond Hill, Brampton, and Mississauga—where half or more of the population consists of visible minorities, there are some low-income pockets but overall income levels are above average. And in each of those municipalities there are subdivisions of single-family houses similar to Morningside Heights where 70 or 80 percent of the population consists of visible minorities and the average income is well over that of the region. In other words, while there is a trend toward increasing income polarization in the City of Toronto, and there are some indications of that in the outer suburbs, a substantial proportion of immigrants of color in the region do not find themselves in the bottom half of the hourglass.[29]

Low incomes do, however, appear to be associated with clusters of apartment towers. A 2011 United Way study called "Vertical Poverty" found evidence that poverty is intensifying in the clusters of high-rise buildings in the inner suburbs as incomes decline and rents rise. On the other hand, it also found that while many of these buildings are now forty or more years old and need substantial renovations, three-quarters of the 2,100 residents who were interviewed considered high-rise apartments to be good places to live, and two-thirds thought they were good places for raising children. In spite of drug dealing and gangs, most residents consider their neighborhoods reasonably safe. There was no significant difference in responses to the survey between the experiences of immigrants and those of Canadian-born tenants. The study concludes that although there are clearly serious problems that need to be attended to, "this housing stock still provides a valued living environment for thousands of low and moderate income households."[30]

Indeed, in the extensive inner suburbs of City 3 there is remarkably little overt evidence of deep poverty. The most obvious signs of low-income neighborhoods are perhaps check-cashing shops, Walmarts and similar discount stores, and rather shabby plazas. There, few obvious signs on the streets or in the appearance of the clusters of apartment blocks support the statistical evidence that income levels in City 3 are declining. The low-rise residential areas of the inner suburbs consist mostly of modest tract houses built in the 1950s and 1960s for white, blue-collar, and lower middle-class families. Many of the owners now are South Asian, Chinese, Vietnamese, Filipino, Caribbean, or members of other visible minority groups, but there are no signs in the maintenance of houses and gardens that pride of ownership has diminished. Furthermore, the spaces left over in the original development of the inner suburbs are being steadily filled in with new projects, especially townhouses, as a result of the post-suburban City of Toronto's commitment to intensification, so in spite of relatively declining incomes inner-city neighborhoods are continually being renewed and upgraded.

Wealth, too, in Toronto is mostly discreet. Though there are some pockets of conspicuous consumption where there are modern 10,000-square-foot houses with ballrooms and a dozen bathrooms on spacious lots with private tennis courts, much of City 1 consists of the nonstreetcar, not very ostentatious affluent suburbs built in the early twentieth century. It also includes more modest streetcar suburbs of houses on narrow lots (such as those shown in Figure 3.2), which, even though they may have been entirely renovated inside and extended at the back, have modest street façades that do not reveal the wealth of their current owners. In short, the increasing polarization of incomes is not very obvious in Toronto's urban landscapes.

Nevertheless, there is no question that the statistical evidence of a persistent and intensifying trend toward income polarization is strong, as is the evidence that the growing affluence is in primarily white parts of the City, while incomes are falling in the nonwhite inner suburbs. Thus far, multiculturalism and public reasonableness, which generally challenge racial hierarchies and marginalization, seem to have prevailed, and income polarization has been accommodated without spilling into landscapes. If crime rates can be taken as an indication, it has also not manifested itself in social frictions—the Canadian Crime Severity Index for 2011 ranks the City of Toronto 117th out of about 250 communities, and its incidence of violent crime is below Victoria, Vancouver, Edmonton, and Montreal. Furthermore crime rates have steadily declined by about 20 percent over the last decade. Nevertheless, the trend to income polarization and the persistent underrepresentation of persons of color in positions of authority do show that there is a long way to go to achieve full integration, and unless ways are found to mitigate these Toronto's rosy reputations as a multicultural urban region and as a preferred destination for immigrants are likely to be sorely tested.[31]

Coping with Transformations

Since Toronto was founded in 1793 it has been caught up in global processes that have grown remarkably in intensity over the last forty years as it
has undergone a transformation from being a major Canadian city to being
a leading world city region in a global economy driven by finance and
information. In spite of a decline in manufacturing and the apparent indifference of successive federal and provincial governments it has managed to
increase and then maintain its status relative to metropolitan areas in North
America and on other continents. And while these economic changes were
under way, the Toronto region has accommodated a veritable tsunami of
immigration from all parts of the world and now has the highest proportion
of foreign-born residents of any city in the developed world.

Given the sheer scale of all these changes, and the fact that Toronto is
by far the largest city in Canada, it is hardly surprising that arguments have
been made for making it a province in its own right, a sort of twenty-first-
century city-state. A Province of Toronto is exceedingly unlikely, but there
have been some important initiatives that have begun to find ways to deal
with the symbiotic and pressing issues of economic development and growing social injustice. The most promising of these initiatives is, I think, the
formation of Civic Action, an organization that has public, private, non-
profit and community support, and is addressing at a regional scale a wide
range of issues that local governments and the Province of Ontario seem to
be unable to resolve. Civic Action is filling a vacuum created by the lack of
effective regional governments.[32]

It is nevertheless difficult to contest the OECD conclusion that the
region suffers economically because of confusion about regional governance. The response of all three levels of government to the need for the
integration of new immigrants into the workforce, especially recognition of
professional qualifications, and to the combined pressures of globalization,
technological change, and economic restructuring, has been, according to
a recent assessment of the situation, "hesitant, uneven and disjointed."
Indeed, there is not even much agreement on just what the economic
region is, and it is frequently not clear whether reports with a title indicating that they are addressing issues in "Toronto" are referring to the City of
Toronto, the Census Metropolitan Area, the Greater Toronto Area, the
Greater Toronto and Hamilton Area, or the Greater Golden Horseshoe.
What is clear is that Toronto, however defined, mostly does rather well in

measures made by outside organizations, whether for economic perform-
ance, foreign investment, social programs, safety and low levels of violence,
programs to integrate immigrants, quality of education, lively streets, quality of neighborhoods, or almost everything else. And it has managed this
while accommodating three million immigrants from many different parts
of the world over the last forty years. Thus far, public reasonableness has
generally prevailed in Toronto, and though it is by no means a cosmopolis,
it has, to borrow an apposite phrase from Leonie Sandercock, for the most
part managed to become a place where "stroppy strangers" seem to be able
to live together without doing too much violence to one another.[33]

Chapter 9

Containing Growth

If growth is a measure of success, then in the last fifty years Toronto has been very successful. A relatively small city that was almost stereotypically white, Anglo-Saxon, and Protestant and contained within a single metropolitan municipality has been transformed into a multicultural, polychrome, and polycentric urban region a hundred miles across. This remarkable growth has almost all been accommodated in new suburban developments that have been carefully regulated by zoning and planning controls to ensure that there was no leapfrogging, the watercourses were protected, a mix of housing was provided, and there were appropriate hierarchies of schools, shops, and roads.

There are three problems with this apparent success. First is the issue pointed out by Jane Jacobs and others that new developments lack the organized complexity and walkability of older areas. Second, during most of this half century of urban expansion little attention was paid to regional coordination. In effect, while the urban growth was tightly regulated in detail it was laissez-faire on the large scale, and it didn't help that it was fragmented between about thirty municipalities. Third, the Toronto conurbation has grown much faster than any other urban area in Ontario; it had about a quarter of the province's population in 1961, but in 2011 it had half the population.[1]

After several decades of apparent indifference the Province of Ontario has, since the start of the present century, taken Toronto's growth in hand by putting in place an ambitious triad of regional plans—the Greenbelt Plan, the Growth Plan to guide urban development, and the Big Move for transportation. The overall aim is that these will determine the patterns of development in and around Toronto until at least 2031, essentially by containing and constraining growth. It is too soon for them to have had a major effect on urban landscapes, but there is no question that that they have altered ways of thinking about the Toronto urban region and will direct its future urban structure both on a large scale and in detail.

Precedents for Urban Regional Planning

The importance of regulating development beyond city boundaries has been recognized since 1912, when the old City was given control over subdivisions in a zone that extended five miles beyond its municipal borders in order to reduce problems of providing water supply and sewers to speculative developments that were hoping to piggyback on city services. This extension of the city's planning authority beyond its borders endured in various guises until regional municipalities were established in the 1970s and it no longer was necessary. Its practical effect was to limit the building of isolated subdivisions, but it also had the incidental effect of promoting the centrist view that Toronto had responsibility for managing regional urban growth. This was certainly apparent in the unofficial 1943 Master Plan, prepared by the Toronto City Planning Board, which looked far beyond the city's borders with its visions of future greenbelts and expressway networks.[2]

At that time there was no political structure for turning those visions into reality, and there was, for instance, none of the spirit of intermunicipal cooperation in the Lower Mainland that led in the 1940s to regional planning initiatives around Vancouver. Nevertheless, they subsequently filtered into plans prepared by Metropolitan Toronto, and Metro had the authority to implement them. Indeed, Metro was, according to the urban historian Richard White, "the only true regional planning body the region has ever known." Within its boundaries it had responsibility for water, sewerage, parks, transportation, land-use control, roads, policing, and education. In an extension of the 1912 bylaw, Metro was given control over development proposals in townships adjacent to its boundaries. This allowed it to apply the planning principle of urban contiguity even beyond its boundaries. No leapfrog subdivisions and no isolated new towns were permitted because all new development had to be serviced efficiently by water and sewer lines connecting to lakeshore treatment plants.[3]

Even though Metro was legally a creature of the province it was in most respects its own boss, and until about 1970 the province paid relatively little attention to patterns of urban growth either within or around Toronto. Then, as Metro filled up with people and the urban area began to outgrow its boundaries, it became clear that the scale of regional planning had to be extended, and the Province of Ontario began to take an increasing interest in the way the built-up area of Toronto would expand, an interest that has culminated in the current three regional plans. The clearest indication of this change came in the early 1970s with the creation of the four new regional municipalities around Metro. These took over the planning controls Metro had previously had beyond its boundaries, and responsibility for regional urban development effectively shifted from the center to the edge.[4]

Then, almost as though the province's politicians and mandarins didn't know quite what to do next, there followed what Richard White calls "an age of non-planning" for the Toronto urban region. This lasted almost three decades and occurred at precisely the same time that immigration and urban growth surged. In spite of, or perhaps because of, this absence of formal planning, this was also a period of intense discussion about future options for the region.[5]

By the late 1980s persistently high levels of growth around Toronto had begun to ring alarm bells, some associated with environmental concerns and the loss of agricultural land, and others with the cost of servicing new developments. In 1988 the province responded by creating the Office of the Greater Toronto Area to assess what was happening in Metro and the surrounding regional municipalities. Consultants were commissioned to assess the implications of various forms of urban growth, and they identified three possible urban futures. "Spread" meant low-density, business-as-usual development; "Central" would contain all future development within existing built-up zones; and "Nodal" would concentrate development within a number of growth centers. A key recommendation, which has filtered into current plans, was that some sort of concentration based on a combination of Central plus Nodal would lead to substantial savings both for the province and for municipalities compared with the business-as-usual Spread because it would involve much lower costs for servicing and transportation.[6]

As these reports were being prepared, ideas were being independently advanced about the environmental merits of compact, sustainable forms of urban development for the Toronto bioregion. At about the same time, an independent and broad-based popular movement arose to argue for protection of the Oak Ridges Moraine from large-scale, low-density projects that were then being proposed by developers. This convergence of interest in the Toronto region as opposed to Metro was followed by a flurry of research that generated several shelf-feet of reports from consultants, agencies, planning departments, and universities, and the provincial government appointed a task force to examine possibilities for the future governance of the Greater Toronto Area. None of these had a direct outcome. What did happen was that a provincial election brought in a neo-Conservative government with strong support in the outer suburbs and rural Ontario, and almost none in Metro Toronto, which brushed aside the idea of a regional form of government for the Greater Toronto Area. Apparently an entirely different and more expansive regional strategy about smart growth was being fermented.[7]

The notion of smart growth was widely discussed in North America in the 1990s; the basic idea was that economic growth could be balanced against social and environmental concerns, with the aim of achieving sustainability by curtailing automobile-oriented subdivisions and promoting transit-oriented development. The right-wing Conservative government in Ontario appropriated the term, and it created smart growth panels to develop programs for "positive growth" in a Central Ontario region. This region was far more extensive than the Greater Toronto Area, the first incarnation of what is now called the Greater Golden Horseshoe, and it included rural areas of long-established Conservative support that counterbalanced the mostly Liberal areas in urban Toronto. By distributing smart growth across a broad region the government had simultaneously asserted the Province of Ontario's authority over urban growth and diluted the Toronto-based political power of the Liberal Party. It had also set in motion the wheels of regional planning.[8]

In 2001, as the smart growth panels were being set up, the province passed legislation to create a conservation plan for the Oak Ridges Moraine (which lies mostly in long-standing Conservative ridings). This multiuse environmental management plan protects agricultural, recreational, and natural heritage areas, and it restricts large-scale subdivisions. In 2005 it became an integral part of the province's more extensive Greenbelt Plan, which was brought into effect by a Liberal government that had replaced

Figure 9.1. "Entering The Greenbelt" sign. There are no signs to indicate when you are leaving the greenbelt. The result is a topological paradox: an area that can be entered many times but never exited.

the Conservative one. Regional planning for Toronto had finally become an established part of provincial thinking, regardless of party politics.[9]

Enclosing the City: The Greenbelt Plan

The Greenbelt Plan was the first of the three regional plans to be implemented. It established a huge section of south-central Ontario as a greenbelt, claimed by the province to include 1.8 million acres and to be the largest greenbelt in the world. The Ontario Greenbelt is defined as "where urbanization should not occur in order to provide permanent protection to the agricultural land base and the ecological features and function." Its boundaries are precisely demarcated on large-scale maps and within landscapes by large blue and white signs (Figure 9.1). Its most notable ecological

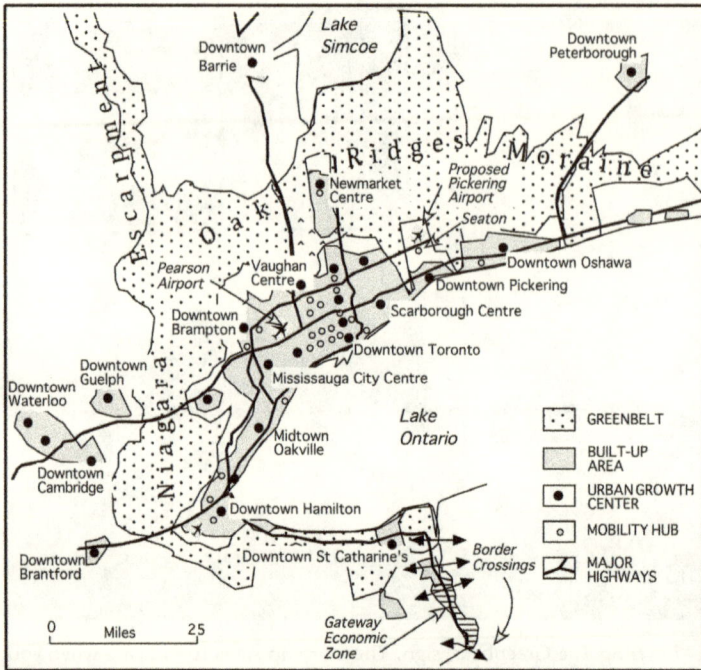

Figure 9.2. Urban growth centers, mobility hubs, and the Greenbelt in the Greater Golden Horseshoe. The narrow, unshaded strip between the built-up area and the Greenbelt is the zone remaining for possible urban expansion of Toronto. Some growth centers are not named. Sources: The Growth Plan, Schedules 4 and 6; The Big Move, Schedule 3.

features are the two that embrace Toronto—the Niagara Escarpment and the Oak Ridges Moraine (see Figure 9.2). In addition, the plan protects large areas of "working countryside," including the Niagara soft fruit and wine-producing area and Holland Marsh, where vegetables are grown. It also includes quarries and sand and gravel pits that provide building materials for Toronto, as well as numerous towns, villages, and hamlets that are to be maintained and revitalized and may even experience "modest growth." However, and this is the key from the perspective of Toronto, "settlement areas outside the Greenbelt are not permitted to expand into it." A strip of land between its southern boundary and the edge of the existing built-up area is the undeveloped space left for urban growth. In short, the Greenbelt is an urban growth boundary zone that is intended to permanently enclose the conurbation of Toronto. It creates the sort of urban containment that, for example, surrounding mountains have always imposed on Vancouver.[10]

An important aspect of the Greenbelt is that it protects "natural heritage," a notion that has been widely adopted in Ontario as a reinterpretation of the value of natural environments and that has become an integral aspect of almost everything to do with land and water management in the Toronto region. The idea of natural heritage probably originated in the United States during the 1950s in its discussions about National Parks, then received international recognition in the UNESCO Convention in 1972 for the Protection of Cultural and Natural Heritage that led to the creation of World Heritage Sites. Following this lead, in 1974 the Ontario Heritage Foundation (now the Ontario Heritage Trust) was established as an arm's-length agency of the provincial government to identify, protect, renew, and promote "Ontario's rich and diverse built, cultural and natural heritage . . . for the benefit of present and future generations."[11]

David Lowenthal, a geographer and historian who has written generally about the concept of heritage, suggests that natural heritage is considered significant both because it is not human made and because it is local and cannot be exported. In an implicit recognition of such significance the 1992 report of the Royal Commission on Toronto's Waterfront claimed that natural heritage is critical for regional and individual identity. Yet in spite of the great value accorded to it, natural heritage evades clear definition. The Ontario Natural Heritage Information Centre—a data bank for what it refers to as "spaces of conservation concern"—suggests that it consists of "all living organisms, natural areas and ecological communities which we inherit and leave to future generations," in effect, everything not made by humans. Neither the Greenbelt Plan nor the legislation behind it offers a definition, even though one of the four schedules of the plan is a detailed map of a "natural heritage system" that demarcates areas with "the highest concentration of the most sensitive and/or significant natural features and function." This system is a discontinuous band of 535,000 acres within the Greenbelt that has been immunized against any form of economic activity. Most local municipalities in the region also identify and protect natural heritage. For example, the City of Toronto Official Plan defines it obscurely as "an evolving mosaic of natural habitats that supports the variety of nature in the City." I am not sure what this means, but a map in the Official Plan identifies natural heritage areas and, as in the Greenbelt Plan, these are rigorously protected from development. In other words, even though it cannot be precisely defined, the idea of natural heritage has been applied in the Greenbelt and elsewhere in material ways that will play an important role in confining and directing future change and growth, urban and otherwise, in the Toronto region.[12]

A practical criticism of the Greenbelt Plan is that even though it protects the environmentally sensitive zones of the Escarpment and the Moraine, and more specifically the natural heritage system within those, it is still insufficient because it does not include substantial areas of prime agricultural land, much of it in the narrow band between the urban edge and the Greenbelt that is intended for urban growth. A further concern is that when this narrow band fills up, future projects will simply jump over the Greenbelt to the other side, and in fact there are already indications of land assemblies north of the Moraine. To reduce this likelihood, the Greenbelt Alliance, a quango established by the province to promote all aspects of the Greenbelt, has developed the idea of Greenbelt 2.0, which recommends the addition of 1.2 million acres in order to make the greenbelt so wide that possible leapfrog projects would be well beyond any commuting range to Toronto. In this environmentalist perspective all forms of urban expansion are apparently bad and must be strictly confined.[13]

Growing Inward: The Growth Plan

The Greenbelt Plan does not mention Toronto once, yet it is clearly intended to create a straitjacket, loose-fitting but a straitjacket nonetheless, that will limit the expansion of Toronto's built-up area. Because Toronto has not stopped growing outward since it was founded in 1793, this poses a problem. If the region's population is to continue to grow in the foreseeable future as it has over the last forty years, and there are no indications of a significant slowdown in immigration, then other urban development strategies are needed. These are outlined in the second element of the regional planning triad, "Places to Grow: The Growth Plan for the Greater Golden Horseshoe" (usually referred to just as the Growth Plan). The Greater Golden Horseshoe is the name the Growth Plan invented for a region that extends well beyond the Greenbelt and that corresponds to the former Central Ontario smart growth area. The reasons for its boundaries are not explained, though in terms of distances people drive to get to Pearson Airport, or the range of day trips, for instance, from Toronto to Niagara Falls, they do not seem unreasonable. The Greater Golden Horseshoe is far larger than the still widely referred to but, for planning purposes at least, now obsolete Greater Toronto Area (see Figure 2.4). It is a polycentric region in which the City of Toronto is the largest urban center among twenty-four other cities that have more than fifty thousand residents.[14]

Unlike the Greenbelt Plan, which apparently will be applicable in perpetuity, the Growth Plan has a target date of 2031 for achieving its goals of accommodating an additional 2.4 million people in the Greater Golden Horseshoe over the 2011 population (for a total of about 11.5 million) and providing almost a million more jobs. These goals are to be achieved by building "compact, vibrant and complete communities," which are to have a diverse mix of land uses, employment, housing, and easy access to local stores. Because land supply is now restricted to the band between the urban edge and the Greenbelt, this will be done by encouraging intensification everywhere, and specifically by concentrating growth within twenty-five urban growth centers (Figure 9.2). These measures, the Growth Plan claims, will promote forms of development that support a strong and competitive economy, conserve natural resources for current and future generations, and optimize use of infrastructure. One indirect aim of the Growth Plan is also "to promote collaboration," a euphemistic way of stating that the province is overcoming current jurisdictional fragmentation by imposing development standards that local municipalities will have to follow.[15]

The Growth Plan requires that, beginning in 2015, 40 percent of the new dwellings built each year in each regional municipality must be in existing developed areas; in other words, conventional suburban development on greenfield sites is to be restricted. This will have to be achieved by rehabilitating brownfield sites, building on unused lots, and redeveloping at greater densities. Longer-term goals are based on density targets for urban areas that combine jobs and population; the target for 2031 is twenty residents and/or jobs per acre (the Growth Plan uses metric measurements so the stated number is fifty per hectare). To put that in perspective, the post-suburban City of Toronto, which has been landlocked by regional municipalities but intensifying since about 1975, currently has about twenty-five people and jobs per acre, while the supersuburb of the City of Mississauga, which is almost built out and has about 720,000 people and 420,000 jobs, has an average of about sixteen people and jobs per acre, so these goals are not out of line with the current situation. What this all boils down to is that from now on urban development in the region has to be as much about filling in as spreading out, so that job creation can offset people accommodation and so that the density of developments on greenfield sites has to be about double what it has been. If all these aims are achieved, the anticipated population growth in the Greater Golden Horseshoe to 2031 should be accommodated inside the constraint imposed by the Greenbelt, with room to spare. This will require a substantial shift away from many of the development habits of the last half century.

The identification of twenty-five urban growth centers amounts to a policy of deconcentrated concentration. It is expected that all of these centers will have transit stations, and many will be linked by corridors of intensification along transit lines such as those already in place in Markham and proposed for Hurontario Street in Mississauga and Brampton (discussed in Chapter 6). They are mostly based on existing nodes, and some are already highly developed and intensified. Five are in the City of Toronto, including the downtown core and the suburban downtowns of North York and Scarborough, where a standard of one hundred and sixty residents and jobs per acre (four hundred per hectare) is applied; others are based on downtowns in smaller cities and towns in the region, and in these the standard is either eighty or sixty residents and jobs per acre (two hundred or one hundred and fifty per hectare), depending on local circumstances. Individual municipalities have to figure out ways to achieve these standards that will fit with their particular circumstances, but the province paternalistically monitors how well the targets are being achieved and, given its constitutional authority over local municipalities, has numerous sticks at its disposal to ensure compliance.

Although the Growth Plan is clearly triggered by the relentless expansion of the conurbation of Toronto, and although it sets by far the highest density standards for urban growth centers in the City of Toronto, it continues the province's petulant disavowal of Toronto by scarcely mentioning the City except to note that its downtown will continue to be a major international center of finance. This omission is especially remarkable because the City of Toronto's transit-oriented developments will provide the best local models for urban growth centers.

The Growth Plan and the Greenbelt Plan both represent a remarkable shift in possibilities for urban development. On the face of it, it seems as if the polycentric character of the urban region will be dramatically reinforced and that the automobile dependence of the inner and outer suburbs will be challenged. Indeed, it seems possible that the urban growth centers, with a little attention to the details of urban form, could meet the four conditions that Jane Jacobs identified as necessary for cities to flourish: they must mingle different uses, such as work and residence, because this leads to people on the streets; they must have short, small blocks so that people on foot can navigate easily between different areas; they need to have a mixture of types, sizes, and ages of buildings; and they must have a high concentration of population.[16]

The Growth Plan does not, however, go into such details. And it may have set its sights too low. The Neptis Foundation, an independent organization that has funded some of the most valuable research into the planning of the Toronto region, considers that the target of twenty people and jobs per acre needs to be closer to thirty-five people and jobs per acre in order to support transit. There are also significant issues, not clearly dealt with in the Growth Plan, with the dispersal of office and other employment to business parks in the outer suburbs that are separated from residential areas and poorly served by transit. These concerns are compounded by what seems to be a continuing commitment in the region to large-format retailing in plazas and power centers located for easy access by driving, mostly several miles away from the proposed urban growth centers. If urban growth centers really are to become high-density, walkable urban nodes that meet Jacobs's criteria, it will be essential to find ways to concentrate shopping and other activities in them, in addition to apartments, townhouses, and offices.[17]

Intensification, Transportation, and the Big Move

In 2006 the Province of Ontario created the Greater Toronto Transportation Authority to address transportation planning. In 2007 this was snappily rebranded as Metrolinx, a change that completed the pattern of removing references to Toronto from the titles of plans for the Toronto region. Strictly speaking, Metrolinx is responsible for the improvement and coordination of all forms of transportation only in the Greater Toronto and Hamilton Area (GTHA); however, because it also has responsibility for GO Transit, whose network of rail and bus lines extends throughout most of the Greater Golden Horseshoe, the boundaries of the GTHA presumably don't matter much.

The Big Move is the transportation and transit plan prepared by Metrolinx. It considers all modes of ground transportation, including the movement of goods, but its main aim is to promote transit-supportive development that will advance the initiatives of the Greenbelt Plan and Growth Plan and which "will lead to the development of more compact and complete communities that make walking, cycling and transit part of everyday life." The Big Move takes a broad perspective that pays attention to the fact that there is often poor transit service in areas of social and economic need, considers relationships between lack of walkability and obesity, and discusses the importance of reducing carbon emissions in the context of climate change. Its proposals are a remarkable reversal of the practices of the previous half century that gave priority to highways, and it mentions highways only in terms of management improvements such as implementing more high-occupancy vehicle lanes.[18]

Metrolinx will focus on the development or enhancement of fifty "mobility hubs," where different modes of transportation interconnect and where people can begin and end trips or make transfers. These are seen as places where the urban form can be intensified. The largest hubs are associated with urban growth centers and with both Union Station in downtown Toronto and Pearson Airport. Intensification in the other smaller mobility hubs will happen in different ways and obviously on a more modest scale. Many of these already exist in nascent form (for instance, around some subway stations in the City of Toronto), but all of them have been identified because they are considered to have considerable development potential as "attractive, intensive concentration[s] of employment, living, shopping and enjoyment around a major transit station." Mobility hubs could have a major impact on future urban form, and several municipalities—Mississauga, Brampton, Richmond Hill, Markham—are moving quickly to implement them in association with the development of light rapid transit and bus rapid-transit systems and intensification along corridors (Figure 9.3).[19]

The emphasis on transit is considered to be the best way to address chronic traffic congestion in the region, which is expected to worsen because car ownership and the number of trips made by car are growing faster than the population. Furthermore, commuting by bus in both the

Figure 9.3. A poster in 2012 for the construction of the Rapidway, a dedicated right-of-way for Viva bus rapid transit along Highway 7. The poster shows views of before and after development in Richmond Hill. Some sections of the route have already been developed at about the intensity shown in the picture on the right. Even after intensification there appear to be three moving lanes and turning lanes for car traffic in each direction, though other renderings show only two. It is not legible at this scale, but the contribution of Metrolinx is acknowledged at the bottom right.

inner and outer suburbs is slow and has not been helped by poor coordination of different municipal transit systems. Aims of the Big Move include improvements to bus services by increasing bus-only lanes, installing preferential signals for transit, and achieving full integration between all systems, including GO Transit, at the mobility hubs, with a single ticketing system for the whole region. The vision of the Big Move is that, by 2031, 30 percent of trips in the region will be by transit and 20 percent by walking or cycling (compared with the current levels of about 23 percent and 6 percent, respectively) and that the majority of the regional population will live within a few minutes' walk of rapid transit.

The Big Move reinforces and fills in the details of the broad picture spelled out in the Growth Plan. From another perspective, it is an attempt to catch up with other North American and European cities that have new light-rail and other public transit systems, though its regional scale and commitment to changing suburban-built forms in mobility hubs and along transportation corridors are unusually ambitious. Given the scale of the proposals it is not surprising that a long section in the Big Move discusses the "investment strategy" needed to reverse several decades of underfunding for transit from all levels of government. Although the Province of Ontario has committed to provide substantial capital funds for transportation projects in the region and has set up Metrolinx as the agency responsible for allocating those funds, the fact is that the province is struggling economically. Additional funds may not be forthcoming for capital projects, and operating costs will have to be covered from the fare box or by municipalities. Furthermore, transportation plans can be upended by local politics. A plan for an extensive light-rail system in the City of Toronto, designed in part to service disadvantaged areas and with financial commitments from Metrolinx, was summarily dismissed in 2010 by a newly elected mayor who declared on his first day in office that roads are for cars and the only good form of transit is underground in subways. Subways cost much more to construct than light rail, and the new mayor's bluster has been reversed, but it has delayed implementation of the light-rail plan by at least two years.

A New Airport and a New Town

The three provincial plans represent a radical change in the context for urban growth in the Toronto region. There is little doubt that they will have a big influence on the forms of future urban development, not least because they build on municipal initiatives, such as the development of high-density suburban centers, transit projects, and brownfield rehabilitation that are already well advanced, and also because they have the province's constitutional authority standing behind them. There is, however, one set of very significant regional initiatives that they scarcely mention. This has to do with airports.

Airports fall under federal rather than provincial jurisdiction, and while Pearson International Airport is recognized in the Big Move as an anchor mobility hub, it is discussed mostly in terms of transit and future rail access. It is scarcely mentioned in the Growth Plan. These are significant omissions because the airport district is one of Canada's largest employment districts, with 12,500 businesses, according to a report by the Greater Toronto Airports Authority in 2011. Of greater significance for the region is that the master plan for Pearson has projected that airport use will double by 2030 from its 2007 levels to about sixty million passengers and eight hundred thousand aircraft movements a year. At this rate of increase in demand, the existing airport will run out of capacity by 2017 and air traffic will have to be moved to a network of "reliever airports." One such airport, now mostly used for cargo, is located near Hamilton, and there is a small intercity airport on the islands close to the center of the City of Toronto. But the main reliever airport is planned for a site in the municipality of Pickering, northeast of the City of Toronto, which was expropriated in the 1970s by the federal government for that purpose. At that time there was a vigorous popular protest and development did not occur (though the reason might have had to do with lack of demand as much as the protest). Nevertheless, a draft master plan has been prepared for the proposed Pickering airport, including details of runways and flight paths. As capacity at Pearson becomes increasingly strained, pressure for the construction of the Pickering airport will certainly grow. This will be contentious for the area's residents and the Big Move circumspectly does little more than note the airport's location on a map. It does, however, identify the nearby site of a proposed new town as a mobility hub.[20]

New towns as a means of handling urban growth have never been popular in Canada, and except perhaps in India and China, they are now not popular anywhere, so the proposed new town of Seaton to the east of the City of Toronto is something of an anachronism. Its site was expropriated by the Province of Ontario in the 1970s with the intention of creating a new city of two hundred thousand that would be adjacent to the proposed Pickering airport. When the airport was put on hold, plans for the new town were scaled back and then went into limbo until the late 1990s. In order to facilitate the Oak Ridges Moraine Conservation Plan, the province swapped some of the land it held at Seaton for areas in the Moraine owned by private developers where development is no longer permitted, and an updated plan was prepared for the new town. The town is now projected to have a population of seventy thousand with thirty-five thousand jobs, and its design has been brought into line with the Greenbelt and Growth

Plans. Seaton is envisaged as "a sustainable urban community," integrated with an extensive local natural heritage system and an adjacent agricultural reserve. It is to have fifteen compact neighborhoods, each with the sort of modified grid-street pattern and mixed land use favored in new urbanist developments, and each one will open onto "forests, fields and streams" because every creek and woodlot will be protected and the neighborhoods will be separated by greenways. Densities within the built areas of those neighborhoods will be transit-supportive (which presumably means buses, although the Big Move does propose a rail link to Toronto) and most shops and other daily-use facilities are to be no more than a five-minute walk away for residents.[21]

In 2012, forty years after the land was expropriated, development still had not begun either at Seaton or the proposed international airport. The airport site occupies several square miles where there are some desultory attempts at cash crop farming, boarded-up buildings, and a few federal government signs that give little indication of the planned future. On adjacent farms and roadsides there are "No Airport" signs that are harbingers of the protests that can be expected when development becomes a real rather than a planned possibility. On the site of Seaton there is no indication at all that a new town might be built—not a single sign. Together the two sites cover a vast area, almost as big as the old City of Toronto, where everything is in limbo. This standstill is a reminder than urban development can be a very long, slow, and uncertain process.

Limitations of Planning for a World City Region

The Greenbelt Plan, the Growth Plan, and the Big Move constitute a huge advance in planning for the Toronto region, both because they follow a period of nonplanning and because they are ambitious in scope. In North America they are regarded as major initiatives; in 2007 the Daniel Burnham Award, the most prestigious award of the American Planning Association, was given for the first time outside the United States to the Growth Plan because "it provides a strategic, innovative and coordinated approach to sustainable growth and development."[22]

Nevertheless, both by comparison with the powers of regional planning that Metro Toronto had in the 1950s and in terms of issues confronting world city regions in the early twenty-first century, the three regional plans are limited. As a single municipality with control over its territory, Metro Toronto had a wide range of powers, including raising bonds to pay for capital projects such as subway construction. The Task Force on the Governance of the Greater Toronto Area in the 1990s recognized that such powers would be equally invaluable for planning and developing the more globally interconnected and multicultural region that Toronto has become. In its report the task force acknowledged "the essential role of city-regions as primary and increasingly important generators of wealth in the new global economy," and it emphasized the need for a government structure that facilitates coordination of planning, transit, infrastructure, economic development, and environmental quality. But instead of creating such a structure the Province of Ontario has opted for the three plans, which, although they are impressive and innovative, really only deal with physical aspects of planning. It is a serious question whether they are up to the task of providing the degree of direction and the flexibility that is needed to manage change and to deal with critical issues for Toronto as a world city region.[23]

For example, although the lack of coordinated economic development in the region has been repeatedly raised both inside and outside it, there is no regional plan for economic development to parallel and reinforce the targets for people and jobs in the Growth Plan. Urban growth centers are apparently expected to compete with one another for their share of the regional pie. Moreover, even though the Greenbelt covers an enormous area, it is still spatially and conceptually constrained as an environmental plan for the Greater Golden Horseshoe because it does not come to terms with what is happening in cities, towns, and suburbs. The Toronto and Region Conservation Authority is trying to correct this by advancing the idea of "the Living City" for the watersheds under its purview, which include most of the built-up area of Toronto. The Living City is defined as "a new kind of community . . . where human settlement can flourish forever as part of nature's beauty and diversity." Yet even this proposal is mostly about land, plants, and rivers, and it does not grapple with the processes, for example, of air pollution and climate change, which respect neither political nor watershed boundaries.[24]

This is a significant local omission. It was at a conference of climatologists held in Toronto in 1988 that attention was first brought to the likelihood that human-generated pollution was having substantial climatic consequences. In the language of the conference report, "Humanity is

conducting an unintended, uncontrolled, globally pervasive experiment."
At the federal level, in both the United States and Canada, climate change
has become embroiled in ideological disputes, with accusations about bad
science accompanied by intense lobbying from oil and coal groups whose
profits could be threatened by attempts to reduce emissions. At the provincial level it has been claimed that the Greenbelt Plan and the Growth Plan
promote a more compact urban form for Toronto that is environmentally
beneficial but there are few other signs of effective policies dealing with
climate change. In spite of this high-level political dithering, substantial
actions are being taken by lower levels of government. As far as I know,
every municipality in the Greater Golden Horseshoe has adopted strategies
to reduce greenhouse gas emissions by promoting green roofs, converting
their fleets to low-emission vehicles, adopting LEED standards for institutional buildings, or increasing the size of the urban forest because of its
importance in providing shade and its value for carbon sequestration.
There is some voluntary coordination of these efforts but an effective
regional environmental plan, equivalent to the Growth Plan, is needed to
ensure consistency, establish common standards, share knowledge about
best practices, and achieve effective results.[25]

In *The Death and Life of Great American Cities* Jane Jacobs observed
wryly that "in real life we lack strategies and tactics for making large scale
metropolitan and regional planning work." Real life in metropolitan
regions is now always open to global influences, of which one is climate
change. The consequences that can accrue when there is a lack of effective
regional planning and coordination in the context of globalization were
made strikingly apparent in Toronto in 2003 with the outbreak of SARS
(Severe Acute Respiratory Syndrome). SARS arrived by air, via aircraft to
be precise, on a flight from China in 2003 and caused an epidemic in the
region in which about four hundred people were infected and forty-four
died. It was a sharp lesson that demonstrated that globalization involves
more than economics and migration. In that instance, there was a systemic
failure of emergency procedures, in part because of strained relationships
between the three levels of government, which competed to take charge of
the situation, and also because both patients and hospital workers who may
have carried the virus crossed municipal borders within the region without
thinking about them. Then it turned out that health records were a municipal responsibility and not shared electronically, and the people working to
find ways to contain the epidemic had to thumb through paper files from

different municipalities in order to find information about patients. It was a distressing illustration of the mismatch between assumptions about political jurisdiction and global processes and of the inadequacy of parochial approaches for addressing the local consequences of living in a global village. It's not exactly what McLuhan meant, but it serves as an object lesson that, with electric speeds and international communications, everywhere can be a center and margins cease to exist. It was also an object lesson for planning in the Toronto region (indeed, for all metropolitan regions) that no matter how widely regional boundaries are drawn, they are inevitably porous.[26]

Chapter 10

A City for Everybody

Toronto has always had difficulty finding its identity. There was the name change to York and back again; then in the late nineteenth century it was nicknamed alternatively Toronto the Good for its moral rectitude and Hogtown for its slaughterhouses. It left Ernest Hemingway, who was a reporter there in the 1920s, at a loss for words: "It couldn't be any worse," he wrote to Ezra Pound. "You can't imagine it. I'm not going to describe it." What the name represents was stretched first to the borders of Metropolitan Toronto, which has now fallen by the wayside, then to the Greater Toronto Area, which has been transcended by the Greater Golden Horseshoe, a region that nominally ignores Toronto altogether. When he was filming *Blues Brothers 2000* in the city in the late 1990s, the Canadian movie actor and producer Dan Aykroyd claimed that "Toronto doubles for anywhere you want it to be . . . that includes the Louisiana bayous." Other movie directors have said similar things. Although Toronto is said to be the third most important center of movie and TV production in North America, it infrequently plays itself. Parts of it regularly pass for neighborhoods in Chicago or New York; the suburban campus where I work was once turned into "The New Pacific Institute of Technology" for a film set.[1]

Perhaps the elusiveness of Toronto's identity has something to do with the fact that there is little in the city or the region that might be said either to inspire or to have been inspired by imagination—no mountains, oceans, or grand urban design; nothing that is either sublime or exceptionally picturesque. There is nothing that has generated a local equivalent of what the planner Carl Abbott referred to as Portland's conceit of "the satisfaction of self-sufficiency" that comes from its amazing natural setting and its reputation for urban design and intelligent planning. Most of Toronto's human landscapes and the things in them, including the CN Tower, seem to express the conviction that it is better to have them engineered to work rather than designed to impress. At the time of the much-lauded World Exposition in Montreal in 1967 the first chairman of Metro, Fred Gardiner, remarked that he would never have agreed to it being in Toronto because "it would have cost us millions of dollars that are a damn sight better invested in sewers and water pipes and roads which are a permanent value instead of a one year's bust." This attitude might explain why Toronto has never been the site of a world expo or an Olympics, in spite of its long urban dominance in Canada and several attempts to become the Olympic committee's choice (the inexplicable lack of a rapid-transit connection to the airport might also have something to do with that).[2]

A character in the novel *The Diary of Samuel Marchbanks* by the Toronto author Robertson Davies says, "I always think of Toronto as a big fat rich girl who has lots of money, but no idea of how to make herself attractive." That was in the 1940s. Other novelists have not been much kinder. The most favorable characterizations in fiction are that it is a reserved, practical sort of place. Michael Ondaatje's novel *In the Skin of a Lion* is set in the early twentieth century and is tellingly told within the context of the construction of public works projects. In Margaret Atwood's novels, Toronto appears mostly as the background for various forms of angst; in *Cat's Eye* she writes of "the old city, street after street of thick red brick houses, with the front porch pillars like the off-white stems of toadstools, and their watchful, calculating windows." And she seems equally unhappy both with the old, pretransformation Toronto and the new version: "The old emptiness of Toronto is gone. Now it is chockfull; Toronto is bloating itself to death." In the preface to their anthology *Toronto Short Stories*, Wolfe and Daymond write: " From a distance Toronto looks like a magical place . . . a place where people whose roots and pasts are elsewhere believe they can make a new beginning. Up close, however, it becomes just another failed dream."[3]

I have scoured anthologies and books of quotations for statements that praise Toronto, but there are not many. Ray Bradbury offered what may be the sole instance of an unqualified compliment when he exclaimed that "Toronto is the most perfect city in the Western hemisphere." Umberto Eco, who studied semiotics there, was a little more guarded when he wrote that Toronto is "a marvelous cocktail between New York and London, at a human size." Buckminster Fuller, who maintained that he had circled the world forty-four times, was somewhat less effusive when he said that he considered Toronto to be the most comfortable city in the world to live in: "It's the cleanest city and it works." The British actor Peter Ustinov once described Toronto as "a kind of New York operated by the Swiss," slightly backhanded but a sort of compliment nonetheless.[4]

These moments of praise all date from the 1970s and 1980s, which suggests that Toronto was then realizing the hopes for the future of cities that Jane Jacobs had expressed in the conclusion to *The Economy of Cities*, which was published in 1970. Future cities, she speculated, "will not be smaller, simpler or more specialized than the cities of today. Rather, they will be more intricate, diversified, and larger than today's, and will have even more complicated jumbles of old and new things than ours do." And indeed the intricate streets of the old City of Toronto, where she had just moved when that book was published, have become more vibrant and diversified than they were then, partly because of practices that integrated heritage preservation with new developments, but also because of immigration, which has dramatically changed the character of populations and streetscapes. For Jacobs this improvement in Toronto was not to last. In her final book, *Dark Age Ahead*, written when she had lived in the city for thirty-five years, she reveals that, for her, Toronto had indeed become just another failed dream. The specific cause of her disillusionment was the amalgamation of the old City with the inner suburbs that had been imposed in 1998. Since then she thought Toronto's deterioration had become "visible and enraging"; it was no longer neat and clean, the transit was deteriorating, there was no new subsidized housing, and there was a crisis of public poverty. More generally she saw Toronto being drawn down, like many other cities, into a spiral of decline, not least because of suburban sprawl "with its murders of communities and wastes of land, time and energy." Toronto's suburban growth was apparently leading it into a dark age.[5]

Marshall McLuhan's sense of the urban future was entirely different from that of Jacobs, and not specifically concerned with Toronto, yet in the end he was scarcely less pessimistic. He anticipated the emergence of "an information megalopolis," in which the functions and meanings of cities would be fundamentally changed as electronic communications sweeping around the world make metropolitan space irrelevant and borders obsolete. "The city becomes terrestrial in its scope," he predicted, "and the planet, in turn, becomes a global village." To the extent that the skyline of Toronto is dominated by the CN Tower and punctuated by thousands of cell phone towers and relays, and its streets, supermarkets, and buses are filled with transnational citizens detached from their present places because they are using personal communication devices to text and tweet, it is already well on the way to becoming an integral part of the information megalopolis. McLuhan would not have been enthusiastic. "Our electric extensions of ourselves simply by-pass space and time," he wrote, "and create problems of human involvement and organization for which there is no precedent. We may yet yearn for the simple days of the automobile and the super-highway."[6]

Civic Self-deprecation and Toronto as a Rustbelt/Sunbelt City

"Civic self-deprecation" is the phrase used by the urban journalist Shawn Micaleff to describe the persistent negativity about Toronto adopted by so many local commentators. He thinks that it is a consequence of not looking at the city in the right way, and he claims that "any Toronto flaneur knows that exploring this city makes the burden of civic self-deprecation disappear." He demonstrates how this can happen by offering descriptions of his explorations of diverse districts of the city, including suburban downtowns, Pearson Airport, the underground PATH system in the financial district, shopping malls, trendy streets in the central city, and Dorset Park, an immigrant reception area in the inner suburbs consisting of unlovely apartment blocks built in the boom era of Metro, where he found residents who love their neighborhood and have a strong commitment to improving it. By looking closely and with clear eyes at landscapes that most writers about Toronto have ignored or not seen, Micaleff reveals a strong, varied, and cumulative sense of place.[7]

From an entirely different perspective and at an altogether larger scale, negativity about Toronto is also belied by the manifest reality of a city that has rarely stopped growing and renewing itself, a process that shows no signs of abating or becoming a spiral of decline leading to a local dark age. Reyner Banham once argued of Los Angeles that insofar as it performs the functions of a great city by being cosmopolitan and filled with creative energy, "to that extent the most admired theorists of the present century, from the Futurists and Le Corbusier to Jane Jacobs . . . have been wrong. The belief that certain densities of population, and certain physical forms . . . are essential to the workings of a great city . . . must to that same extent be false." His remark applies no less to cosmopolitan, multicultural, constantly expanding Toronto. Its role in the global economy; its major events that range from the Toronto International Film Festival to the West Indian celebration of Caribana and its hugely popular Gay Pride Parade; its contributions to science, medicine, and stem cell research; its manifest attractiveness for new immigrants; its transnational ethnoburbs; its implementation of new suburban forms—these all indicate that Toronto is also a great city, not quite on the scale of Los Angeles or New York perhaps, but not that far behind them. The problem seems to be that Torontonians cannot bring themselves to acknowledge this because civic self-deprecation gets in the way.[8]

Larry Ford has written of San Diego that "even outrageous housing costs and egregious traffic congestion do not dissuade people from coming." One of Toronto's defining characteristics as a city and an urban region is that, although housing costs and traffic congestion are probably even more outrageous and egregious than San Diego, and although there are problems of social deprivation and a lack of regional coordination, people keep coming, and Toronto is for the most part thriving and growing both in its center and its suburbs. This is remarkable for a city that in the 1950s and 1960s was part of the rustbelt, with a large manufacturing industry and major automobile plants. Yet unlike Philadelphia and Detroit, the center did not hollow out as manufacturing and residents moved away. On the contrary, the population of Toronto's downtown area, which includes both the financial district and the residential area where Jacobs had lived, has steadily increased since the 1970s, and this increase has unquestionably contributed to old Toronto's transformation from an inward-turned city to one strongly oriented to street life, with patio cafés and busy sidewalks in diverse neighborhoods. At the same time this was happening, the outer suburbs were growing at an average of about eighty thousand people per year, a sustained rate that has been close to the peak population growth of the most prosperous sunbelt cities, yet without their problems of low-density overbuilding. This expansion of Toronto's outer suburbs may not have reproduced the pedestrian-friendly environments of the old streetcar city, but neither has it created undifferentiated sprawl. On the contrary, greenways have been preserved along rivers and creeks, there are numerous new urbanist developments, growth has been structured around a variety of old and new centers, and regional plans have been put in place to promote intensification and the use of rapid transit. There are certainly things that could have been done better in the suburbs, especially locating stores so that almost everyone is in reasonable walking distance of them, but there is little of the "thinking small and living big" sprawl that characterizes Phoenix and other sunbelt cities.[9]

The reasons for this successful transformation from a rustbelt city to a relatively compact northern equivalent of a sunbelt city may have something to do with stronger planning controls, different political systems, and the relative absence of racial divisions. Perhaps the practices of Metro contributed to it. But I suspect that the main reasons have to do with the fact that at about the same time that manufacturing went into decline, the federal government increased immigration into Canada and there was a flight of capital out of Montreal because of a separatist crisis in Québec. Toronto was the largest and most southerly city in Canada, and it simultaneously attracted both new immigrants and old money. Whatever the reasons, most indications are that Toronto is a successful city region that, regardless of theoretical criticisms, has managed to experience sunbelt levels of growth while avoiding rustbelt decline.

Management and Restraint in a City for Everybody

If the indications are that Toronto is, in several senses, a great city in North America, then it's a puzzle as to why its citizens have so often regarded it negatively. The answer to this was, I think, provided by Jim Lemon, a historical geographer who identified "management and restraint" as the two key principles that have guided Toronto's development. Management, because so much of the making of the city and its region has been controlled from above: first by colonial officials and then by a family compact of wealthy businessmen in the nineteenth century, and more recently by Metro and by the Province of Ontario to ensure that everything works in an orderly way. Restraint, because management has always been imbued with the sort of frugal utilitarian ethic that Fred Gardiner expressed so clearly in his preference for improving sewers rather than hosting a World's Fair. Consider, for example, Simcoe's second-hand canvas house, a grid that could be easily subdivided into neat rectangular lots, the utilitarian plans of Metro that balanced urban development against municipal income, and most recently a sensible regional plan for urban growth centers that barely mentions urban design presumably because it is regarded as a frill. They all convey an attitude that admires nothing excessive or wasteful. Management, restraint, and utilitarianism are not, however, the sorts of ideas and practices that lift the soul or inspire imagination, which is probably why novelists and artists do not seem to have viewed Toronto as inspiring.[10]

Shawn Micaleff, in his psychogeographic strolls around the city, sees something similar though he gives it a different spin. "Since Toronto seems to exist without design or reason," he has written, "we don't expect to turn the corner and see beauty or be amazed." If there is one consistent theme in the personality of the regional urban landscapes, it is the frugal practicality of its planning and design. There are no grand urban avenues, no remarkable examples of deliberate urban design, no internationally acclaimed works of modern architecture. It is telling that most buildings in Toronto that have been designed by celebrity architects—Daniel Libeskind's crystal extension to the Royal Ontario Museum, Frank Gehry's addition to the Art Gallery of Ontario, Santiago Calatrava's atrium at BCE Place—are additions to older structures. While these additions acknowledge the importance of international architectural excellence for a world city, they do it in a restrained way. Originality has been kept under control.[11]

On the other hand, the unpretentious streets that you usually encounter when you turn the corner—regardless of whether they are in the old City, the inner suburbs, or the outer suburbs, and regardless of whether they are in districts of condominium towers, bay and gable Victorian houses, Metro Toronto slab apartment blocks, or suburban subdivisions—are mostly pleasant places for everyday life. They have the same sort of practical, straightforward value as things that were invented or discovered in the Toronto region, which include insulin, business improvement districts, the Robertson screwdriver, the commercial use of phones, and Cineplex cinemas. Utilitarian urban management may not amaze, but it does reduce the likelihood of extreme low points. In Toronto there are neither ghettos nor areas of abandoned housing, no equivalents of Superfund sites, no leapfrog developments with inadequate services. In spite of limited municipal budgets and chronic underfunding by higher levels of government, old areas of the city have been adaptively reused, the hundreds of aging apartment towers are slowly being renovated, and the outer suburbs are installing rapid transit systems and continue to expand and to absorb new immigrants.

Of course, Toronto does have problems, including the persistently widening income gap, the racialization of poverty, an underrepresentation of visible minorities in leadership positions, traffic congestion, and evidence that the region's economy is insufficiently productive and innovative. Thus far, ways have been found to mitigate the worst manifestations of these. There have been relatively few instances of the sort of political corruption and racial conflict that, for example, Jan Nijman writes about as being instrumental in the development of Miami. Instead innovative coalitions have been developed, such as the one between United Way and the City of Toronto to provide assistance to the most disadvantaged priority neighborhoods. Civic Action and other organizations, which involve some sort of public/private/nonprofit cooperation, are finding ways to address a range of economic, social, and environmental problems in the region. At a larger scale, the plans for the Greater Golden Horseshoe recently instituted by the Province of Ontario promise to put an end to the city's inexorable expansion and to promote widespread intensification in growth centers and along transit corridors.[12]

It is, of course, possible that these various coping strategies will not be sufficient to prevent some sort of spiral of decline for Toronto, such as the one that Jacobs foresaw, and it is wise to remember that in the 1950s nobody could have imagined the decline of Detroit or Philadelphia. Nevertheless, and perhaps I am missing something obvious to others, it seems to me that these initiatives are evidence that deep-seated traditions of management and restraint are still working to ensure that both the City of Toronto and the region as a whole will continue to be renewed and to diversify, grow, intensify, and adapt to as-yet-unforeseen challenges. These traits have facilitated what seems to be Toronto's capacity of providing something for everybody (Figure 10.1). Not because it is created by everyone, which is an impossible dream, but because of the more modest reason that it has somehow come to provide reasonable spaces in all its different parts for almost all its citizens and because, in an unassuming way, it embodies most urban practices and values. I do not think Toronto can be said to have one especially distinctive character trait. Instead it combines a little of most urban qualities. Toronto is simultaneously a streetcar city of walkable neighborhoods, a skyscraper city of offices and apartments, a network of expressways, a world city, a multicultural cosmopolis of diverse ethnic communities that speak many languages and worship in many faiths, a planned city with fragments of unplanned suburbs, a neoliberal city, a post-suburban city, a series of automobile-oriented suburbs, a little bit of this, some of that, nothing too exceptional, all coexisting in a polycentric region

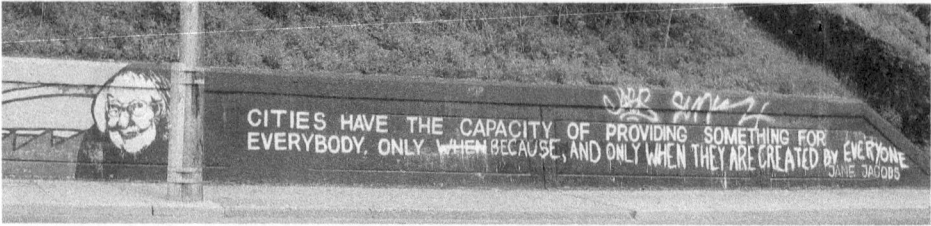

Figure 10.1. "Cities have the capacity of providing something for everybody, only ~~when~~ because, and only when they are created by everyone"—attributed to Jane Jacobs by an anonymous street artist (who presumably also provided the portrait of her on the left) and modified by a street editor. Graffito on Christie Street at Davenport in the City of Toronto, 2012.

of fifty distinct centers that is being turned into an experiment in constraining urban growth. Toronto is both literally and figuratively an urban region of many different cities. For the most part it is not beautiful, and there may be little in its urban landscapes that can be said to be truly inspiring, but by and large it works well in its own managed and restrained way, and to that extent it provides something for almost everybody.

Notes

Chapter 1

1. R. Fulford, *Accidental City: The Transformation of Toronto* (Toronto: Mac-Farlane, Walter and Ross, 1995), 1–2.

2. SkyscraperPage.com has a database that lists skyscrapers that are more than twelve stories or thirty-five meters high in all the major cities in the world. New York has about 5,800 completed high-rises; the City of Toronto, 1,900; Shanghai, 1,170; followed by Tokyo, Chicago, and Hong Kong. The source for the population figure for Toronto and for the ranking of cities in North America by urban agglomeration is Demographia, *World Urban Areas 2012* at http://www.demographia.com/db-worldua.pdf, which assesses the populations of built-up areas rather than metropolitan areas as defined in respective censuses. The urban agglomeration of Toronto now includes the three census metropolitan areas of Hamilton, Toronto, and Oshawa, each of which incorporates outlying towns and exurban zones, and it had a combined population of almost 6.6 million when the Canadian Census was taken in 2011. Different definitions of Toronto are discussed in Chapter 2, skyscrapers in Chapter 5, density and different measures of urban areas in Chapter 6, expressways in Chapter 7, and immigration and multiculturalism in Chapter 8.

3. H. Lefebvre, *The Urban Revolution* (Minneapolis: University of Minnesota Press, 2003; original French version, 1970), 16. "Cities are dead" is the first sentence in J. Friedmann, *The Prospect of Cities* (Minneapolis: University of Minnesota Press, 2002), 1.

4. The quote from Aneurin Bevan is something I have carried with me for many years, but the precise source has sunk into the swamps of time. Nadia Tazi has suggested that the end of the city is one of the commonplaces of postmodernity, and the concept of the city has lost all its validity and force. See N. Tazi, "Fragments of Net Theory," in R. Koolhaas, ed., *Mutations: Project on the City* (Bordeaux, France: Actar, 2000), 42.

5. "City region" is from J. Jacobs, *Cities and the Wealth of Nations* (New York: Vintage, 1985), 45. "Post-war suburbs" is from J. Jacobs, "Preface," in J. Sewell, *The Shape of the City: Toronto Struggles with Modern Planning* (Toronto: University of Toronto Press, 1993), x.

6. R. Bruegmann, *Sprawl: A Compact History* (Chicago: University of Chicago Press, 2005), 7, 9.

7. P. Lewis, "Axioms for Reading the Landscape: Some Guides to the American Scene," in D. W. Meinig, ed., *The Interpretation of Ordinary Landscapes* (New York: Oxford University Press, 1979), 15.

8. J. Jacobs, *The Death and Life of Great American Cities* (New York: Vintage, 1961). In this portrait of Toronto I have drawn on most of Jacobs's books. Jane's Walks are described at http//:www.janeswalk.net/. An annual conference dedicated to her ideas that is called "Ideas That Matter" is held in Toronto. R. White, "Jane Jacobs and Toronto: 1968–1978," *Journal of Planning History* 10, no. 2 (2011): 114–138 (online at http://jph.sagepub.com/content/10/2/114), provides a thoughtful discussion of Jacobs's impact on Toronto.

9. J. Lemon, *Liberal Dreams and Nature's Limits: Great Cities of North America since 1600* (Toronto: Oxford University Press, 1996), 20–24.

10. While I have taken ideas from most of McLuhan's books, the most useful has been *Understanding Media: The Extensions of Man* (Toronto: Signet Press, 1964).

11. McLuhan, *Understanding Media*, 92–93. "Every city a suburb of every other city" is from M. McLuhan and E. McLuhan, *Laws of Media* (Toronto: University of Toronto Press, 1988), 202. McLuhan was profoundly influenced by the ideas of Harold Innis, a political economist at the University of Toronto, whose ideas are most clearly expressed in H. Innis, *The Bias of Communication* (Toronto: University of Toronto ress, 1951).

12. R. Banham, *Los Angeles: The Architecture of the Four Ecologies* (London: Penguin, 1971), 173.

Chapter 2

1. H. Scadding, *Toronto of Old: Collections and Recollections,* (Toronto: Adam Stevenson, 1873), 73–74. The origins of the name "Toronto" are discussed in A. Rayburn, "The Real Story of How Toronto Got Its Name," originally published in *Canadian Geographic*, September/October 1994, 68–70, available at Natural Resources Canada, http://geonames.nrcan.gc.ca/education/toronto_e.php. Salmon's map can be found in *Salmon's Geographical and Astronomical Grammar, including the ancient and present state of the World* (London: Printed for C. Bathurst et al., 1785).

2. The land claim is discussed in "Mississaugas of the New Credit First Nation, Toronto Purchase Specific Claim: Arriving at an Agreement," 2010, at www.new creditfirstnation.com, and the settlement is described at Aboriginal Affairs and Northern Development Canada, "Canada and the Mississaugas of the New Credit First Nation Celebrate Historic Claim Settlement," October 2010, at http://www.aadnc-aandc .gc.ca/eng/1292349280146/1292349332936. The settlement, paid by the Canadian federal government, was $145 million.

3. This summary of the founding of Toronto is based on several sources, including *The Diary of Mrs. John Graves Simcoe, with Notes and a Biography by J. Ross Robertson*

(Toronto: William Briggs, 1911) and W. Careless, *Toronto to 1918: An Illustrated History* (Toronto: Lorimer, 1984).

4. J. Jacobs, *The Economy of Cities* (New York: Vintage, 1970), especially chapter 1. The argument that the founding of Pittsburgh, Cincinnati, Louisville, and St. Louis preceded rural settlement west of the Appalachians is made by R. Wade, *The Urban Frontier: Pioneer Life in Early Pittsburgh, Cincinnati, Lexington, Louisville and St. Louis* (Chicago: University of Chicago Press, 1959).

5. The reasons for changing the name of York to Toronto are given in J. E. Middleton, *The Municipality of Toronto: A History*, vol. 1 (Toronto: Dominion, 1923), 30.

6. This definition of "city" is from *The Canadian Oxford Dictionary* (Toronto: Oxford University Press, 1998). For Jacobs's definition see her *Economy of Cities*, Appendix VI, 262. Jacobs's idea of a city as a problem in organized complexity is expressed throughout *The Death and Life of Great American Cities* (New York: Vintage, 1961), especially chapter 22. The shift in language in the Canadian Census is noted in Statistics Canada, "From Urban Areas to Population Centres," 2011, at http://www.statcan.gc.ca/subjects-sujets/standard-norme/sgc-cgt/urban-urbain-eng.htm.

7. Margaret Atwood's novels set in the old City of Toronto include *Cat's Eye*, *The Edible Woman*, and *Life Before Man*; Michael Ondaatje's novel is *In the Skin of a Lion*.

8. The creation of the regional municipalities reduced the number of upper- and lower-tier municipalities from sixty-six to thirty. The creation of a Greater Toronto Council was recommended by the Greater Toronto Area Task Force, in *Report of the GTA Task Force* (Toronto: Queen's Printer for Ontario, 1996), available at http://www.scribd.com/doc/99998119/English; this is often referred to as the Golden Report after its chair, Ann Golden, and has nothing to do with the Greater Golden Horseshoe. F. Frisken, *The Public Metropolis: The Political Dynamics of Urban Expansion in the Toronto Region, 1924–2003* (Toronto: Canadian Scholars Press, 2007), has detailed accounts of processes that led to the creation of regional municipalities and of the demise of the task force's recommendations.

9. There is some confusion about the appropriate abbreviation for the Greater Toronto and Hamilton Area. It is mostly written as GTHA, but sometimes as GTAH or GTA + H. Whatever the abbreviation, it now corresponds more closely to the built-up agglomeration of Toronto than the GTA. H. Puderer, "Defining and Measuring Metropolitan Areas: A Comparison between Canada and the United States," Geography Working Paper Series, Statistics Canada, 2008, PDF at http://www5.statcan.gc.ca.

10. Royal Commission on Toronto's Waterfront, *Regeneration: Toronto's Waterfront and the Sustainable City* (Toronto: Queen's Printer of Ontario, 1992).

11. Ontario, Ministry of Public Infrastructural Renewal, "Places to Grow: Growth Plan for the Greater Golden Horseshoe," 2006, accessible at https://www.placestogrow.ca/index.php?option=com_content&task=view&id=9&Itemid=14.

12. Regional Institute, State University of New York at Buffalo, "The Region's Edge: Policy Brief," 2006, PDF at http://www.regional-institute.buffalo.edu.

13. The Regional Planning Association's discussions of megaregions are at http://www.america2050.org/images/2050_Map_Megaregions2008_150. Eleven urban mega-regions in North America are identified. The others are Southern California, Northern California, Cascadia, the Arizona Sun Corridor, the Front Range of Denver and Boulder, the Texas Triangle, the Gulf Coast, Florida, the Piedmont Atlantic, the Great Lakes, and the Northeast (the original megalopolis). The one-day and one-hour distances from Toronto are at Greater Toronto Marketing Alliance, http://www.greater toronto.org/why-greater-toronto/top-ten-reasons/. Similar claims about Toronto's economic reach, often with similar maps, have been made, for instance, by the Toronto Region Research Alliance, which is a branch of Toronto Civic Action, and by economic development departments of the City of Vaughan, the City of Toronto, and several other municipalities in the region

14. M. McLuhan, *Understanding Media: The Extensions of Man* (Toronto: Signet Press, 1964): "abolish the spatial dimension," 225; "implosion," 93; J. Friedmann, "The World City Hypothesis," *Development and Change* 17 (1986): 69–83. His comment that "cities are dead," cited in Chapter 1, is from J. Friedmann, *The Prospect of Cities* (Minneapolis: University of Minnesota Press, 2002), 1. The Globalization and World Cities material is at http://www.lboro.ac.uk/gawc/world2010t.html.

Chapter 3

1. J. Jacobs, *The Economy of Cities* (New York: Vintage, 1970), chapter 5. She lived on Albany Street, in a late nineteenth-century neighborhood called the Annex.

2. M. McLuhan, *Understanding Media* (Toronto: Signet Press, 1964): "urban structure," 103. He lived in Wychwood Park, which remains an idiosyncratic fragment of the old City. Sam Bass Warner, in *Streetcar Suburbs: The Process of Growth in Boston, 1870–1900* (Cambridge, MA: Harvard University Press, 1962), had previously demonstrated the role of streetcars in changing urban form and society. More generally, the idea that cities are influenced by transportation was well stated by John Borchert, a geographer at the University of Minnesota, in "America's Metropolitan Evolution," *Geographical Review* 57, no. 3 (1967), 301–332. He proposed "a model of urban evolution" in America, based on five phases: sail and wagon, 1790–1830; iron horse, 1830–1870; steel rail, 1870–1920; automobile and air, 1920–1970; and satellite and electronic communication, 1970 to present. For Toronto's urban form the periods might be sail, foot and wagon, 1790 to 1850; rail and horse-drawn streetcar, 1850 to 1900; electric streetcar, 1900 to 1940; automobile, 1940 to 1970; and automobile and electronic devices, 1970 to present.

3. R. Wade, *The Urban Frontier: Pioneer Life in Early Pittsburgh, Cincinnati, Lexington, Louisville and St. Louis* (Chicago: University of Chicago Press, 1959), 1. Henry Scadding, in his partially autobiographical history of Toronto written in the 1870s, notes that in the decades after 1800, there was one mail delivery a year from England "mockingly called the Express Post." H. Scadding, *Toronto of Old: Collections and Recollections* (Toronto: Adam Stevenson, 1873), 58.

4. McLuhan's argument about the connection between grids and print technology is discussed in R. Cavell, *McLuhan in Space: A Cultural Geography* (Toronto: University of Toronto Press, 2002), 89–90; Wade, *The Urban Frontier*, 24; L. Mumford, *The City in History* (New York: Harcourt, Brace and World, 1961), 421–422.

5. An additional base line was created to the west of Toronto, also parallel to the shore of Lake Ontario where it turns southwest, and the two master grids meet in a series of triangles and wedges, once referred to as Toronto Gore, at the western border of the current City of Toronto.

6. M. O'Brien, *The Journals of Mary O'Brien 1828–1838*, ed. A. Saunders Miller (Toronto: Macmillan, 1968), 34–35.

7. A. Jameson, *Winter Studies and Summer Rambles in Canada* (London: Saunders and Otley, 1838), 2, 98; D. McLeod, *A Brief Review of the Settlement of Upper Canada* (Cleveland: printed for the author by F. B. Penniman, 1841), 10.

8. C. Dickens, "American Notes 1842," in *The Writings of Charles Dickens*, vol. 11 (Boston: Houghton Mifflin, 1894), 556–557. The installation of gas lighting and paving is noted in J. E. Middleton, *The Municipality of Toronto: A History* (Toronto: Dominion Publishing, 1923), vol. 1.

9. Jacobs, *The Economy of Cities*: "stagnant little cities," 143; urban growth and import replacement is discussed throughout, but see 223–224. Middleton, *The Municipality of Toronto*, 1: 234, describes a census in Toronto in 1848 that gave the total population as 23,500: of these, 3,800 were English, 1,600 Scottish, and 9,000 were Irish. About 35,000 Irish refugees passed through Toronto in 1847 at the height of the famine on their way to other parts of Upper Canada.

10. The telegraph line to Buffalo is discussed in Middleton, *The Municipality of Toronto*, 1: 230. McLuhan, *Understanding Media*, chapter 25: powerful voice to the weak, 223; subordination of the telegraph to railway, 220.

11. Middleton discusses the railway line and Roebling's bridge at Niagara Falls in *The Municipality of Toronto*, 1: 249–250, 474. D. Kerr and J. Spelt, *The Changing Face of Toronto* (Ottawa: Queen's Printer for Canada, 1965), 44, note that U.S. federal legislation passed in 1846 had allowed Toronto merchants to ship through New York without paying tariffs, which presumably facilitated the subsequent telegraph and railway connections.

12. McLuhan, *Understanding Media*, 163–164.

13. The reasons why so many town and city halls in Ontario are oriented to the south are obscure, but as an empirical generalization it certainly applies in the Toronto region.

14. The details about pollution and sewage are from Kerr and Spelt, *Changing Face of Toronto*. The quote is from p. 72.

15. Sandford Fleming's contribution to standardized time is discussed in S. Kern, *The Culture of Time and Space, 1880–1918* (Cambridge, MA: Harvard University Press, 1983), 11. Information on Bell's phone call is from the Bell Homestead in Brantford. The comments about implosion are based on McLuhan, *Understanding Media*, 237.

16. Kerr and Spelt, *Changing Face of Toronto*, 69.

17. R. Harris, *Unplanned Suburbs: Toronto's American Tragedy* (Baltimore: Johns Hopkins University Press, 1996).

18. A. Duany, E. Plater-Zyberk, and J. Speck, *Suburban Nation: The Rise of Sprawl and the Decline of the American Dream* (New York: North Point Press, 2001), 159.

19. Some of the working-class history of Toronto in the 1920s and 1930s is well documented at "Mapping Our Work: Toronto Labour History Walking Tours," a PDF at http://www.labourcouncil.ca/uploads/8/8/6/1/8861416/labourhistorymap.pdf. H. Rasky, *Nobody Swings on a Sunday* (Toronto: Collier Macmillan, 1980). The Grove quote is from J. R. Colombo, ed., *Colombo's Canadian Quotations* (Edmonton: Hurtig Publishers, 1974); L. Infeld, *Quest: The Evolution of a Scientist* (New York: Doubleday, 1941), 341. The Harry Rasky quote I took from a public service advertisement on the Toronto subway; his sort of caustic observation is now locally celebrated as an indication of just how much things have improved. Jameson, *Winter Studies and Summer Rambles in Canada*, 2

20. The history of the Queen Elizabeth Way is described in J. Sewell, *The Shape of the Suburbs: Understanding Toronto's Sprawl* (Toronto: University of Toronto Press, 2009), 50–60. The Toronto Island Airport was originally named for King George, but that seems to have been completely forgotten.

Chapter 4

1. The 1943 plan is described, illustrated, and discussed in both J. Lemon, *Toronto since 1918: An Illustrated History* (Toronto: Lorimer, 1985), 103, and R. White, *The Growth Plan for the Greater Golden Horseshoe in Historical Perspective* (Toronto: Neptis Foundation, 2007), 8–10. Lemon and White reproduce slightly different illustrations of the original plan. The only other comprehensive development plans at a regional scale are those implemented by the Province of Ontario between 2006 and 2008, which are discussed in Chapter 9.

2. J. Jacobs, *The Death and Life of Great American Cities* (New York: Vintage, 1961): "city planning," 167; "bustles but does not advance," 439; "dull, inert cities," 448 (the last paragraph in the book).

3. J. Sewell, *The Shape of the Suburbs: Understanding Toronto's Sprawl* (Toronto: University of Toronto Press, 2009), 80–96, describes the development of Don Mills in detail. See also the Don Mills iTour at http://heritagetoronto.org/183/.

4. The comments about Don Mills creating true communities and amorphous developments are from D. Kerr and J. Spelt, *The Changing Face of Toronto* (Ottawa: Queen's Printer for Canada, 1965), 126.

5. Metro also controlled subdivisions in the townships outside but adjacent to its borders in order to ensure reasonable integration of services with what was happening inside Metro. Annexations over the next twenty years reduced the number of municipalities within Metro to six, including the old City of Toronto.

6. The deliberate attempt in Vancouver not to copy Metro is noted by Z. Taylor and M. Burchfield, *Growing Cities: Comparing Urban Growth Patterns and Regional Growth Policies in Calgary, Toronto and Vancouver* (Toronto: Neptis Foundation, 2010), 65.

7. "The only symphony" is cited in W. Kilbourn, ed., *The Toronto Book: An Anthology of Writings Past and Present* (Toronto: Macmillan, 1976), 250. The origins and responsibilities of Metro Toronto are described in F. Frisken, *The Public Metropolis* (Toronto: Canadian Scholars Press, 2007), 70–102.

8. Metropolitan Toronto Planning Board, *The Official Plan of the Metropolitan Toronto Planning Area* (Municipality of Metropolitan Toronto, 1959). This was technically a draft plan, not formally approved until 1966, by which time most of it had been implemented. The "first plan in North America" is discussed on p. 2; "balance all the costs," 253.

9. Metropolitan Toronto Planning Board, *Official Plan*, 1959: raising densities with high-rises, S5; "judicious mix," 62–63.

10. Metropolitan Toronto Planning Board, *Official Plan*, 1959: regional plan and attractive symbol, S4.

11. D. B. Kirkup, *Boomtown: Metropolitan Toronto—A Photographic Record of Two Decades of Growth* (published by the author in cooperation with Lockwood Survey, undated but probably 1969): "monumental expansion," 1; "boomtown," 8; "good thoughtful planning," 75.

12. The 1944 report is discussed in Kerr and Spelt, *Changing Face of Toronto*, 113.

13. The data on employment and vehicle ownership are from Kerr and Spelt, *Changing Face of Toronto*, 141, 107.

14. Ibid.: "beauty of the city," 12; Jacobs, *Death and Life of Great American Cities*; J. Gottman, *Megalopolis: The Urbanized North-Eastern Seaboard of the United States* (New York: Twentieth Century Fund, 1961).

15. L. Mumford, *The City in History: Its Origins, Its Transformations and Its Prospects* (New York: Harcourt, Brace and World, 1961).

16. Jacobs, *Death and Life*: "pseudoscience," 13; "unurban urbanization," 7; "suburbanized anti-city," 343; basket weaving and pottery, 374.

17. Gottman, *Megalopolis*: "nebulous structure" and related quotes, 5, 7, 9; polynuclear system of flows, 692; see also 736 for comments about flow, flux, and "nebulous and colloidal" patterns. The McLuhan comments are from *Understanding Media*, 94, 267.

18. J. Jacobs, "Preface," in J. Sewell, *The Shape of the City: Toronto Struggles with Modern Planning* (Toronto: University of Toronto Press, 1993), x.

19. Gottman, *Megalopolis*: "tidal currents," 21; "manifold concentrations," 24.

Chapter 5

1. W. I. Thompson, *At the Edge of History* (New York: Harper and Row, 1971), 74. The "urban crisis" is discussed, for instance, in E. Soja, *Postmetropolis: Critical Studies of Cities and Regions* (Oxford: Blackwell, 2000), 95–100.

2. Stop Spadina and the protest that saved Old City Hall are discussed in J. Lemon, *Toronto since 1918: An Illustrated History* (Toronto: Lorimer, 1985), 146–156.

3. The origins of policies of deconcentration and decentralization that have been so important in the subsequent development of the Toronto region are City of Toronto, *Central Area Plan Review: Part 1 General Plan* (City of Toronto Planning Board, 1975), B1–B8; Metropolitan Toronto, *The Central Area and Sub-Centres* (Long Range Planning Division, Municipality of Metropolitan Toronto, 1976); and Metropolitan Toronto, *Plan for the Urban Structure of Metropolitan Toronto: Concepts, Objectives* (Municipality of Metropolitan Toronto, 1976).

4. The key ideas and failed planning process for the Toronto Centred Region are discussed in F. Frisken, *The Public Metropolis: The Political Dynamics of Urban Expansion in the Toronto Region, 1924–2003* (Toronto: Canadian Scholars Press, 2007), 126–130. J. Sewell, in *The Shape of the Suburbs: Understanding Toronto's Sprawl* (Toronto: University of Toronto Press, 2009), also discusses the Toronto Centred Region proposals and devotes chapter 3 to the Big Pipe: see especially the maps on pp. 112 and 117. R. White, in *Urban Infrastructure and Urban Growth in the Toronto Region: 1950s to the 1990s* (Toronto: Neptis Foundation, 2003), offers a well-illustrated history of the Big Pipe and similar infrastructure projects.

5. Frisken, *The Public Metropolis*, 138–140, discusses the background to regional government reorganization, as does Sewell in *Shape of the Suburbs*, chapter 7.

6. The CN in CN Tower originally stood for Canadian National because it was developed by Canadian National Railways. Though they no longer own it, the name has stuck.

7. The old industrial/commercial areas that were re-zoned are often referred to as "the two kings" because they were centered on the intersections of King Street and Spadina Avenue, and King and Parliament Streets, respectively; a summary and review of re-zoning and reinvestment in these areas are available at http://www.toronto.ca/ planning/pdf/kingsmonit.pdf. The increase in the number of people living downtown is from City of Toronto, "Living Downtown" (October 2007), available at http:// www.toronto.ca/planning/living_downtown.htm.

8. The city rankings for skyscrapers are from http://skyscraperpage.com/cities; elsewhere on its site it identifies more than 2300 high-rises in the City of Toronto built or under construction, with a further 250 proposed; in the outer suburbs of the rest of the Greater Toronto Area there are another 510. Skyscraperpage also has thumbnail sketches of most of Toronto's tall buildings, including the CN Tower. The Emporis site at http://www.emporis.com/statistics/skyline-ranking rates what it calls the "visual impact of skylines" by awarding points for the total number of floors per building, and it has a database of high-rise buildings that is broadly consistent with Skyscraperpage.com. It defines skyscrapers as buildings more than one hundred meters tall, by which measure Toronto with 155 such buildings ranks seventh in the world. Data from these websites were used in an intriguing interactive graphic called "Vertical

Toronto" in the *Toronto Star*, November 17, 2011, at http://www.thestar.com/news/article/1089426—vertical-toronto-going-going-up?bn = 1.

9. This account of Flemingdon Park is pieced together from J. Sewell, *The Shape of the City: Toronto Struggles with Modern Planning* (Toronto: University of Toronto Press, 1993), 98–102; D. Kerr and J. Spelt, *The Changing Face of Toronto* (Ottawa: Queen's Printer for Canada, 1965), 115; and Metropolitan Toronto Planning Board, *The Official Plan of the Metropolitan Toronto Planning Area* (Municipality of Metropolitan Toronto, 1959), 62–72; and the insights of Noreen Khimani, a former student of mine who grew up in Flemingdon Park. It should be noted that although the intention of distributing apartment towers in clusters was to reduce the likelihood of social issues, many of them now are the poorest parts of the city.

10. The origins of the Bloor West Village BIA, which appears to have been the first business improvement area/district in the world, are given at http://www.bloor westvillagebia.com/about-us/history-of-the-bloor-west-village. M. Atwood, *Cat's Eye* (Toronto: Seal Books, 1989), 55; Risley's comment about districts was triggered by the renaming of the garment area of the old City as the Fashion District.

11. On reurbanization, see Berridge, Lewinberg, Greenberg Ltd, *Guidelines for the Reurbanization of Metropolitan Toronto: A Draft for Discussion* (Toronto: Berridge, Lewinberg, Greenberg, 1991); and "Avenues: Reurbanizing Arterial Corridors," section 2.2.3, City of Toronto, in *Toronto Official Plan* (2010 consolidation), a PDF available at http://www.toronto.ca/planning/official_plan/introduction.htm.

12. Metro's deconcentration strategy for Scarborough and North York is described in Metropolitan Toronto, *The Central Area and Sub-Centres*, Long Range Planning Division (Municipality of Metropolitan Toronto, 1976), 83. I gave a brief general account of the subcenters as they had subsequently developed in E. Relph, "Suburban Downtowns of the Greater Toronto Area," *Canadian Geographer* 35, no. 4 (1991): 421–425.

13. The City of Toronto's 2007 report "Living Downtown" (map 2, p. 7) shows that 81 percent of the residents of the new condominiums in the city center had moved from a zone within three miles of the financial district. Moreover, the number of dwellings increased by 36,000 between 2001 and 2006, but the number of households with children decreased by 4,500. "Living Downtown" indicates a population growth of 70,000 from 1970 to 2006, but because condominium construction has continued apace since then, it is reasonable to assume that another 15,000 or more people have now been added to the central area population, for a total of about 185,000.

Chapter 6

1. "416 and 905: We're More Alike than We Think," *Toronto Star*, April 18, 2010. The poll found that in the City of Toronto 27 percent knew many neighbors and 10 percent knew few; in Vaughan, the respective percentages were 24 percent and 9 percent, and in Mississauga, 27 percent and 11 percent. In Toronto 85 percent did not find it hard to walk around their neighborhood; in Vaughan, the numbers were 83

percent and in Mississauga, 78 percent. The former neat distinction between the 416 and 905 area codes is being blurred by the addition of other area codes to meet the demand for cell phones.

2. J. Jacobs, *The Death and Life of Great American Cities* (New York: Vintage, 1961) 13; J. R. Forman, *Urban Regions: Ecology and Planning beyond the City* (New York: Cambridge University Press, 2008).

3. L. Mumford, *The City in History* (New York: Harcourt Brace and World, 1961): "formless urban exudation . . . semi-urban tissue" is pieced together from pp. 505 and 508. Also see J. Sewell, *The Shape of the Suburbs: Understanding Toronto's Sprawl* (Toronto: University of Toronto Press, 2009), 229.

4. J. Gottman, *Megalopolis:* The Urbanized North-Eastern Seaboard of the United States (New York: Twentieth Century Fund, 1961), 13–16; P. Lewis, "The Galactic Metropolis," in R. H. Pratt and G. Macinko, eds., *Beyond the Urban Fringe* (Minneapolis: University of Minnesota Press, 1983), 34–35; R. Fishman, "Beyond Sprawl," in W. Saunders, ed., *Sprawl and Suburbia* (Minneapolis: University of Minnesota Press, 2005), xi.

5. The report that found evidence of overall intensification is GHK, *Growing Together: Prospects for Renewal in the Toronto Region*, a report prepared for the City of Toronto Department of Works and Oak Ridges Moraine Steering Committee (2002), see 5–6; Z. Taylor and M. Burchfield, *Growing Cities: Comparing Urban Growth Patterns and Regional Growth Policies in Calgary, Toronto and Vancouver* (Toronto: Neptis Foundation, 2010), 15, 25. My analysis shows 3 percent faster growth of the area than the population in the outer suburbs and 1 percent in the core; this is based on data in their tables 3.1 and 3.2. They do note on p. 21 that the totals for population and area changes in these two tables do not correspond, which presumably accounts for these inconsistent conclusions about rates of growth.

6. Sewell, *The Shape of the Suburbs*, 8; City Mayors Foundation, http://www.city mayors.com/statistics/largest-cities-density-125.html; and "Largest 850 World Urban Areas: Density," a PDF at Demographia, http://www.demographia.com/.

7. Other conservation authorities in the Toronto region, such as the one for the Credit River that flows through Mississauga, have similar policies and practices. Conservation authorities have a broad range of responsibilities for managing development in river valleys and monitoring and managing water quality, fisheries, recreation, and environmental education. See, for instance, the Toronto and Region Conservation Authority website at http://www.trca.on.ca/. The reintroduced salmon are Chinook from the Pacific coast, which apparently fare better than Atlantic salmon.

8. A. Sorensen, "Toronto Megacity," in A. Sorensen and J. Okata, eds., *Megacities: Urban Form, Governance and Sustainability* (New York: Springer, 2011), 259–260; R. Banham, *Los Angeles: The Architecture of the Four Ecologies* (London: Penguin, 1971), 217. Patricia Gober, in *Metropolitan Phoenix: Place-Making and Community Building in the Desert* (Philadelphia: University of Pennsylvania Press, 2005), 139–140, makes a

similar point, suggesting that the grid of roads there makes it easy to get from place to place.

9. Sewell, *The Shape of the Suburbs*, 98–105, provides a history of the assembly and development at Bramalea and also of another early outer suburban development at Erin Mills in the City of Mississauga.

10. My comment about high-rise apartments in the outer suburbs is based on numbers given for the municipalities shown in Figure 6.1 and listed at http://skyscrap erpage.com/cities. In January 2013 Mississauga had 252; Brampton, 65; Markham, 36; Burlington, 43; Oakville, 33; the others, fewer than 30 each. I have not included Hamil-ton, which had 114 high-rise buildings. As far as I could determine, fewer than 20 of the 530 high-rises were commercial and office buildings.

11. J. Jacobs, *Dark Age Ahead* (New York: Random House, 2004), 39. My compar-ative comment about European and American cities is based on the densities for cities around the world at Demographia, http://www.demographia.com/.

12. Information about Cornell and Markham's commitment to new urbanism is available at Markham, "New Communities Profile," Development Services Commit-tee, 2007, a PDF available at http://www.markham.ca/Markham/coveo/search.aspx?; and Markham, "Built Form, Height and Massing Study: Built Form Principles," 2010, a PDF available at http://www.markham.ca/Markham/Departments/Planning/Major PlanStudyOverview.htm. The figure of 150,000 people accommodated and the claim that Markham has the highest concentration of new-urbanist developments in North America are found in D. Gordon and S. Vipond, "Gross Density and New Urbanism: Comparing Conventional and New Urbanist Suburbs in Markham, Ontario," *Journal of the American Planning Association* 71 (2005): 1.

13. Data in the 2006 Canadian Census indicate 1.4 million jobs in outer suburbs and 1.25 million in the City of Toronto.

14. The quote about Unionville is from http://www.guidingstar.ca/Virtual_ Tour_of_Main_Street_Unionville.htm. The comments about urban design in small towns are based on Ontario, Ministry of Housing, *Main Street: Planning and Design Guidelines* (Project Planning Branch, Ministry of Housing, 1980).

15. Jacobs, *Dark Age Ahead*, 90. A summary of the downtown development plan for Brampton is at http://www.brampton.ca/en/City-Hall/SWQ-Renewal/Pages/Wel come.aspx.

16. The new centers I identify are Pickering, Markham, Beaver Creek, Vaughan, Bramalea, and Mississauga; there are slightly different types of new centers appended to old towns at Whitby, Newmarket, Maple, and Oakville. Plans for the City of Vaughan Metropolitan Centre are described at http://www.vaughantomorrow.ca/ OPR/VCC/index.html. The Markham Centre (or Downtown Markham) development is described at http://www.markham.ca/ under the tab "Business and Development, Markham Centre," in the drop-down menu.

17. The quote "shore up an urban landscape" is from I. Charney, "Two Visions of Suburbia: Mississauga City Centre and the Heartland Business Community," *Cana-dian Geographer* 42, no. 2 (2005): 219.

18. *Downtown 21: Creating an Urban Place in the Heart of Mississauga*, 2011, is accessible at http://www.mississauga.ca/portal/residents/downtown21.

19. The plan for this light-rapid transit intensification corridor is "Hurontario-Main Street Master Plan LRT Project," 2011, accessible from the links at http://lrt-mississauga.brampton.ca/EN/Pages/Welcome.aspx.

20. Renderings of the imagined future corridors along Viva routes are at vivaNext, 2011, http://www.vivanext.com/. See also York Region, "Making It Happen: The York Region Centres + Corridors Study," 2002, a PDF accessible at http://www.york.ca/De partments/Planning + and + Development/Long + Range + Planning/Centres + Corri dors + and + Subways.htm. Peter Calthorpe's plan is a PDF most easily accessed at http://www.markham.ca and then searching for "Langstaff Master Plan Project."

21. Taylor and Burchfield, *Growing Cities*, 2010. They used satellite and GIS information to reach this conclusion. R. White, *The Growth Plan for the Greater Golden Horseshoe in Historical Perspective* (Toronto: Neptis Foundation, 2007), 278.

22. In 2005 the Province of Ontario made the Niagara Escarpment and the Oak Ridges Moraine part of a greenbelt in which additional exurban developments will be strictly regulated. This is discussed in Chapter 9 of this book.

23. The divergence of views about cities that is expressed through the writings of Jacobs and Gottman is discussed at the end of Chapter 4.

24. Mumford, *City in History*, 505; Jacobs, *Death and Life of Great American Cities*, 343. Spiro Kostoff, in *The City Assembled: Elements of Urban Form through History* (London: Thames and Hudson, 1992), 67, wrote that "there has always been some vestigial pretense that suburbia is not complete in itself, that the umbilical cord which connects it to the city center cannot be totally severed. That symbolic bond has become meaningless to the new edge-dweller." This general observation clearly applies to the Toronto region.

Chapter 7

1. P. Lewis, "The Galactic Metropolis," in R. H. Pratt and G. Macinko, eds., *Beyond the Urban Fringe* (Minneapolis: University of Minnesota Press, 1983), 34–35.

2. The idea of the urban revolution was developed by Henri Lefebvre; see Chapter 1 for a discussion.

3. Vance conceived the idea of urban realms in 1968, and an updated account is provided in J. Vance, *The Continuing City: Urban Morphology in Western Civilization* (Baltimore: Johns Hopkins University Press, 1990), 502–508. "Evolving urban form challenges conventional wisdom" is from L. S. Bourne, J. N. H. Britton, and D. Leslie, "The Greater Toronto Region: Restructuring, Social Diversity and Globalization," in L. S. Bourne et al., eds. *Canadian Urban Regions: Trajectories of Growth and Change* (Toronto: Oxford University Press, 2011), 237. "Centers everywhere" is from M. McLuhan, *Understanding Media* (Toronto: Signet Press, 1964), 92.

4. The major centers in the City of Toronto are North York, Scarborough, Yonge/ St. Clair, Yonge/Eglinton, and Islington/Kipling. The municipal centers and downtowns in the conurbation are at Oshawa, Whitby, Ajax, Pickering, Markham, Richmond Hill, Aurora, Newmarket, Vaughan, Bramalea, Brampton, Mississauga, Oakville, Burlington, and Hamilton. Centers in the exurban belt are Bowmanville, Uxbridge, Stouffville, King City, Bolton, and Georgetown. Urban centers in the Greater Golden Horseshoe are Peterborough, Lindsay, Barrie, Milton, Collingwood, Orangeville, Guelph, Kitchener/Waterloo, Cambridge, Brantford, St. Catharine's, Niagara Falls, Welland, and Fort Erie.

5. Metropolitan Toronto, "Metroplan: The Official Plan for Metropolitan Toronto," 1981, 15; Ontario, Ministry of Public Infrastructural Renewal, "Places to Grow: Growth Plan for the Greater Golden Horseshoe," 2006, a PDF at https://www .placestogrow.ca/index.php?option = com_content&task = view&id = 9&Itemid = 14, pp. 10, 12.

6. York Region, "Official Plan: Office Consolidation," 2008, a PDF available at http://www.york.ca/Departments/Planning + and + Development/Long; plRange + Pla nning/ROP.htm.

7. P. Hall, "Looking Backward: Looking Forward—The City Region of the Mid-21st Century," in M. Neuman and A. Hull, eds., *The Futures of the City Region* (London: Routledge, 2011), 27.

8. D. Sudjic, *The 100 Mile City* (London: André Deutsch, 1992), 305. The argument for recognizing the continuing importance of old downtown cores in regional, polycentric cities is presented both in P. Calthorpe and W. Fulton, *The Regional City* (Washington, DC: Island Press, 2002), especially xvii, and in W. Bogart, *Don't Call It Sprawl: Metropolitan Structure in the Twenty-first Century* (New York: Cambridge University Press, 2006), 89–90.

9. B. Fuller, *Project Toronto: A Study and Proposal for the Future Development of the City and the Region of Toronto* (Cambridge, MA: Fuller-Sadao/Geometrics, 1968), 14; OECD, *OECD Territorial Reviews: Toronto, Canada*, 2010, a PDF available at http:// www.oecdbookshop.org/oecd/; Greater Toronto Civic Action Alliance, "Breaking Boundaries: Time to Think and Act Like a Region," July 2011, a PDF accessible at http://www.civicaction.ca/breakingboundaries. Toronto is mentioned just twice in Ontario, "Places to Grow," in section.1.21, p. 9, and in section 2.26, p. 18.

10. M. Castells, *The Rise of the Network Society* (Oxford: Blackwell, 1996), 385–386. D. Watts, in *Six Degrees: The Science of a Connected Age* (New York: W. W. Norton, 2003), 27, observes that "network" is a slippery term, easily misunderstood as a fixed rather than a dynamic structure.

11. The carrier hotel at 151 Front Street West is described at http://www.151front street.com/.

12. The most reliable data on transit ridership are those at American Public Transportation Association, http://www.apta.com/resources/statistics/Pages/ridership

report.aspx, which put the City of Toronto slightly lower than Montreal for subway ridership in 2011 yet slightly higher for overall public transit ridership (including buses) at 2.6 million. The term "anchor hub" is from Metrolinx, "The Big Move: Transforming Transportation in the Greater Toronto and Hamilton Area" (Government of Ontario, 2008), a PDF at http://www.metrolinx.com/thebigmove/en/default .aspx, which is a regional transportation plan discussed in Chapter 9.

13. Sudjic, *100 Mile City*, 144–145, also suggests that most citizens visit their city airports more times each year than they go to its galleries and museums. This seems to be the case in Toronto, where no gallery or museum has more than a million visitors annually. The number of jobs at Pearson International Airport is from http:// www.torontopearson.com/PearsonContent.aspx?id = 1011.

14. Sudjic, *100 Mile City*, 297.

15. Toronto with the longest section of ten-lane highway is from Inautonews, "List of World Record Highways," 2011, at http://www.inautonews.com/list-of-world-record-highways.

16. Traffic flows on Highway 401 is from Ontario, Ministry of Transportation, "Ontario Provincial Highways Traffic Volumes on Demand," 2007, http://www.raq sa.mto.gov.on.ca/techpubs/TrafficVolumes.nsf/tvweb?OpenForm&Seq = 1.

17. Sudjic, *100 Mile City*, 304. This sort of vision in motion is a fundamental aspect of the experience of the urbanized regions of hundred-mile cities. It is important to note that it is impossible to convey this sense of constant motion with maps, diagrams, or photographs, a limitation that biases illustrations of cities in favor of static things such as buildings.

18. J. Jacobs, *The Economy of Cities* (New York: Vintage, 1970), 105; IBM, "IBM Global Commuter Pain Study Reveals Traffic Crisis in Key International Cities," 2010, at http://www-03.ibm.com/press/us/en/pressrelease/32017.wss; Toronto Board of Trade, "Toronto as a Global City: Scorecard on Prosperity—2012," at http://www.bot .com/AM/Template.cfm?Section = Scorecard&Template = /CM/HTMLDisplay.cfm& ContentID = 4449; M. Turcotte, *The Time It Takes to Get to Work and Back: General Social Survey on Time Use* (Ottawa: Statistics Canada, 2005), and M. Turcotte, *Commuting to Work: Results of the 2010 General Social Survey* (Ottawa: Statistics Canada, 2011), at http://www.statcan.gc.ca/pub/11-008-x/2011002/article/11531-eng.htm.

19. OECD, *OECD Territorial Reviews*, 23, 93–96; Council of Ministers Responsible for Transportation and Highway Safety, "The High Costs of Congestion in Canadian Cities," 2012, a PDF at http://www.comt.ca/english/uttf-congestion-2012.pdf; Metrolinx, "The Big Move," 6.

20. Second Cup originated in Scarborough Town Centre in 1975, Pizza Pizza in downtown Toronto in 1967, Harvey's in Richmond Hill in 1959, and Swiss Chalet in downtown in 1954. The approximate counts of Tim Horton's, Starbucks, and Home Depot are based on Internet searches.

21. McLuhan, *Understanding Media*: "the medium is the message," ix; "metropolitan space," 103–104; "abolish the spatial dimension," 225; "any place to be a center,"

47. The full sentence is "Electric power, equally available in the farmhouse and the Executive Suite, permits any place to be a center and does not require large aggregations."

22. H. Rheingold, *Smart Mobs: The Next Social Revolution* (New York: Basic Books, 2003), xii, 207. R. E. Lang, *Edgeless Cities: Exploring the Elusive Metropolis* (Washington, DC: Brookings Institution, 2003), 17, discusses the idea of post-polycentric cities.

23. Cell phone towers across North America are mapped on Google Earth at http://loxcel.com/celltower.

Chapter 8

1. Price Waterhouse Coopers, "Cities of the Future: Global Competition, Local Leadership," 2010, 156, a PDF at http://www.pwc.com/gx/en/government-public-ser vices/issues-trends/index.jhtml. My comments about globalization in this chapter are informed by A. Appadurai, *Modernity at Large: Cultural Dimensions of Globalization* (Minnesota: University of Minneapolis Press, 1996).

2. D. Kerr and J. Spelt, *The Changing Face of Toronto: A Study in Urban Geography* (Ottawa: Queen's Printer for Canada, 1965), 75, 77. All percentages of employment are for Metro/New City of Toronto, and 2006 percentages are from Statistics Canada, Census 2006, http://www12.statcan.ca/census-recensement/2006/dp-pd/prof/92–591/ index.cfm?Lang = E.

3. J. Jacobs, *The Economy of Cities* (New York: Vintage, 1970). She reinforced this idea in *Cities and the Wealth of Nations* (New York: Vintage, 1985). See also M. Castells and P. Hall, *Technopoles of the World: The Making of Twenty-first Century Industrial Complexes* (London: Routledge, 1994), 2 and 6–7; and *Forbes*, 2008, "World's Most Economically Powerful Cities," http://www.forbes.com/2008/07/15/economic-growth-gdp-biz-cx_jz_0715powercities.html.

4. Forbes ranks Toronto tenth on its 2008 list of the world's most economically powerful cities. FDI Intelligence, "Foreign Direct Investment: Global Insight from the Financial Times," 2011, ranks Toronto fourth among North American cities for qual-ity of life and fourth for economic potential (http://www.fdiintelligence.com).Mercer Human Resource Consulting, "Quality of Living Worldwide City Rankings," 2012, puts Toronto fifteenth in the world and third in North America (after Vancouver and Ottawa) as a recommended place to live (http://www.mercer.com/qualityofliving pr#city-rankings). The most recent account of Global and World Cities rankings is at http://www.lboro.ac.uk/gawc/world2010t.html.

5. Greater Toronto Marketing Alliance, "Top 10 Reasons to Invest in the GTA," 2011, http://www.greatertoronto.org/why-greater-toronto/top-ten-reasons/; OECD, *OECD Territorial Reviews: Toronto, Canada 2009*, 2010, a PDF at http://www.oecd bookshop.org/oecd/.

6. J-A. Boudreau, R. Keil, and D. Young, *Changing Toronto: Governing Neo-Imperialism* (Toronto: University of Toronto Press, 2009).

7. "Toronto the Not-so-good," *Economist*, June 29, 2010, http://www.economist .com/blogs/americasview/2010/06/toronto_after_g20_summit.

8. Boudreau, Keil, and Young, *Changing Toronto*, 163. The "extraordinarily diverse" economy is discussed in L. S. Bourne, J. N. H. Britton, and D. Leslie, "The Greater Toronto Region: Restructuring, Social Diversity and Globalization," in L. S. Bourne et al., eds., *Canadian Urban Regions: Trajectories of Growth and Change* (Toronto: Oxford University Press, 2011), 236.

9. The constitutional relationships between municipalities, provinces, and the federal government are described in M. Dewing, W. R Young, and E. Tolley, "Municipalities, the Constitution, and the Canadian Federal System," Library of Parliament, Parliamentary Information and Research Service, 2006, at http://www2.parl.gc.ca/con tent/lop/researchpublications/bp276-e.htm.

10. As of 2012 the Province of Ontario was suffering the economic problems of many parts of the developed world, with a high deficit and debt. John Ibbitson has pointed out that the evidence of these problems is not very obvious in Toronto because of its relative insulation from the rest of the province. See J. Ibbitson, "Other Provinces Have No Cause to Gloat over Ontario's Economic Woes," *Globe and Mail*, February 20, 2012.

11. Greater Toronto Marketing Alliance, "Top 10 Reasons."

12. Greater Toronto Civic Action Alliance, 2011, http://www.civicaction.ca/ (before the 2011 Toronto City Summit Alliance). See Boudreau, Keil, and Young, *Changing Toronto*, 213; TRRA (Toronto Region Research Alliance), 2011; Toronto Board of Trade, "Toronto as a Global City: Scorecard on Prosperity—2012," a PDF at http://www.bot.com/AM/Template.cfm?Section = Scorecard&Template = /CM/HTML Display.cfm&ContentID = 4712.

13. The branding claims of various local development offices were taken from their websites in April 2012. This sort of branding is ephemeral and has probably changed since then.

14. The 2006 Census counted 501,685 Chinese and 710,235 South Asians in the Greater Toronto and Hamilton Area, together almost exactly one-fifth of the total population of 6,135,954.

15. L. Sandercock, *Cosmopolis II: Mongrel Cities of the 21st Century* (London: Continuum, 2003): "urban political regimes," 2; term "mongrel," xiii; "marginalized, displaced," 110.

16. The numbers and percentages of immigrants and visible minorities are based on the counts in the 2006 Census for the Toronto CMA; equivalent data from the 2011 Census had not been released at the time of this writing, but annual rates of immigration have not changed much since 2006 so it is possible to make a reasoned guess about current percentages. The comment that Toronto has a higher percentage of foreign-born residents than all other cities in North America and Europe is based on OECD, *OECD Territorial Reviews*, 40. The U.S. cities with the highest numbers of foreign-born residents are listed as Miami at 37 percent and Los Angeles at 34 percent.

Cities in other parts of the world, notably Dubai at more than 80 percent, are higher than Toronto. Information on visible minorities is from the community profile for Toronto CMA in Statistics Canada, Census 2006, http://www12.statcan.ca/census-recensement/2006/dp-pd/prof/92-591/index.cfm?Lang=E. While immigrant inflow to Toronto is about one hundred thousand per year, there is an outflow of around fifteen thousand: hence the average annual population growth for the CMA that is shown in Table 8.1 is eighty-four thousand.

17. The comment about Chinese plazas is in OECD, *OECD Territorial Reviews*, 70. See also D. Brand, "Ossington to Christie, Toronto," in *A Map to the Door of No Return* (Toronto: Vintage Canada, 2001), 110–111.

18. The comment about ethnic heritage in American cities is based on J. Lin, *The Power of Urban Ethnic Places: Cultural Heritage and Urban Ethnic Life* (London: Routledge, 2011). See also Appadurai, *Modernity at Large*, 172.

19. M. McLuhan, "The Later Innis," *Queens Quarterly* 60 (1953): 391. The phrase "jumbled, malleable, amalgam" is from D. Lowenthal, "Natural and Cultural Heritage," *International Journal of Heritage Studies* 11, no. 1 (March 2005): 81. See also D. Lowenthal, *Possessed by the Past: The Heritage Crusade and the Spoils of History* (New York: Free Press, 1996), in which he argues that heritage now all but defies definition.

20. W. Kymlicka, *Multicultural Citizenship: A Liberal Theory of Minority Rights* (New York: Oxford University Press, 1995). "Public reasonableness" is in W. Kymlicka, "Multicultural Citizenship," in *The Citizenship Debates: A Reader*, ed. G. Shafir (Minneapolis: University of Minnesota Press, 1998), 171.

21. OECD, *OECD Territorial Reviews*, 90. See also TRIEC (Toronto Region Immigrant Employment Council), http://www.triec.ca/; the Maytree Foundation, http://maytree.com.

22. M. Castells, *The Rise of the Network Society* (Oxford: Blackwell, 1996), 415.

23. D. Hulchanski et al., *The Three Cities within Toronto: Income Polarization among Toronto's Neighbourhoods, 1970–2005*, Centre for Urban and Community Studies [now the Cities Centre], Research Bulletin No. 41, first published 2007, updated 2010, available at http://www.urbancentre.utoronto.ca/redirects/3citiesDec2010Report.html.

24. The suburbanization of poverty is discussed in Bourne, Britton, and Leslie, "The Greater Toronto Region," 251. In a separate chapter in the same volume, Alan Walks, one of the coauthors of the *Three Cities* study (cited in n. 23), discusses income polarization in several Canadian cities and notes specifically that average per capita income of recent immigrants in Toronto and Vancouver has declined steadily since the 1990s. See also R. A. Walks, "Economic Restructuring and Trajectories of Socio-spatial Polarization in the Twenty-first-century Canadian City," in L. S. Bourne et al., eds., *Canadian Urban Regions: Trajectories of Growth and Change* (Toronto: Oxford University Press, 2011), 125–159.

25. United Way, "Poverty by Postal Code: The Geography of Neighbourhood Poverty, 1981–2001," prepared jointly by the United Way of Greater Toronto and the

Canadian Council on Social Development, 2004, table 1.4, p. 66, a PDF available at http://www.unitedwaytoronto.com/whatWeDo/reports/povertyByPostalCode.php. See also Daily Bread Food Bank, "Who's Hungry—Fighting Hunger: 2012 Profile of Hunger in the GTA," 8, a PDF at http://www.dailybread.ca/learning-centre/hunger-statistics

26. City of Toronto and United Way of Greater Toronto, "Strong Neighbourhoods: A Call to Action," 2005, a PDF at http://www.toronto.ca/demographics/priorit yareas.htm.

27. Hulchanski et al., *Three Cities*, 20; United Way, "Poverty by Postal Code," 50. The Colour of Poverty fact sheets, 2007, are available at http://www.colourofpoverty .ca. See also Children's Aid Society of Toronto, "Greater Trouble in Greater Toronto: Child Poverty in the GTA," 12, a PDF at http://www.torontocas.ca/wp-content/. . . / castchildpovertyreportdec2008.pdf.

28. DiverseCity, "DiverseCity Counts: The Greater Toronto Leadership Project," 2010, at http://www.diversecitytoronto.ca.

29. A. Walks and L. S. Bourne, "Ghettos in Canada's Cities: Racial Segregation, Ethnic Enclaves and Poverty Concentration in Canadian Urban Areas," *Canadian Geographer* 50, no. 3 (2006): 272–297. I know of no comprehensive study of visible minority immigrants and income levels in the Toronto region. However, a sample of Census tract information from the 2006 Canadian Census confirms that in the following neighborhoods both the proportions of visible minorities and median household income levels were above the respective averages of 42 percent and $64,000 for the Toronto CMA: in Brampton, Castlemore (80 percent, $90,000) and Malton (73 percent, $80,000); in Markham, near the Civic Center (66 percent, $98,000), and Cornell (66 percent, $86,000); in Mississauga between Meadowvale and Highway 401 (75 percent, $84,000), the Erin Mills area (64 percent, $116,000); Bayview Hills in Richmond Hill (68 percent, $117,000); in the City of Toronto, Highland Creek in the eastern inner suburbs (70 percent, $89,000); North York, downtown (53 percent, $110,000), or, at the average, near Islington Avenue in Rexdale in Etobicoke (52 percent, $62,000).

30. Walks and Bourne, "Ghettos in Canada's Cities," concluded that low-income areas are concentrated within clusters of high-rise apartments. See also United Way, "Vertical Poverty: Poverty by Postal Code 2," 2011, 170, a PDF at http://www.united waytoronto.com/verticalpoverty/.

31. The Crime Severity Index for Communities with more than ten thousand residents for 2011 is based on police data summarized by Statistics Canada and is available at http://www.statcan.gc.ca/pub/85-002-x/2012001/article/11692/tbl/csi value-igcvaleurs-2011-eng.htm. The regional municipalities ranked even lower: Peel, 103rd; Durham, 135th; York, 177th; Halton, 216th. In 2011 there were eighty-six homicides in the Toronto CMA. A separate ranking of one hundred urban areas, with each having more than fifty thousand residents, by the Canadian magazine *Macleans* is based on crimes per one hundred thousand residents, and it puts Toronto thirteenth

for violent crime and eighty-sixth for nonviolent crime (http://www2.macleans.ca/crime-chart).

32. Arguments for making Toronto a province, including an essay by Jane Jacobs, are presented in M. W. Rowe, ed., *Toronto: Considering Self-Government* (Owen Sound, ON: Ginger Press, 2000), and in A. Broadbent, *Urban Nation: Why We Need to Give Power Back to the Cities to Make Canada Strong* (Toronto: HarperCollins, 2008). A thoughtful counterargument is made by the political scientist A. Sancton in *The Limits of Boundaries: Why City-Regions Cannot Be Self-Governing* (Montreal: McGill Queens, 2008).

33. Responses to change as "hesitant, uneven and disjointed" are from Bourne, Britton, and Leslie, "Greater Toronto Region," 268. "Stroppy strangers" is from Sandercock, *Cosmopolis II*, 105.

Chapter 9

1. Toronto's share of Ontario's population in 1961 is based on the population of Metro; the 2011 figure is based on the population of the Greater Toronto and Hamilton Area.

2. The urban zone is discussed in J. Lemon, "Plans for Early 20th-century Toronto: Lost in Management," *Urban History Review* 18, no. 1 (1989): 11–31. The 1943 Master Plan was described in Chapter 4.

3. R. White, *The Growth Plan for the Greater Golden Horseshoe in Historical Perspective* (Toronto: Neptis Foundation, 2007): "only true regional planning body," 12; urban contiguity, 16. Municipal cooperation and regional planning around Vancouver is discussed in Z. Taylor and M. Burchfield, *Growing Cities: Comparing Urban Growth Patterns and Regional Growth Policies in Calgary, Toronto and Vancouver* (Toronto: Neptis Foundation, 2010), 62.

4. These proposals and the decision to service northward growth were described in Chapter 5.

5. White, *Growth Plan in Historical Perspective*, 32–42.

6. Greater Toronto Coordinating Committee and IBI Group, *Greater Toronto Area Urban Structure Concepts Study: Background Report 7—Comparison of Urban Structure Concepts* (Toronto: Greater Toronto Coordinating Committee, 1990). This summarizes the Spread, Nodal, and Central options that had been discussed in detail in six preceding reports.

7. The Toronto bioregion was identified in the report of the Royal Commission on Toronto's Waterfront, *Regeneration: Toronto's Waterfront and the Sustainable City* (Toronto: Queen's Printer of Ontario, 1992). The main lobby organization for the Moraine was STORM (Save the Oak Ridges Moraine), a coalition of environmental lobby groups formed in 1989, including some from the old City of Toronto because the Don and Humber rivers have their headwaters in the Moraine. The recommendation for regional governance was in the Greater Toronto Area Task Force, *Report of the GTA Task Force* (Toronto: Queen's Printer of Ontario, 1996).

8. The final report of the Central Ontario Smart Growth Panel, "Shape the Future," 2003 (accessible at https://www.placestogrow.ca), includes many elements that were incorporated into the Growth Plan and the Big Move.

9. Ontario, Ministry of Municipal Affairs and Housing, "Oak Ridges Moraine Conservation Plan," 2001, available at http://www.mah.gov.on.ca/Page1707.aspx.

10. Ontario, Ministry of Municipal Affairs and Housing, "The Greenbelt Plan (2005)," http://www.mah.gov.on.ca/Page189.aspx#greenbelt: "where urbanization should not occur," section 1.1; "settlement areas not permitted to expand," section 3.4.2.

11. I derived the history of "natural heritage," including a reference to President Kennedy's cross-county trip to save it in 1963, from Google's Timeline for Natural Heritage in October 2010. Google discontinued this Timeline feature in October 2011. See the Ontario Heritage Trust, http://www.heritagetrust.on.ca/About-us/Who-we-are.aspx.

12. D. Lowenthal, "Natural and Cultural Heritage," *International Journal of Heritage Studies* 11, no. 1 (March 2005): "not human made," 86–87. See also Royal Commission on Toronto's Waterfront, *Regeneration*, 57, see also 42; Ontario Natural Heritage Information Centre, http://nhic.mnr.gov.on.ca/MNR/nhic/glossary.cfm; City of Toronto, "Toronto Official Plan," 2002 (2009 consolidation), section 3.4, a PDF at http://www.toronto.ca/planning/official_plan/introduction.htm.

13. A "quango" is a quasi-autonomous nongovernmental organization. Ontario Greenbelt Alliance, "Greenbelt 2.0 Backgrounder," 2011, http://greenbeltalliance.ca. I can no longer find this report on the website, but Greenbelt 2.0 is discussed in the report "Green amongst the Grey: Fifth Anniversary Progress Report on the Greater Golden Horseshoe Greenbelt," 2010, a PDF available on that website in April 2012.

14. Ontario, Ministry of Public Infrastructural Renewal, "Places to Grow: Growth Plan for the Greater Golden Horseshoe, 2006," https://www.placestogrow.ca/index .php?option = com_content&task = view&id = 9&Itemid = 14.

15. The Growth Plan's target population is in Schedule 3: "compact, vibrant and complete communities," 10; urban growth centers, especially on 16–17; "promote collaboration," 10.

16. J. Jacobs, *The Economy of Cities* (New York: Vintage, 1970), 100. She acknowledges that these are based on her ideas in *Death and Life of Great American Cities*.

17. The Neptis report criticizing density targets as too low was written about a draft of the final plan: "A Response to the Ontario Government's Discussion Paper 'Places to Grow,'" September 2004, a PDF at http://www.neptis.org/library/show.cfm ?id = 66&cat_id = 30. The criticism about retailing is from another Neptis report: R. Buliung and T. Hernandez, *Places to Shop and Places to Grow: Power Retail Consumer Travel Behaviour, and Urban Growth Management in the Greater Toronto Area* (Toronto: Neptis Foundation, 2009), 5, 42, 50.

18. Metrolinx, "The Big Move: Transforming Transportation in the Greater Toronto and Hamilton Area," 2008, a PDF at http://www.metrolinx.com/thebigmove/en/default.aspx: "compact and complete communities," 1; areas of social need, climate change, and so on are discussed on 5–12.

19. On mobility hubs, see Metrolinx, "Mobility Hub Guidelines for the Greater Toronto and Hamilton Area," September 2011, accessible through the Metrolinx website.

20. The number of 12,500 businesses is from "Partners in Project Green: Greening the Bottom-line in the Pearson Eco-Business Zone," a brochure describing a joint project for addressing environmental issues that involves the Greater Toronto Airports Authority, Toronto Region Conservation Authority, Toronto, Mississauga, Brampton, and the Region of Peel. The brochure and other information are available at http://www.partnersinprojectgreen.com/. See also Greater Toronto Airports Authority, "Taking Flight: The Airport Master Plan 2008–2030," 2007, http://www.torontopearson.com/GTAAContent.aspx?id = 788.

21. Seaton is discussed in Ontario, Ministry of Municipal Affairs and Housing, "Central Pickering Development Plan," 2006, a PDF at http://www.mah.gov.on.ca/Page1726.aspx: "sustainable urban community" and "forests, field and streams," 17; see also map of Planning Area Neighbourhoods, 79.

22. American Planning Association, "APA Recognizes Ontario's Greater Golden Horseshoe Plan," 2006, at http://www.planning.org/newsreleases/2006/dec19–10.htm.

23. Greater Toronto Area Task Force, *Report*, especially 159.

24. The lack of coordinated economic planning was discussed in Chapter 8, but see, for example, Greater Toronto Civic Action Alliance, "Breaking Boundaries: Time to Think and Act like a Region," 2011, a PDF at http://www.civicaction.ca/breaking boundaries. The Living City is described at Toronto and Region Conservation Authority, http://trca.on.ca/about.

25. The 1988 climate change meeting in Toronto is discussed in American Institute of Physics, "The Discovery of Global Warming," by Spencer Weart, 2009, http://www.aip.org/history/climate/index.htm. A very brief summary of some of Ontario's policies about climate change is in Ontario, Ministry of Municipal Affairs and Housing, "Info Sheet: Planning for Climate Change," 2009, a PDF at www.mah.gov.on.ca/AssetFactory.aspx?did = 7234, which refers to the Greenbelt and Growth Plans as contributing to mitigation.

26. J. Jacobs, *The Death and Life of Great American Cities* (New York: Vintage, 1961), 417. The SARS epidemic, and the confused response to it, is analyzed in the report of the commission that was set up to find out what went wrong: Ontario, Ministry of Health and Long Term Care, SARS Commission, "Spring of Fear," 2006, a PDF at http://www.health.gov.on.ca/en/common/ministry/publications/reports/campbell06 /campbell06.aspx. The comment about systemic failure is from the "Interim Report: SARS and Public Health in Ontario," 7, available at the same website.

Chapter 10

1. The Hemingway quote is in J. R. Colombo, *New Canadian Quotations* (Edmonton: Hurtig Publishers, 1987), 383. Dan Aykroyd was cited in the Toronto newspaper *Globe and Mail,* February 6, 1998, section C5.

2. C. Abbott, *Greater Portland: Urban Life and Landscape in the Pacific North-West* (Philadelphia: University of Pennsylvania Press, 2001), 201. Gardiner's comment is cited in J. Lemon, *Toronto since 1918* (Toronto: Lorimer, 1985), 149.

3. R. Davies, *The Diary of Samuel Marchbanks* (Toronto: Totem Press, 1947), 268; M. Ondaatje, *In the Skin of a Lion* (Toronto: McClelland and Stewart, 1987); M. Atwood, *Cat's Eye* (Toronto: Seal Books, 1989), 13–14 and 55; M. Wolfe and D. Daymond, *Toronto Short Stories* (Toronto: Doubleday, 1977), x.

4. Ray Bradbury, Buckminster Fuller, and Peter Ustinov are cited in Colombo, *New Canadian Quotations,* 384, 428, and 569. Umberto Eco is cited in G. Gatenby, ed., *The Wild Is Always There* (Toronto: Alfred Knopf, 1993), 428.

5. J. Jacobs, *The Economy of Cities* (New York: Vintage, 1970), 250; J. Jacobs, *Dark Age Ahead* (New York: Harper, 2003): "visible and enraging," 119; public poverty, 107–108; suburbs as a part of a spiral of decline and "murders of communities," 169–170.

6. The term "information megalopolis" is from M. McLuhan and Q. Fiore, *The Medium Is the Massage: An Inventory of Effects* (Toronto: Bantam Books, 1967), unpaginated but the discussion is toward the middle of the book. "The city becomes terrestrial in its scope" is from McLuhan's lecture at Fordham University, included in S. McLuhan and D. Staines, eds., *Understanding Me: Lectures and Interviews/Marshall McLuhan* (Toronto: McClelland and Stewart, 2003), 141. "Yearn for the simple days of the automobile" is from M. McLuhan, *Understanding Media* (Toronto: Signet Press, 1964), 103–104.

7. S. Micaleff, *Stroll: Psychogeographic Walking Tours of Toronto* (Toronto: Coach House Press, 2010): Toronto "flaneur," 11; Dorset Park, 220ff.

8. R. Banham, *Los Angeles: The Architecture of the Four Ecologies* (London: Penguin, 1971), 236.

9. L. Ford, *Metropolitan San Diego: How Geography and Lifestyle Shape a New Urban Environment* (Philadelphia: University of Pennsylvania Press, 2004), 223. The hollowing out of Philadelphia is discussed in S. Conn, *Metropolitan Philadelphia: Living with the Presence of the Past* (Philadelphia: University of Pennsylvania Press, 2006), 247ff. The expression "thinking small and living big" is from P. Gober, *Metropolitan Phoenix: Place-Making and Community Building in the Desert* (Philadelphia: University of Pennsylvania Press, 2006), 207.

10. Restraint and management constitute the central theme in J. Lemon, *Liberal Dreams and Nature's Limits: Great Cities of North America since 1600* (Toronto: Oxford University Press 1996), chapter 7, which provides an account of Toronto. Incidentally and in the tradition of negativity, Lemon believed that by 1995 Toronto's golden years had already passed.

11. Micaleff, *Stroll,* 11. For the record, although University Avenue, which leads to the provincial legislature, does have the appearance of a city beautiful grand avenue, its width is the result of the fact that in the early nineteenth century it was where Toronto's aristocrats would parade in carriages and on horseback. The fact that it looks like a grand axial avenue is a happy accident rather than a deliberate design.

12. J. Nijman, *Miami: Mistress of the Americas* (Philadelphia: University of Pennsylvania Press, 2011).

Index

www.ingramcontent.com/pod-product-compliance
Lightning Source LLC
Chambersburg PA
CBHW031534260326
41914CB00032B/1808/J